LITTLE BROTHER

ALSO BY BEN WESTHOFF

*Fentanyl, Inc.: How Rogue Chemists Created
the Deadliest Wave of the Opioid Epidemic*

*Original Gangstas: Tupac Shakur, Dr. Dre, Eazy-E, Ice Cube,
and the Birth of West Coast Rap*

*Dirty South: OutKast, Lil Wayne, Soulja Boy, and the
Southern Rappers Who Reinvented Hip-Hop*

LITTLE BROTHER

LOVE, TRAGEDY, AND
MY SEARCH FOR THE TRUTH

BEN WESTHOFF

hachette
BOOKS

NEW YORK

Hachette Books
Hachette Book Group
1290 Avenue of the Americas
New York, NY 10104
HachetteBooks.com
Twitter.com/HachetteBooks
Instagram.com/HachetteBooks

First Edition: May 2022

Published by Hachette Books, an imprint of Perseus Books, LLC, a subsidiary of Hachette Book Group, Inc. The Hachette Books name and logo is a trademark of the Hachette Book Group.

The Hachette Speakers Bureau provides a wide range of authors for speaking events.

To find out more, go to www.hachettespeakersbureau.com or call (866) 376-6591.

The publisher is not responsible for websites (or their content) that are not owned by the publisher.

Print book interior design by Abby Reilly.

Library of Congress Cataloging-in-Publication Data has been applied for.

ISBNs: 9780306923173 (hardcover), 9780306923166 (ebook)

Printed in the United States of America

LSC-C

Printing 1, 2022

Jorell Cleveland in 2015

CONTENTS

INTRODUCTION

I hadn't seen Jorell in a couple months. It was August 2016, and he'd stopped returning my texts. This was a bit frustrating, but I didn't take it personally. After all, he'd turned nineteen that year, and I figured this was typical teenager stuff.

Jorell Cleveland was my little brother. The Big Brothers Big Sisters program had paired us eleven years earlier, and I had watched him grow from a shy kid with a big afro who barely stood as high as my chest to a confident, muscled young man people looked up to. We didn't share blood, but as far as I was concerned he was my family.

Our backgrounds could have hardly been more different. I grew up in a tree-canopied St. Paul neighborhood near the University of Minnesota. My mother was an entomologist and my father a doctor. Jorell lived his early years in a poor Arkansas town, and when we first met, his single-parent father was a roofer raising eight children in St. Louis, Missouri. His mother was in prison, back in Arkansas.

I first moved to St. Louis to attend Washington University. I developed an affinity for the city, and moved back there at age twenty-six for my new job at a weekly paper. Before long I felt a need to get involved in a public service program, one where I could actually make a difference. I read a news story about a Big Brothers Big Sisters program focused on children of incarcerated parents. "For many children, a parent's incarceration often marks the beginning of a generational cycle of crime," the article said.

"Having a mother in prison often disrupts a child's environment more than having a father in prison."

The article touched me, and at Big Brothers Big Sisters, they had an immediate, pressing need, particularly for male volunteers. And so after going through a background check I was assigned a match. In the early evening of June 30, 2005, I went to the Big Brothers Big Sisters' offices and met my "Little," a tiny eight-year-old who possessed a gigawatt smile.

"What's your name?" I asked.

"Jorell Marsay Cleveland," he said.

"It's great to meet you," I said, extending my hand.

"Nice to meet you too," he said, shaking it without making eye contact. I thought: There must be some mistake. This kid is so charming and adorable that he couldn't possibly need mentorship. People must fall at his feet. I was also introduced to his father, Joe, who seemed gregarious and appreciative of my efforts.

For our first outing together, Jorell and I ate dinner at an old-fashioned Italian restaurant called Rossino's, where the wait staff melted for him, refilling his 7UP glass continually. He couldn't have been more than fifty pounds.

"Where do you go to school?" I asked.

"Adams," he said.

"Do you like your teacher?"

"Yes."

"What grade are you in?"

"Second."

It continued like this. He politely answered my questions with one-word answers, an upward inflection on the last syllable. When we said goodbye he asked when I'd pick him up again and suggested, "Monday?" which was that same day.

Jorell craved undivided adult attention. He lived in a crowded household, in a dodgy St. Louis neighborhood called Forest Park Southeast. When I drove through the area at night, guys standing on the side of the street tried to flag me down to sell drugs. One time, when Jorell's dog got off its leash, police shot and killed it.

Despite our biographical differences, we found plenty in common as we explored St. Louis together, trying new burger stands and bowling alleys, and seeing bad movies. I took him to his first Cardinals game at Busch Stadium, and got him swimming lessons at the YMCA.

Jorell could be cripplingly shy, his answers to my questions often barely audible. But he had bright eyes, an insatiable curiosity, and relentless positivity. He liked to feel the stubble on my face with both of his hands. He was game to do anything, even if it was just hanging out by the pool, listening to rap albums, or watching TV in my apartment with my tuxedo cat, Nora.

Not long after we met I went to pick him up at his home, and upon being invited inside was shocked by what I saw. "He sleeps on a bare mattress," I wrote in my journal. "The bedroom door is a frayed blue tarp, and his windows have been broken but never replaced." But Jorell almost never complained. One time he found a Books-A-Million gift card in his backyard, and I took him to the mall to redeem it, but the card had no value. Later, his bike was stolen. Still he didn't get angry or rant about unfairness. He just accepted life as it was. He never wanted to discuss his mother in prison, or any other hardships. I didn't press him.

A year into our pairing, Jorell told me that his family was moving to a new house in the St. Louis suburb of Ferguson. This was a chance for them to get away from the violence and poverty of their city neighborhood. I visited when they moved in, and I was surprised by the size of their six-bedroom home. The backyard was as big as a football field. This was late 2006, the go-go era for real estate, and Jorell's dad also invested in another house in the area, which he rented out.

This seemed to be a step up for the Cleveland family. Though I didn't know much about Ferguson, a municipality of twenty-one thousand people, I had middle-class friends who'd been raised in that part of the metro area, known as North County. It was the suburbs, so it had to be safer than the city, right? As I looked around, I saw an area in flux. Some houses on the block were run down, others well maintained. A cute downtown business district was just a short walk away.

Most of the Clevelands' neighbors were white, but, as I would later learn, Ferguson's population was changing quickly. In the years leading up to Black teenager Michael Brown's killing by a white police officer in 2014, the city would become majority Black for the first time, even as the power structure—the lawmakers, the police, the school board—remained white.

It was all part of the evolving demographics of North County, which includes dozens of small towns north of St. Louis. Black families (like the Clevelands) were arriving from the city, while white families were fleeing for suburbs even more distant.

"What do you think?" Jorell asked, showing off his bedroom. I took stock: its only piece of furniture was a blow-up bed, which he shared with three siblings. But the possibilities were endless.

"It's awesome," I said.

As a staff writer at the local weekly, the *Riverfront Times*, I wrote about everything from news to sports to restaurants. But my primary beat was hip-hop music, which was blowing up in St. Louis thanks to the success of multiplatinum rapper Nelly, famous for his song "Hot In Herre." Rap music was also the soundtrack to Jorell's life and a big part of how we connected. We listened to CDs together and shared notes on albums. Jorell introduced me to new rappers, and I wowed him with stories of interviewing artists whose songs he loved.

Many found it amusing that I, a straightlaced white guy, covered hip-hop, especially considering I neither looked nor acted the part. But it was the music I loved. Plus, it was a great topic for a journalist, as it wielded enormous cultural influence. Rock stars tend to be boringly middle class, but the rappers I interviewed often had cinematic, rags-to-riches stories. Very few journalists were telling their stories, and covering hip-hop gave me a chance to meet people from different backgrounds, as well as an entrée to parts of St. Louis I never would have known otherwise.

Nonetheless, by 2007 St. Louis started feeling small. I wanted to advance my career as a writer and decided the best place to do that was New York City. I rented a small apartment in Brooklyn, and began hustling up freelance gigs.

Jorell and I stayed in touch, and we spoke on the phone regularly. I soon began spending time with a woman named Anna, eventually moving in with her in Hoboken, New Jersey. In 2008 ten-year-old Jorell boarded a plane for the first time in his life to visit us for a long weekend. "He enjoyed the flight, watching the cars on the ground turn to ants and drinking Sprite," I wrote in my journal.

He and Anna got along well. We looked out from the top of the Empire State Building. We explored art galleries in Chelsea. He tried sushi for the first time. He wanted to buy an oversized, novelty $100 bill at a tourist shop, but I talked him out of it. The next summer he came back and stayed with us for five weeks, sleeping on the couch in our duplex and attending a YMCA day camp. Jorell quickly made friends with the other kids in the neighborhood, and even started a dog-walking business with the boy next door, posting signs around the neighborhood.

In these years I saw Jorell searching for an identity, not unlike young people anywhere. One time he sported an afro; the next time cornrows; the next time, his head was shaved. Kids made fun of him at school because of how small he was, and he sometimes got into fights. But I never saw that, and he didn't want to talk about the tougher parts of his life. He often relied on small scowls or pursed smiles to express his emotions, except in those rare situations where he felt completely comfortable, when he would explode with waves of roaring laughter.

During a visit to the Museum of Natural History on his first trip to New York, I snapped a photo of him standing next to a tiger, stuffed and roaring in a glass cage. Jorell posed with his hands up in the air, cowering and pretending to be petrified of the tiger. When I look at the photo now, I see the ideal image of childhood: a happy boy, carefree, totally at ease, unguarded.

In 2014 I moved back to St. Louis yet again, this time with Anna and our two young boys. Anna had never lived there, but I'd gone to college at Washington University and worked at the *Riverfront Times*. We moved to be closer to our families; plus, Jorell lived there, and we were thrilled to reconnect.

But upon our October 2014 arrival, St. Louis was in flames. It was the 250th anniversary of the city's founding, but no one was celebrating. Just two months earlier, Michael Brown had been shot dead in Ferguson. Images of Brown's body in the street went viral, and local businesses were burned to the ground. Jorell joined the protests and looting on Ferguson's main thoroughfare. A Justice Department report later detailed how the Ferguson police department targeted African Americans.

Brown's killing shook me because in him I saw Jorell. Michael Brown was only a year older and he lived nearby. They were acquaintances; Jorell could have been him.

During this time I wanted more than ever to be there for Jorell, and through early 2016 I saw him regularly, hanging out and tutoring him with his classwork. But by that summer, when he was nineteen, he'd grown increasingly difficult to reach. He didn't have a phone of his own, so I had to go through his dad, his sister Iesha, or his girlfriend Danielle. They usually told me he was busy. He had just returned for his fifth year of high school, and spent long hours frying chicken at his job.

When we did get together I often smelled marijuana on him, and his energy level varied wildly. Sometimes he was practically lifeless, barely listening when I talked and falling asleep in my car. Other times he bounced with uncharacteristic pep. Though I worried there were things he wasn't telling me, I figured he probably wasn't up to anything more scandalous than I'd done at that age.

Plus, I was busy too. That summer I prepared for the release of my third book, *Original Gangstas*, a history of Los Angeles gangsta rap in the 1980s and 1990s, as well as the LA riots, gangs, police brutality, and crack epidemic that also defined the era. I got to talk to my West Coast childhood heroes, guys like Snoop Dogg, Dr. Dre, and Ice Cube. Jorell was excited about the book. Though he tended to prefer newer rappers, I'd gotten him into the old West Coast stuff, particularly Snoop Dogg, who was a wiry, menacing Long Beach Crip when he was young. It was striking how much Jorell resembled him, right down to the wispy mustache.

I was working on my book promotion on a Saturday afternoon in August 2016, when I received a phone call from a number I didn't recognize.

"Hello, Ben? Are you sitting down?"

"Who is this?"

"This is Danielle's mother."

This woman—the mother of Jorell's girlfriend—was someone I'd never spoken with in my life.

"What happened?"

"Jorell has been shot," she said. "He's dead."

After Jorell's death I went numb. I remained so through his funeral, which was attended by dozens of friends and family members, and for weeks to come. I had no idea why he was killed, and it appeared that the police didn't either.

Weeks turned into months, and my shock turned to anger. As the killer continued to go unnamed, that anger turned to guilt. Without knowing why he was killed, I focused the blame on myself. To this day the guilt hasn't subsided. I was his Big Brother, after all. The Big Brothers Big Sisters program had no specific requirements for the program—it was our bond that kept us together for over a decade, not any formal obligations—but I believed it was my job to keep him safe. And at that I failed.

One thing seemed certain: his shooting must have been random. The killer must have mistaken him for another person, or he must have accidentally gotten in the middle of someone else's dispute. He was so good-hearted he couldn't possibly be tied up in any dangerous business. There was no denying that he had a lot going against him in his life, but he had a big heart and a winning attitude, and didn't seem to possess an ounce of cynicism.

Who could possibly want him dead?

That's the question I set out to answer in this book. Doing so required me to find out what was happening behind the scenes in his life—the stuff he never told me. It required me to reconstruct his last months and speak with almost everyone he knew well.

When the police investigation into his death stalled, leaving Jorell's family desperate for answers, I took matters into my own hands, employing my skill set as an investigative journalist to find the truth. I retraced his steps through dangerous North County streets, tracked down underworld figures, and pored over reams of police records.

In the end, what I discovered challenged almost everything I believed about Jorell. It turns out he wasn't the happy-go-lucky kid I'd always believed he was. He'd grown paranoid in his final months, answering his front door while clutching his gun. He also had real enemies I never imagined.

This story is much more than a whodunnit. Seeking the truth about Jorell's killer required me to understand the troubled history of St. Louis, how discrimination and pervasive poverty has shaped life for millions. It also required me to examine my own choices and mistakes.

I conducted this investigation for Jorell's family and friends and for myself, to help those who knew him heal. But I held in mind those who live on the margins, whose deaths are seen as insignificant. St. Louis now experiences more violent crime than any other major American city. As measured by per capita homicides per year, it's thirteenth in the world—with the top twelve all located in Mexico, Venezuela, and Brazil.

We process these deaths through ninety-second news clips, if at all. But there's a lifetime of pain behind each killing. Mothers who lose their children, and then lose themselves. Kids who never learn to trust again after their fathers are taken.

I wanted to know what was causing so many homicides. And I wanted to understand something we all know exists but rarely interrogate ourselves: Why can't people in places like Ferguson live in peace?

As a reporter, I had investigated other homicides, but Jorell's death happened so close to home that I failed to see the full scope for some time. Going after criminals wasn't new to me, but doing so had never felt so personal, or presented such challenges to my family. I considered the potential repercussions for my wife and children, chasing an at-large suspect who had killed and could kill again. But I just couldn't let it go. Jorell's family needed to know who did this, and so did I.

There were times I was terrified, and considered abandoning this quest altogether. But ultimately this book became the most rewarding project I've ever taken on. Because, though it's a story of tragedy, it's also one of hope. My research taught me more about Jorell than I'd known during his life, and it helped me understand what made him such a remarkable kid. It brought me closer to his family, and closer to my own.

Investigating Jorell's death also helped me understand the dual worlds that exist in all cities: how wealthy people rarely cross paths with those living in poverty amidst violence. It helped me see, with my own eyes, the inequalities I'd taken for granted. I learned about the systems that conspired against Jorell, and how they might be torn down.

PART I

CHAPTER ONE

I grew up near the University of Minnesota's St. Paul campus, an area where, legend has it, you can throw a rock in any direction and hit a PhD. My dad's medical clinic was close; my mom's lab was even closer. At the local hardware store, just behind the gas station, I earned $4.25 an hour cutting glass to replace broken windows and helping old-timers with their home-improvement projects. My best friend, Eric, lived literally across the street. His parents didn't mind when I barged right in without knocking.

The high school I attended with my siblings, St. Paul Central, was located in a mostly Black neighborhood. We attended as part of a unique desegregation program, with white students from other districts bused in for an advanced curriculum called International Baccalaureate. As a freshman I found the place intimidating. From the outside, Central resembled a prison, and, during school hours, kept its doors locked with electromagnets. Inside, the bottom two floors housed the "regular" classes, while the advanced, mostly white classes were on the top two floors. The annual coronation to crown a homecoming king and queen usually pitted Black candidates versus white candidates, and you could count on plenty of booing in the crowded gym.

This was the early '90s, and my friends and I appropriated our identities from Black culture coming out of South Los Angeles: *The Chronic*, *Boyz n the Hood*, *Menace II Society*. We'd drive to the Mall of America in Eric's minivan, bumping Snoop Dogg's *Doggystyle* and trying (and failing) to pick up girls. After practicing tennis on our school's dilapidated courts, my teammates and I would use fake IDs to buy forty-ounce bottles of Olde English 800, and then pick up bathroom tissue multipacks. We'd put on Eazy-E, drink, and blanket the trees of our rivals' homes with toilet paper.

My adolescence was full of small rebellions. I once took a date to the local zoo—after hours, hopping the fence when it was closed. My teenage friends and I roamed the neighborhood at night, bored, sometimes breaking into unlocked parked cars and stealing their CDs. We devised elaborate schemes to get out of paying bills in restaurants. In high school I skipped Spanish almost every day, and instead I'd go out to grab fast food with my friends and occasionally get drunk. Despite this I got into a good college, with all the assumed ease people of my world expected, ready to start the next stage of my life.

My family is half WASPs, half scrappy European immigrants.

My grandmother's Orthodox Jewish family arrived a hundred years ago from Romania to Lower East Side tenements. After falling in love with a Christian man originally from Germany—my Grandpa Richard— Grandma Doris ran away from home. Some family members never spoke to her again, and her marriage with my grandfather didn't work out too well either. They had a messy divorce, and Grandpa Richard basically kidnapped my dad when he was thirteen and took him to Europe for a year.

My mom's family includes *Mayflower* descendants. Her dad, Grandpa Shelly, was short and bald, but a baller in the academic world, a celebrated University of Minnesota genetics professor who invented the discipline known as genetic counseling. He advised the Pope and appeared in hundreds of newspaper stories. Grandma Elizabeth was a talented biologist, but, due to the sexist norms of the time, was not permitted to be a professor at the university because her husband was one.

My mom skipped her senior year in high school to enroll at Cornell University, where she met my dad in the choir. Neither could sing much, but they began dating and attended an ROTC ball together. It's funny to see that picture, with my mom in a ball gown and my dad's hair shorn short, considering my dad soon abandoned his military training as their hippie instincts kicked in. My mom stopped shaving her legs and helped organize grape pickers with Cesar Chavez in California. After college she taught English for two years in Ghana. My father avoided Vietnam by volunteering in the VISTA program, where he taught GED classes in Mason City, Iowa.

He became an occupational medicine doctor, and my mother an entomologist, studying bugs. In our home's basement she kept an aquarium crawling with long, creepy, South American cockroaches. Their shelves held Bob Dylan; Joan Baez; *Free to Be You and Me*; *Our Bodies, Ourselves*; and *Earth First!* journals.

For my brother, sister, and me, public service was a critical part of our upbringing. My mom's parents opened their home to Hmong refugees, and when Grandpa Shelly retired he taught Hmong children how to write their language. My mom tutored a Vietnamese refugee named Quang for years; he'd fled his country by boat, forced to leave his wife and two small boys behind. We built houses with Habitat for Humanity, and in high school I organized a volunteer program at a Minneapolis soup kitchen. We attended summer solstice celebrations, called Pagan Parties; vacationed in foreign countries; and ventured into deep wilderness for camping trips. Even as my dad drew a doctor's salary, he bought his clothes from Goodwill and volunteered at a co-op grocery store so hardcore that it didn't sell chocolate or coffee.

Rejecting the conservative establishment was paramount, my parents taught me. Getting a corporate job and a McMansion was a fate comparable to death.

The summer after eighth grade, my church confirmation class journeyed five hundred miles south to St. Louis for a service trip.

The twenty members of this coed group wore ozone-depleting hair products and roamed the humid metro area in a state of high hormones. There was making out, petty rivalries, and anguished breakdowns. I can't think of greater torture for our youth minister and parental chaperone. We visited the famous inverted catenary made of Pennsylvania stainless steel (aka the Gateway Arch), and then the Budweiser brewery, where we got free soda and hard pretzels. We also volunteered at a day camp in the city, and at night slept on the floor of a church in the suburbs.

Four years later, as I considered colleges, I returned to St. Louis to visit Washington University. I'd chosen the right weekend, as one of my favorite rap groups, The Pharcyde, performed a free show in the quad for a bash called WILD, which stands for Walk In Lay Down theater. Frat guys lugged over couches and kegs for the occasion, and somehow this university-sanctioned event permitted underage students to get nauseous on warm Natural Light beer and Jell-O shots.

My college choice now cemented, my dad deposited me in my dorm that fall. I still knew very little about St. Louis. A snobby East Coast floormate decried the local cultural offerings and called our new home state "Misery." His roommate sold me a quarter ounce of marijuana for $35, which turned out to be mostly sticks and seeds.

The school's campus offered the full elite college experience, with collegiate gothic architecture and luxurious lawns in every direction. "This is like heaven," Jorell said when he visited with me years later. He had been born in Arkansas during my sophomore year, and would move to St. Louis as a kid. But in college I had absolutely no idea how the other half lived. I rarely traversed into the city other than for subpar Italian meals at The Old Spaghetti Factory. Instead I stayed on campus, started a humor magazine, and tried to read *Infinite Jest*.

I come from a family of academics and doctors, but I could not cut it as a premed. I dropped my chemistry major and took writing classes, mesmerized by the brutal short fiction of Raymond Carver. But I couldn't hack it as a fiction writer either, at least as evidenced by the failure of my literary magazine, called *Undershorts*. "Short, Orgasmic Fiction" was its slogan, but it went underwater with the first issue and continued sinking from there. I won a resident advisor job after my mother wrote me a letter of recommendation—I think the hiring committee thought the fact that my mom penned it was funny—but then I was nearly fired when I got caught smoking weed with my freshman charges.

I found my footing in journalism, however, scoring an internship at the *St. Louis Post-Dispatch*, where I covered a speech by homegrown broadcaster Bob Costas, who criticized the manner in which St. Louis had acquired its new football team, the Rams. "St. Louis felt such an inferiority complex that it forsook roads and schools…just to feel big league?" he asked.

During another incarnation of WILD, I was drunk and threw a nearly full can of beer at the band performing, called The Samples, whose brand of easy-going rock I detested. The can hit the bassist, temporarily shutting down the concert. They shone a spotlight on the crowd to try to find the culprit, but I ducked into the night.

I was no model student, or citizen, but could charm my way in and out of situations, and I took advantage of the career development network available to me. In a journalism class I connected with my mentor, *St. Louis Post-Dispatch* writer Robert Duffy, who would later get me my first job at the *Riverfront Times*. There, I interviewed the lead singer of The Samples. Without immediately copping to the Washington University beer can incident of a few years earlier, I asked him if he recalled it.

"I do remember that!" he said. "Our bass player was ripped—he was pissed. Man, you're so defenseless on stage because you have lights in your eyes half the time; you can't see. That was probably up there with beating up an old lady—it's really bad."

After I confessed to being the perpetrator, however, his tone changed. "We've all done stupid things. Don't worry about it!"

I laughed. I couldn't believe he'd let me off the hook so easily.

During my many years in St. Louis, I've come to realize it has an odd place in American culture; everyone knows the name, but few outsiders spend much time here. In recent years tourism has slowed to a trickle. Though it was once the economic engine of the Midwest, now it's dwarfed in cultural influence by nearby cities like Chicago, Minneapolis, and Nashville. But it's not dead yet; with nearly three million residents, it has the twentieth biggest metro area nationally, and it attracts small-towners from across the Midwest and South.

The city itself, however, has suffered. On a daily basis St. Louisans behold a grandeur that once was; the crumbled factories, abandoned homes, and painted advertisements on sides of buildings for companies that no longer exist. In lieu of current accomplishments, we recall past glories: the arrival of German beer baron Adolphus Busch in 1857, the World's Fair (and summer Olympics) of 1904, the release of Chuck Berry's pioneering first hit "Maybellene" in 1955, the Rams championship of 2000. It's a city forever looking backward.

St. Louis sits across the Mississippi River from the remains of an ancient Indigenous civilization, called Cahokia, which a thousand years ago housed the most populous settlement north of Mexico, bigger than London at the time. Cahokia's leaders lived atop giant earthen pyramids with flat tops, surrounded by fertile farmland. The civilization was later abandoned, owing in part to floods, and French fur traders established St. Louis in 1764, its location desirable for its proximity to the confluence of the Mississippi and Missouri Rivers.

Named for French King Louis IX, many parts of St. Louis have French names, though their pronunciations are butchered in hilariously Midwestern ways. (North County suburb Bellefontaine Neighbors, for example, is pronounced, "Bell-Fountain Neighbors.") French-born Pierre Laclède and his stepson Auguste Chouteau founded the city on money made from trapping, enlisting the help of local Osage Indians to hunt beavers, whose pelts were all the rage in Europe.

St. Louis was a part of the Louisiana Purchase, and in 1803, Napoleon sold the entire region to the United States for $15 million. A year later Thomas Jefferson dispatched Meriwether Lewis and William Clark to assess the goods, and they departed on their famous voyage from St. Louis. The city is called the "Gateway to the West," and Lewis and Clark's travels remain a foundational aspect of local lore, even if their expedition led to land theft from native people.

As part of the Missouri Compromise, the state of Missouri was admitted to the US as a slave state in 1821, and enslaved people were sold on the steps of downtown St. Louis's Old Courthouse—whose dome is modeled on St. Peter's Basilica in Rome, and is shown on nearly as many local postcards as the Arch. Since free state Illinois was just across the river, the local slave trade was particularly fraught in St. Louis, as its location made it easier both for enslaved people to escape to freedom and for free Black people to be kidnapped into slavery.

St. Louis is a Catholic town, known for its majestic Cathedral Basilica, Lenten fish fries, and a strong tradition of Jesuit schools. The American Catholic Church, scholars agree, was the largest slaveholder in the country, and slave labor was used to build local institutions including the Old Cathedral. In 1833 an enslaved elderly man named Thomas Brown wrote to his owner, St. Louis University president Father Peter J. Verhaegen, requesting to purchase freedom for himself and his wife. "Have pity on us, let us go free for one hundred dollars or else we will surely perish with the cold," he wrote, referring to the unheated loft of an outhouse where Verhaegen was pressuring them to move. "I will pray for you." His request was denied and there is no record of his ultimate fate.

In April 1836 a free boatman from Pittsburgh named Francis McIntosh disembarked in St. Louis, shortly before encountering two sailors fleeing police. For reasons unknown—perhaps McIntosh interfered with their pursuit—the police attempted to arrest him instead, at which time McIntosh produced a knife and severely cut them both. He was thrown in jail, but a gathering mob took the sheriff's keys from his pocket, and McIntosh was dragged back outside and tied to a tree on Chestnut Street. Wood was placed around his feet and set ablaze, and he was burned alive.

McIntosh was likely just defending himself, and he may not have even known the men arresting him were police. His killing was perhaps the first American lynching, but no charges were filed. An abolitionist publisher named Elijah Lovejoy railed against the lynching and its aftermath in his newspaper, the *St. Louis Observer*. The blowback forced him to move across the river to Alton, Illinois, before he was murdered by another mob. Lovejoy's accounts of McIntosh's killing fueled the antislavery movement. In January 1838, decades before being elected president, Abraham Lincoln spoke of him during an address in Springfield, Illinois. He decried the "horror-striking" treatment of McIntosh, "all within a single hour from the time he had been a freeman, attending to his own business, and at peace with the world."

In 1846 a Virginia-born enslaved man, Dred Scott, began legal proceedings in the Old Courthouse, putting the institution of slavery on trial. Scott had lived for years with his owner in Illinois and the Wisconsin Territory before returning to St. Louis, and when the owner died Scott sued for his freedom, arguing that his time in free states qualified him for emancipation. The case went all the way to the Supreme Court, which concluded that slaves weren't US citizens and thus couldn't sue.

This decision helped spark the Civil War, for which Missouri was an important battleground. As a slave state that never joined the Confederacy, it was bitter, contested terrain, where militias and mercenaries often held more sway than governments, and outlaws like Jesse James prospered. Governor Claiborne Jackson, a Democrat, held slaves, yet antislavery sentiment in St. Louis ran strong, spurred by abolitionist German immigrants.

Following emancipation, Black people arrived in St. Louis in huge numbers. Illinois native Annie Malone built her empire of hair care products here, becoming possibly the first female African American millionaire. She set up shop in a downtown well known for its Black entertainment district, Chestnut Valley, where Scott Joplin played his ragtime songs that helped create America's first popular music. Watering holes and brothels were jammed with piano players, helping develop jazz in its infancy. And W. C. Handy's melancholy "St. Louis Blues" became one of America's most enduring songs, later inspiring the name of the local hockey team.

St. Louis has played a critical role in every form of American popular music, from Chuck Berry, who inspired a teen dance revolution and helped invent rock and roll, to Nelly, who led St. Louis's ascent onto the national hip-hop stage. My favorite radio station in the world, midtown St. Louis indie KDHX, plays everything from the barrelhouse blues to alternative country, two more genres with strong roots here. St. Louis's literary contributions have been equally profound, with T. S. Eliot, Kate Chopin, Tennessee Williams, William Burroughs, and Jonathan Franzen each coming of age in the city. Never mind that they all left town as adults.

CHAPTER TWO

By 1999 Jorell's father, Joe Cleveland, had seven children, and his job prospects weren't panning out in Arkansas. "With the minimum wages they were paying, there was no way a single parent could provide without being on government assistance," he told me, after Jorell's death. He believed St. Louis would offer steadier work. He'd already broken up with Jorell's mother, Dianne Robinson, who had been going through tough times, including a serious car accident. Still, taking Jorell and his two daughters with Dianne away from their mother was a difficult choice.

In St. Louis, Joe found a job as a union roofer, sometimes working on the campus of Washington University, my alma mater. His family moved into a hundred-year-old townhouse on Gibson Avenue, with accented brickwork and charming design flourishes. These homes, found throughout the city, look largely as they did in 1900. Their durable, deep-red bricks, made by European immigrants and enslaved workers, came from the rich clay deposits formed at the confluence of the Mississippi and Missouri Rivers.

In 2005, not long after Jorell and I were paired, we brunched with my college friends at an artisanal spot near his house called La Dolce Via, and then, with Jorell riding on my shoulders, we walked past the vibrant gay and lesbian nightclub scene rising on nearby Manchester Avenue. Much of the area remained destitute, however. The neighborhood's name, Forest Park Southeast, was meant to invoke the grandeur of the nearby urban park, St. Louis's crown jewel. But it's a misnomer; to access Forest Park from Jorell's home required traversing an interstate, perhaps bypassing posted-up drug dealers along the way.

In an episode I'm ashamed to recall, after a friend and I had been drinking one night we decided we wanted cocaine, and it was my bright idea to try to procure some on Jorell's block. We pulled up in my car and asked guys on the corner if they had coke. They didn't, but sold us a small crack rock for $20, which we took home, chopped up with a credit card, and snorted. It was dangerous and didn't even really get us high.

Looking back, I'm disappointed in myself for engaging in such destructive behavior. In my desire for cheap thrills I completely ignored the bigger picture. What if this were the block where I grew up and these illicit sales were happening outside my bedroom window? Considering how much I cared about Jorell, I should have realized that my actions were perpetuating the misery on his street.

Jorell's siblings have fond memories of their time in Forest Park Southeast. "We had a lot of fun over there," his older sister Rece told me. "There was a lot to do. We was always outside." The kids walked to nearby Adams Elementary School, which boasted a new facility and dedicated teachers. In one of Jorell's classes—he must have been in third grade—he drew a picture of us standing next to each other, our arms spread wide. I'm wearing a crown, for some reason, and we're surrounded by floating hearts. It's captioned: "Ben-N-Jorell 4 ever." He gifted it to me soon afterward, and to this day I keep it framed in my office.

In the nearby Central West End neighborhood I purchased my first home, a one-bedroom condo in a high-rise, for about $100,000. I was attracted by the restaurant and bar scene in the area, and my condo neighbors were genial old gay men who invited me over for cocktails. Known for its cobblestone streets and mansions dating back to the Gilded Age, the Central West End received national coverage in 2020 when homeowners Mark and Patricia McCloskey brandished firearms at protesters who got too close to their million-dollar estate, once inhabited by an Anheuser-Busch heiress. In the wake of George Floyd's killing in Minneapolis,

Black Lives Matter activists had headed to the St. Louis mayor's house nearby, and pictures of the sixty-something couple on their lawn bearing guns earned them widespread derision, as well as speaking time at the Republican National Convention. Mark later ran for US Senate.

The Central West End was mostly white, while Jorell's neighborhood was mostly Black, despite the fact that they're adjacent. It's like that all over St. Louis, which has one of the highest rates of minority residential segregation in the nation. Black St. Louisans below the poverty line are nearly twenty times more likely to live in concentrated poverty than whites, the highest disparity of any big city in the country.

People in the area use a term called "Delmar divide," referring to Delmar Boulevard, which slices the city in half. Most people to its north are Black, while most to its south are white. This stubborn divide has remained for decades. For most St. Louisans, birthplace determines destiny. As the author Walter Johnson notes, someone born in the tony suburb of Clayton has a full eighteen-year-longer life expectancy than someone born seven miles away in the largely Black Jeff-Vander-Lou neighborhood in St. Louis.

When I was first getting to know Jorell, he'd come over and we'd splash around in the pool at my condo complex. I didn't spend much time considering the inequality of it all. We both were born elsewhere, so why was it that, upon their arrival, Jorell's family ended up in a dangerous part of St. Louis, while I ended up in a posh one? I'd studied inequality in college, and sometimes wrote about it as a young journalist, but when it came to my actual life I was downright incurious on the topic. Looking back, I suspect that, having been born privileged, I was content to let the subject remain strictly theoretical.

A few years ago I brought my sons to see the annual Fourth of July parade downtown. We took in a forty-foot-tall Uncle Sam balloon, a giant shopping cart tricked out with an engine, and a brass band performing on an antebellum-style steamboat-on-wheels. The boys were showered in confetti and candy. Thankfully a fellow parade watcher offered us bottles of water, since I'd come unprepared for the heat.

The most curious aspect of the parade was the first float, featuring a gown-clad teenage girl waving to the crowd, identified as a representative of the Veiled Prophet Society. This organization, which organized the parade, is shrouded in mystery. All I knew at the time was that it featured St. Louis executives and civic leaders operating in semisecrecy, each year crowning a new Veiled Prophet, who appeared in public with a long staff and a piece of white fabric covering his face.

The first Veiled Prophet Parade, I learned, was held in 1878 and featured Mardi Gras–style floats from New Orleans. It served as a "blunt assertion of social hierarchy," according to the *St. Louis Post-Dispatch*, a ruling-class response to a massive general strike a year earlier. The Veiled Prophet that year was announced as John G. Priest, the police commissioner who helped suppress the strike. Since then, however, the Veiled Prophet's identity has been kept secret. At a ball every year he chooses a Queen of Love and Beauty, a young debutante deemed "the fairest maid of his beloved city." She is crowned and sits on a throne beside him at a ceremony, described in a 2016 *St. Louis Magazine* story:

> The whole scene looks like the set of an Aladdin musical. The Bengal Lancers come out to show off their marching skills— and make fools of themselves, to the amusement of all. At one point, a lancer nearly spears a maid by accident, all part of the fun. "At least they're all wearing pants this year," one observer jokes.

In 2021 actress Ellie Kemper, star of *Unbreakable Kimmy Schmidt*, issued an apology for serving as the Queen of Love and Beauty when she was nineteen. (The Kempers are a prominent St. Louis family; Washington University's Mildred Lane Kemper Art Museum is named for Ellie's grandmother.) The organization itself also apologized for "the actions and images from our history," while noting that it places a strong emphasis on community service, and that its young "maids" have logged thousands of volunteer hours.

Yet many believe the organization preserves the status quo and perpetuates a racist power structure. They didn't permit African Americans until 1979, for example, which never sat right with St. Louis civil rights activist Percy Green. He was a McDonnell Aircraft engineer who'd previously climbed the still-being-built Arch to protest racial inequities in its construction contracts. In 1972 he sent in two female protestors to infiltrate the ball: Jane Sauer created a distraction by throwing leaflets off a balcony, while Gina Scott, wearing a ball gown, descended to the stage by a power cable before pulling the mask off the Prophet's face. The women were arrested, and the Prophet was revealed to be Tom K. Smith, a Monsanto executive vice president.

Yet such ceremonial racial antagonism paled in comparison to the institutional racism shaping daily life.

Around 1910 St. Louis real estate agents began administering housing covenants—promises that homeowners would not sell to African Americans. The Black population in St. Louis doubled following World War I, but they were shunted into the most undesirable neighborhoods.

In 1916, by voter referendum, St. Louis banned Black residents from living on blocks that were at least 75 percent white. A year later the US Supreme Court overturned this law, but the decision did little to stop housing segregation in practice. White flight took off around World War II, with families increasingly moving out to St. Louis County. The wealthy suburbs there often only permitted single-family homes with minimum-sized lots unaffordable to Black people. African American neighborhoods, meanwhile, were often zoned alongside commercial and industrial areas. As a result white neighborhoods had well-manicured streets, parks, and big lawns, while Black neighborhoods sat next to bars and factories.

This was the St. Louis region that Jorell and I arrived to, one specifically designed to separate white from Black and preserve the status quo. We almost certainly would have never met, were it not for the Big Brothers Big Sisters program.

CHAPTER THREE

At the dawn of the twentieth century, a New York City court clerk named Ernest Coulter argued against putting young boys into disciplinary systems intended for adult criminals. Founded in 1904, his Big Brother Movement, as it was then known, sent boys to camp, gave them free medical and dental care, and helped with job placement. During this time of great industrialization, Coulter emphasized the importance of acknowledging children's humanity.

Having started his career during the Spanish-American War as a war correspondent in Cuba, Coulter was one of those old-fashioned progressives who might not seem so progressive today. He became a lieutenant colonel in World War I, and later founded an organization to give military training to kids, some very young. Late in life he decried "pinks," "pacifists," and "crackpots" in letters to the *New York Times*.

But he absolutely believed juvenile detention was the wrong approach. Those who instead received committed adult mentorship in their "plastic age"—before twenty-five—were much more likely to become contributing members of society, he believed. Coulter's Protestant-leaning mentorship organization later united with the Catholic Big Sisters and a Jewish Big Brothers organization in Cincinnati. The latter's founder, a distillery salesman named Irvin F. Westheimer, found inspiration after looking out his window one day and seeing a young boy and his dog rummaging through a trash can in the alley. "God did not create all men equal," he said to himself, plopping on his hat and taking the boy to lunch.

Over the decades support for Big Brothers Big Sisters mushroomed. Its presidential patrons have included both Republican Calvin Coolidge and Democrat Franklin D. Roosevelt, and George W. Bush and Barack Obama were supporters as well. Research published in the 1990s ascribed positive benefits to mentorship, while also noting that mentors who abandoned their charges could cause damage. "The child views it as, yet again, they are not a good person and it's their flaw," said Jean Grossman, a senior vice president of Public/Private Ventures, a social research and policy organization. The organization has had controversies. In 2003 the right-wing group Focus on the Family called for a boycott of Big Brothers Big Sisters for permitting gay mentors. In 2013 the Justice Department temporarily froze the organization's funding, after it was found to have improperly comingled into its general fund more than $19 million in taxpayer funds intended for "at-risk" youth and others. Three years later Big Brothers Big Sisters agreed to pay back $1.6 million to resolve the issue.

But by the 2000s the organization had over a thousand national programs and was firmly embedded in the public consciousness. For the 2007 Super Bowl telecast the coaches of both competing teams, the Indianapolis Colts and the Chicago Bears, extolled the benefits of mentorship in a public service announcement. "Many kids don't have someone to help them compete in life," said Colts' coach Tony Dungy. "Change that. Be a mentor. Become a Big Brother or Big Sister." Today Big Brothers Big Sisters maintains an A+ rating from CharityWatch.

Despite its accolades, the group has always lacked sufficient male mentorship. "What we need is more Big Brothers," Coulter said in 1929, on the silver anniversary of the organization's founding. The same was true in 2005 when I inquired about joining. Many male "Littles" in St. Louis would never receive a match at all, I was told.

And so, after a colleague wrote me a testimonial and I went through a background check, I was quickly paired with Jorell. Though Big Brothers offered activity suggestions, the organization was hands off; we were left to do whatever we wanted. It was a blast. We'd shoot baskets at the YMCA and fool around on the weights machines, and I got him swimming lessons for his birthday. "Today, albeit with flippers—he learned to swim!" I wrote in my journal in December 2005. The following spring my then girlfriend, Courtney, and I went to Chicago to see friends for the weekend. We brought Jorell along for the ride, dropping him off with his youthful-looking grandfather, Cordell Cleveland. Before we said goodbye, Cordell took us to lunch at a South Side diner. "When you take time out for somebody it's good karma," he told me.

Jorell often wanted to go shopping. We ventured to the St. Louis Mills mall in the distant suburbs, where we watched the St. Louis Blues practice, drank bottles of retro soda, and played video games in a NASCAR-themed arcade. He eyed the gold chains at the island kiosks and the baggy apparel at sports-themed stores, but lacked the funds to buy much. Plus, he was too short to ride the go-carts, which bummed him out. "Riding go-carts is the only time I feel free," he explained, cryptically.

But his ennui was short lived. Soft spoken but electric in his enthusiasms, he talked up our adventures to his siblings, so much so that his older brother Jovan sometimes wanted to come, though I didn't allow it, since Big Brothers Big Sisters believed one-on-one time with the Little made them feel special. And I do think Jorell felt special. He'd wait outside for hours before my scheduled arrivals, his family told me. When I arrived he smiled with his whole face.

I felt special too; people appreciated my service. My editor Tom, never much for compliments, said I was doing a wonderful thing.

"Dear Ben," Jorell wrote in perfect penmanship, in a letter he sent me in November 2005, as part of one of his classes. "When I first met you I knew that you was nice. I really like your cat. She is black and white, she's cute. You are a fun Big Brother. Your friend, Jorell Cleveland."

Jorell and I were exploring cultures vastly different from our own. He would wander through my condo, examining everything—my books, my framed photos, my reporter's notebooks, my camping gear—while I witnessed for the first time what poverty looked like up close. I was taken aback when he used a plastic garbage bag for a suitcase and when I saw, in the Cleveland kitchen on the stovetop, a cauldron of cold, black grease, likely for making homemade french fries.

Jorell's diet was a constant sticking point. As a twenty-something bachelor I ate plenty of junk, but everything Jorell consumed seemed to be coated in grease or sugar. "I told Jorell not to drink sodas and only have candy once per week," I wrote in my diary. "He has no idea how to floss his teeth (I tried to help him)."

I wasn't allowed soda as a kid; even chocolate was banned in my house for a time. I wasn't suggesting Jorell consume carob—the gross chocolate substitute my dad brought home from his co-op—but I didn't want his teeth to rot. I wished he would at least eat the plate of rice and beans I served him.

Our values clashed in other ways. A few weeks before Christmas 2005, I brought him with me to the Kmart to buy a floor lamp for my condo. Inside the store he eyed a $20 remote-control car—tricked out with giant rims—and asked me to purchase it for him. I declined. Maybe I was feeling broke, maybe it looked cheaply made, maybe I didn't want to set a precedent. When we got back to the car, Jorell broke down crying, telling me his dad said he and his siblings weren't getting Christmas presents that year.

I felt awful. Even worse, that night Jorell called me to apologize. "I'm sorry for complaining about the car," he said.

"What? You don't have to say that," I responded. "I should be the one saying sorry."

I suspected that Jorell's father insisted he make the apology call, after Jorell had explained what happened at the Kmart. It felt like Jorell had been reprimanded simply for wanting a happy Christmas just like anyone else. And it was my fault.

Living in St. Louis during the mid-2000s, it seemed like everyone I knew got their car stolen. Mine wasn't, thankfully, but these crimes made me curious about the evolution of St. Louis. Growing up in the Twin Cities, it felt like the population's quality of life kept improving over the years. Here, however, that was not the case.

At the 1950 census, St. Louis had the fourth-largest population in the country, 850,000, I learned. But since then, the once-prominent city has experienced unprecedented decline, hollowing out from within.

The population loss was spurred by familiar national trends, including industrial pollution, manufacturing decline, and white flight. But locals have always felt that, with a little luck, the ship could right itself. In 1965, Walt Disney almost built a giant theme park here. A decade after opening Disneyland in Southern California, the Missouri-native Disney drew up extensive plans for a downtown St. Louis development called Riverfront Square, an embodiment of his love for Mississippi River culture. The park would have been enclosed in a five-story building two blocks long, but it was shelved at the last minute when city leaders declined to offer Disney the financing he requested. Disney World arrived in Orlando soon after.

But even as St. Louis city residents left for the suburbs, the region's economic growth continued, in industries as varied as engineering, banking, shoes, pharmaceuticals, beer, and pet food. By 1980 the city was home to twenty-three Fortune 500 companies, and per capita income was a respectable 89 percent of that in New York City. But with the relaxation of federal antitrust rules in the 1970s and '80s—which encouraged big coastal corporations to swallow up smaller companies in the Midwest— St. Louis has since been struggling to stay afloat. Today the region is down to nine Fortune 500 companies, and residents make only seventy-nine cents for every New York dollar.

"By almost any objective or subjective standard," wrote the *New York Times*, "St. Louis is still the premier example of urban abandonment in America." This was written in the late 1970s, but the sentiment is even more true today. Detroit gets the headlines, but St. Louis has seen a steeper population decline, to around three hundred thousand. Since the city's housing stock was built for more than twice as many people, and many abandoned homes were never knocked down, once-thriving neighborhoods are now dotted with "doll houses"—century-old homes stripped of their bricks; you can see inside them.

Walking around St. Louis is one of my favorite things to do, for both its splendor and its decay. One block might contain buildings of breathtaking craftsmanship, the next abandoned to prairie grass. In the city's stunning architectural remnants, it's impossible not to imagine grand eras past.

Yet even a casual stroll requires taking stock of your surroundings, considering the crime and the stark neighborhood divisions. St. Louis is an especially hostile place to live for African Americans, more than half of whom reside in poverty, and who comprise the vast majority of murder victims. African American Missourians are murdered at almost triple the national average, and the state imprisons Black people more than five times as often as whites.

It's difficult to lure young professionals to come here, and it's hard to convince promising young talent to stay. At the *Riverfront Times*, when we'd profile an exciting local artist, the premise was often, "Why hasn't she decamped for a coast?"

I've now lived in St. Louis longer than anywhere else. My friends often ask why I don't move back to the Twin Cities, which has a higher standard of living and better public amenities. Minneapolis is on the up-and-up, the kind of place where the building on the corner becomes a new coffee shop. St. Louis, meanwhile, is on the down-and-down, the kind of place where the building on the corner becomes condemned.

I usually cite the weather, but it's more than that. There's something about St. Louis that has seized me and won't let go. The beautiful brick architecture. The musical traditions. As a journalist, there's so much to dig into. Centuries of mismanagement and race and class antagonism—not to mention disease, flood, and fire—have created generational problems so entrenched that understanding them can take a lifetime. St. Louis is full of people who hang on despite long odds. There are so many stories here, suspended in the amber of a deep, murky past. It sometimes feels like you're confronting history just by stepping outside your front door.

In the fall of 2006, there was news: The Cleveland family's landlord had sold their house in Forest Park Southeast. The area was gentrifying, and they had to go.

Looking at the property records today, I see it was listed as "vacant and boarded" immediately after they were kicked out, and then sold for $15,000. "It is certainly possible that there was an illegal eviction involved," St. Louis housing expert Chris Naffziger told me.

Yet the move to Ferguson seemed like a positive development. Since they were buying their own home, they couldn't be displaced.

And in the family's first days, Ferguson held nothing but possibility. Their house on Oak Avenue had 3,300 square feet, enough space for a growing family, as Jorell's older brothers and sisters began having children of their own. Each side of the house had its own driveway, providing the Cleveland men plenty of room to work on their cars.

Joe felt so optimistic that he bought another house nearby, a brick two-bedroom to rent out. "Housing was booming," Joe recalls. It was the height of the real estate bubble, and he may have been victimized by predatory loans; real estate records show he sold the rental house in 2007 at a loss.

But the house on Oak was—and remains—the mothership for generations of Clevelands, always open to extended family members who needed a place to stay. This included Joe's then girlfriend, Tonya, a warm and accommodating caregiver for the elderly who would crack a beer when she got off her shifts. She was like a surrogate mother to Jorell.

In 2006, not long after they moved in, Jorell showed off the new house to me, its six bedrooms, its balcony, its giant backyard. I drove him and his younger sister Peaches to a coffee shop nearby, where we played Monopoly and had milkshakes. We took a circuitous route back to their house, passing the Liquor Doctor package store on Airport Road, the street that led to the local headquarters of the defense contractor Boeing, one of the region's biggest employers. Not far from there lived the white lawyer and lifelong resident whom Anna and I later hired to draw up our wills.

Culturally the place was all over the map, but I dug the vibes. "The neighborhood is much improved over good ol' Forest Park Southeast," I wrote in my journal. That Halloween, my then girlfriend Courtney and I took Jorell and his siblings trick or treating on Oak Avenue. Jorell dressed up as a garbage man, and kids were running around the street. It was a blast.

After Michael Brown's killing in 2014, most Ferguson media coverage focused on the racist local officials, rarely noting that the city, overall, was progressive in many ways. The white flighters were now mostly gone, and the city had large amounts of subsidized housing. A racially mixed crowd shopped in Ferguson's walkable downtown area, which was anchored by a popular farmers market, a bicycle shop, a wine bar, and an art gallery. Every May, thousands participated in 5K and 10K twilight runs, and the annual Ferguson StreetFest had live music and booths selling essential oils.

I loved visiting the Clevelands there, and on my next visit I arrived with my new CD—as in, rap tracks I'd made myself. Though I could not rap in a way you might call competent, I enjoyed filling notebooks with absurdist lyrics, and I recorded a hip-hop album at the marijuana-saturated, in-home studio of a local rap collective. Somehow this collective (whose members were raised Christian Scientists) overlooked my pitiful skills. To my shock Jorell actually enjoyed one of the tracks, called "Ian Has an Internet Girlfriend." The song was about a friend of mine who was catfished, and the melodic beat, from Chicago producer Midas Wells, papered over my lack of rhyme skills. "This one's my favorite," Jorell told me. I told him he could keep the CD.

Jorell's companionship meant a lot to me, at a time when my life was unstable. I drank too much, I could barely afford my mortgage, and I screwed up my relationships with women. But Jorell was always there. He never judged me, and was always glad to see me. Whenever I got knocked off my axis, Jorell pulled me back to center.

When the Clevelands moved in I knew nothing about the history of Ferguson, located twelve miles northwest of St. Louis and one of the biggest cities in North County. As I would later come to learn, it was founded in the late nineteenth century, originally marketed as a bedroom community offering clean air, cheap land, and a modern rail line that quickly delivered commuters downtown.

After the interstate system was built out after World War II, white families began arriving in droves to the burgeoning municipality. Multi-family housing was banned, limiting the Black population. A small section of town was known as Little Africa, where African American families lived in substandard dwellings that included log cabins.

For the white residents the schools were good, the fraternal meetings were well attended, and there was a strong sense of community. "Grocery stores took orders over the telephone and delivered them later that day," remembered one elderly Ferguson resident about the 1940s. "Service stations picked up your car, did any needed work, filled it up with gas and delivered it back to your home. Doctors made house calls, milkmen delivered and the White Bakery Company sold door-to-door. Oh, those yummy cinnamon rolls!"

By 1970 Ferguson had nearly thirty thousand residents. The town had its own newspaper, a thriving commercial center, and neighborhoods of colonial revival and craftsman bungalows. Many workers no longer had to commute to St. Louis as Ferguson had begun drawing industry of its own, such as the Universal Match Company, which made millions of matchbooks per year, and Emerson Electric, now a Fortune 500 company with over seventy-five thousand employees.

Some of my college classmates grew up in Ferguson. Their families came for the same reason people move to the suburbs everywhere—more space, safer streets, better schools. Who could blame them? Ferguson shared a school district with the adjacent suburb of Florissant, St. Louis County's biggest municipality. It's over two hundred years old, with vibrant Catholic schools, VFW halls, and an annual big top circus sponsored by the city.

Sure, Ferguson and Florissant were part of the St. Louis metro area; residents rooted for the Cardinals. But they were North County islands unto themselves. Their families were younger and wealthier. They held classic car shows, crowned beauty queens, and funded dedicated police departments.

They lived above the fray and worked to keep things that way. In 1968 an African American assistant school principal named Larman Williams wanted to buy a house in Ferguson. At first, the homeowner refused to show him the property. Only after the white pastor of Williams's church conducted a prayer meeting with the neighbors did the owner change his mind. Beginning in the 1970s, the demographics of Ferguson began to shift from white to Black.

CHAPTER FOUR

Not long after the Clevelands moved to Ferguson, I began feeling antsy in my professional life.

At the *Riverfront Times* I'd sometimes go weeks without finding a good story. Rather than blaming myself, I often found fault with St. Louis, which began feeling like a cultural black hole.

In late 2006 I flew out to New York City for a freelance story for the *Village Voice*, the country's most famous alternative weekly, about a rapper who'd been shot and was now in a wheelchair. I took the subway into the Bronx for my reporting, and in my free time hung out in Brooklyn bars full of good-looking people. My piece made the cover, and I began dreaming of life in the Big Apple, where I imagined my writing career taking off. Visualizing bylines in magazines like *Rolling Stone*, I put my Central West End condo on the market and gave my notice at the *Riverfront Times*. Perhaps most difficult was telling Jorell the news. He didn't understand why I had to go.

We had one last hurrah before I left town, in February 2007, at an overnight "lock-in" at a local recreation center, sponsored by Big Brothers Big Sisters. We both stayed awake all night, playing basketball, sliding down waterslides, and answering trivia contest questions. We consumed all manner of snacks, which likely contributed to the evening's lowlight, during a competition based on the gross-out hit show *Fear Factor*. Jorell competed against other nine-year-olds in a race to consume a plate of awful-smelling, spreadable pork liver sausage called braunschweiger. No sooner had he taken it down than it came back up. He vomited all over his plate and ran into the bathroom, embarrassed.

He recovered by the time the party ended, at 5:45 a.m. The organizers gave away the uneaten junk food, and Jorell was first in line. He packed up two-liter bottles of orange soda and Little Debbie snack cakes to go. "This is my hope," he said as he put his bounty into my trunk.

I didn't know exactly what he meant. I too hoarded sweets as a child, and could remember their availability (or lack thereof) determining my moods. But something seemed different for Jorell. It was almost like these sweet treats represented light in a cold world.

"I love you," I groggily imparted as I dropped him off in Ferguson. I was almost shocked to hear myself say it; I've never been the type to throw "I love you's" around. But Jorell had been saying it to me, and I'd finally gotten comfortable. He smiled and got out of the car. "See you in New York," he said.

I wasn't the only twenty-something moving to Brooklyn. Almost nothing was affordable in my desired neighborhoods, so I settled in a quasi-industrial zone in an area called Sunset Park. It was walking distance to the subway, and to trendy Park Slope, so I could get a good bagel. But it was directly on a trucking route, and the eighteen-wheelers rumbling over potholes kept me up at night. My roommate was an older guy who didn't keep the place clean. Before long we got bedbugs, which turned my life upside down for months.

I wrote more stories for the *Village Voice*, as well as the *New York Observer* and a glossy magazine called *BlackMen*, which featured voluptuous models and heavily tattooed hip-hop stars. Haggling over payment required me to venture out to the publication's headquarters in Paramus, New Jersey, where they shared a floor with a publisher of niche porn titles like *Plumpers* and *Leg Action*. I hustled hard, but staying afloat was not easy, and a few times I felt sure I'd have to move back home with my parents.

A bright spot was my relationship with Anna. With pale skin and long curly hair, she was quick to laugh and had a fierce intelligence. We'd actually met a decade earlier. She'd attended Northwestern University with my high school friend Sam, and for winter break in 1997 they and two other friends picked me up in St. Louis. We drove down to Anna's hometown of Birmingham, Alabama, where I experienced major culture shock. Anna's father spoke with a thick drawl, and we visited their country club. I'd never spent so much time with actual Republicans. Yet in many ways she was the family's black sheep, and I'd crushed on her even back then. Now she lived in Hoboken and worked for a New Jersey–based commercial real estate finance firm. To visit her I'd catch the PATH train at Ground Zero, where the World Trade Center was being rebuilt.

I deposited my bedbug-infested mattress on the street (along with a warning note), said goodbye to Sunset Park, and moved in with Anna across the state line. Though my cat scratched her furniture, Anna and I gelled, seeing shows at Maxwell's, walking along the Hudson River, and hitting up low-rent watering holes as research for my first book, about New York City's best dive bars. For the gig I was paid the princely sum of $1,000, as well as another thousand in drinking money. It suited my lifestyle, though I could have done without the weeknight visits to deep Queens, where once I was forced to duck into the bathroom to avoid a raging bar fight.

In March 2008 I brought Jorell out for a long weekend. It was his first time on a plane. He was waiting behind the attendant's podium when I arrived at the gate, a plastic lanyard with his ticket around his neck. On the train to my home he said how much he enjoyed the flight, and I told him about my first plane ride, at age five, traveling from Minnesota to Los Angeles. "Were you running away from home?" Jorell asked, in all seriousness. "No," I laughed. "I was going to see my grandfather."

We made the most of our four days together. We rock climbed at Chelsea Piers, perused art galleries, rode an elevator to the top of the Empire State Building, and took a photo with a Johnny Depp impersonator in Times Square. Jorell tried sushi for the first time; he couldn't believe he was eating raw fish. We swung on a tire swing in Central Park and visited the Museum of Natural History. Strolling Wall Street, he wanted to learn about stocks. We even saw a movie star in a diner, Emily Mortimer, from *Lovely & Amazing*, whom Jorell asked for an autograph. She looked flattered.

I asked Jorell: If he was old enough to vote, who would he vote for in the Democratic primary? He said Hillary Clinton, over Barack Obama, though I couldn't draw him out about why he felt this way. He tried to teach me a new dance popularized by a kid rapper from Atlanta named Soulja Boy, hopping from right to left and putting his arms above his head like Superman flying. "You're doing it all wrong!" he laughed as I flailed about hopelessly.

He asked me why I hadn't yet asked Anna to marry me. "Also," he wanted to know, "why don't you have a dog?"

As I wrote in my diary:

> A calm, contented feeling washed over me. Maybe it's because the almost-11 year old is so energetic, or perhaps it's being constantly needed and appreciated. As I've told many, he's a perfect kid, always enthusiastic.

Still, I had concerns about his life back in Ferguson. His left front tooth had recently been chipped, from a "butting" by his brother's BB gun, he said. He couldn't answer the basic math problems I quizzed him on, and didn't know how to tell time. At one point he grew tired of my questioning, telling me he'd rather be a roofer like his father than type on a computer all day like I did.

At the airport we learned his departure flight had been pushed back a couple hours, and we both became irritable. He browsed a gift shop, finally convincing me to buy a packet of overpriced gum for his sister Peaches. Our moods lightened as we played twenty questions.

"Man or woman?" he asked.

"Man," I said.

"Fat Joe," he guessed, a rapper whom I'd recently interviewed.

"Correct," I said. We both cracked up, that he'd been able to guess it so quickly.

In October 2009, when Anna and I got married in Birmingham, Jorell and his dad drove the five hundred miles south from St. Louis, stopping off briefly to see Jorell's mother in Arkansas, who was out of prison and working at McDonald's. They got me a card with a picture of a distraught bride addressing a bridesmaid: "I'm having second thoughts now that I've seen him do the Hokey Pokey."

The wedding week itself was a blur of coconut cream pies, mustard greens, cigars, and martinis, not to mention in-law drama. Relations between our parents had frayed after my mother expressed her enthusiasm for our country's new president. A mixture of tension and excitement kept me up the entire night before our wedding in my hotel room in the Five Points South neighborhood. Per tradition, Anna and I spent the evening after the rehearsal dinner apart, and I was a wreck as I finally arose at dawn. Jorell and Joe were staying down the hall, and I gently rapped on their door.

"Jorell?" I whispered.

"Yeah?" he answered.

"Are you awake?"

"Yeah."

"Do you want to work out?"

"Sure."

I gave him a pair of my baggy running shorts, which he cinched snuggly at the waist. We went downstairs to the hotel gym, and jogged on a pair of side-by-side treadmills.

"This helps calm my nerves," I said.

"Me too," he responded. We both laughed.

I thanked Jorell for the camaraderie, and that day I successfully surfed the logistical snafus, in-law glad-handing, and occasional moments of grace that encompass a wedding day. I walked the aisle with my beautiful bride at the Cathedral Church of the Advent, and later at the reception at the Mountain Brook Country Club Jorell and I posed for photos, him in a crisp polo shirt and me in my rented black and gray tuxedo.

A Dixieland jazz band called the Legendary Pineapple Skinners played our first dance, and I later took over as DJ. I drank Manhattans, danced to Miley Cyrus with my friends, and retired to the club's Cherokee Suite with my Anna, feeling satisfied and loved.

Not long after our wedding, Anna and I ventured farther into New Jersey to be closer to her work, moving into a rented one-bedroom duplex in a bedroom community called Summit. In the summer of 2010 Jorell stayed with us for five weeks.

He was two inches taller than I'd seen him last, with closely cropped hair and a plastic diamond in his right ear. Now thirteen, he was going through puberty right before our eyes. We put sheets on the living room sofa for him, and he was thrilled to meet our new dog, Pippi, a brown Dalmatian mix rescue with boundless energy. He soon began day camp at the YMCA. I was heartened by how quickly he fit into the new environment and made friends.

There was more good news. I'd taken on my first literary agent, and had signed a contract for a book about Southern hip-hop, titled *Dirty South*. The pay was abysmal, and my in-laws were wholly unimpressed. But I was confident of good things to come, and I discussed my writing with Jorell and Anna over long dinners. Afterward we'd have ice cream in the town square or watch a movie.

Jorell was usually well behaved, but not always. He was going through a sarcastic phase, much like myself at that age. "It's like we're suddenly parents...of a 13 year old boy!" I wrote in my journal. We picked out library books for him, but he'd only read for a few minutes before falling asleep in his chair. Anna and I didn't know if we should correct his grammar; we didn't want to impose our culture on him, but we also wanted him to be able to succeed at, say, job interviews. His education seemed shockingly substandard; he couldn't even name what country we lived in. We were also increasingly concerned about his diet. Once I gave him a few dollars to go buy milk, and he instead spent it on french fries.

"I didn't give you the money for junk," I said.

"I didn't spend it on junk," he responded. "I spent it on french fries!"

I complained when he forgot to remove the bathmat from the bathtub's edge when he showered, soaking it. Another time, with the bathroom toilet paper exhausted, he wiped himself with the shower curtain. (We didn't notice this until later, and didn't say anything.) I can only imagine how bizarre it must have been to inhabit our strange world. One afternoon Jorell and I went jogging with Pippi, coming upon a fancy neighborhood west of Summit Avenue. We slowed to walk along the edge of a sprawling, man-made lake, which was essentially in someone's backyard. Jorell was in awe. Ostentatious displays of wealth mesmerized him.

We had long heart-to-hearts. He told me shocking things about himself I'd never known.

"I got jumped a couple of times last year," he said.

"What?" I responded. "Were you hurt?"

"Yeah."

"Did you cry?"

"Yeah."

"Who did it?"

"These teen guys."

"Did you know them?"

"Not really."

"Why did they do it?"

"I don't know."

"You don't know? What happened after that?"

"My family sent out a group of fifty people to catch them."

"Did they beat them up?"

"Yeah, I think so."

I wasn't sure I was getting the full story, and this account got even scarier when my imagination filled in the rest of the details. I probed him further, about the problems at school he'd had for many years. He was held back in second grade for fighting, he said. But his main concern was starting school in the fall, which he dreaded owing to something called "seventh grade beat-down day" at Ferguson Middle School. Apparently it was an annual rite of passage. He'd heard other distressing rumors about the school as well, like that cliques ruled certain hallways, and those who went down the wrong ones got beaten up. To avoid this he wanted to go live with his mother in Arkansas, though that plan never materialized.

One afternoon, Jorell casually mentioned that he had two uncles in prison for murder. I almost didn't believe him when he said this, but later I looked them up. Incredibly, it turned out they both had high-profile cases that reached the US Supreme Court.

On the evening of December 29, 1991, Joe's brother Bennie Cleveland—Jorell's uncle—entered a convenience store in the town of McGehee, Arkansas, just south of Dumas, where Jorell was born. Bennie's girlfriend worked there, but they were on the outs.

Brandishing a loaded .22-caliber pistol, Bennie apparently intended to both rob the store and extract his girlfriend, named Paula Easter. He arrived with an accomplice bearing a shotgun, who promptly fired it into a wall. "I told you that no police could keep me away from you," Bennie told Easter. Another store employee, Michelle Nagle, interceded. Bennie fired upon her from a very short distance, and the bullet entered Nagle's right arm, at which point it traveled along the length of her arm, hitting her heart and killing her.

A customer who just happened to be in the store at the time tried to escape through the back door, but Bennie shot him too; the customer laid on the floor and played dead. Easter tried to hide in the store's cooler, but she came out after Bennie "told her that if she did not do so, she would never see her daughter again," according to court records. Bennie robbed the store, and then, with his accomplice and Easter, drove to Little Rock. The accomplice departed, Bennie procured crack cocaine, and stole a truck. He and Easter then drove all the way to New Jersey before being arrested. Bennie was charged with murder, attempted murder, kidnapping, and theft.

Though Bennie was initially convicted of all the charges, he claimed that Easter was not actually kidnapped—that she remained with him willingly. His conviction was first upheld by the Arkansas Supreme

Court, and then vacated by the US Supreme Court, sparking a new trial in 1995, during which he acted as his own lawyer. He was convicted again of the killing, the nonfatal shooting, and the theft—but not the kidnapping. He appealed again, arguing there was racial bias in the jury selection. The Arkansas Supreme Court disagreed, and Bennie has been incarcerated ever since.

The other imprisoned family member was actually Jorell's great uncle—Joe's uncle—named Tony Thrash. His case involved a prison break.

On July 6, 1980, a Dumas welder named Tommy Gill was murdered. His body wasn't discovered until weeks later, and local detectives had no leads for years. In 1984 they received a call out of the blue from Anchorage, Alaska, police, who said a woman named Deidra Gaddy had confessed. She was brought back to Arkansas, and claimed that, at age sixteen, she'd participated in Gill's killing along with Tony Thrash, who was then twenty-seven.

According to the *Arkansas Times*, Gaddy said she and Thrash had been living together in Dumas when they decided they wanted to take a trip. Since they didn't have a car, Thrash decided to steal a vehicle, hatching a convoluted plan involving both of them dressing up as prostitutes. They put on makeup and dresses and solicited a ride at a nearby carnival, where Gill picked them up. Thrash soon produced a sawed-off shotgun and shot Gill twice, Gaddy said, and they hid his body by a farmhouse. Not long afterward they robbed a pool hall and drove to Kansas City, where the truck broke down and they were soon arrested after holding up a liquor store. They were convicted of the robbery, but at this point authorities were unaware of any connection to the Gill murder.

Gaddy was released from prison first, and she made her way up to Alaska. It's not clear why she finally decided to confess, but she and Thrash were charged with murder. Before their trials Gaddy made a secret deal with the prosecution guaranteeing her testimony could not be used against her. The jury was not made aware of this, however, which hurt Thrash's case, and may have been unlawful. Though he claimed he had nothing to do with the murder, he received life without parole. Gaddy served only about five years.

A full decade passed, until in 1996 news broke that Thrash had escaped from his prison, just north of Dumas. From an *Arkansas Times* account quoting an Arkansas Department of Correction spokesman:

> Thrash put on a blue jumpsuit, which was what new officer recruits wore during training. He then mixed with a group of the recruits and officers during a shift change "and simply walked through the front gate with them." He was found six months later, living in Pennsylvania, and surrendered peacefully.

During his time on the lamb, Thrash committed no new crimes, instead focusing on uncovering information about his case. Working with confidants, including Deloris Robertson—the mother of Jorell's sister Iesha—Thrash learned of Gaddy's secret deal with the prosecution.

Even more stunningly, Gaddy soon decided to recant her entire testimony, claiming she'd implicated Thrash to save herself. "It was all a lie," she wrote in a sworn affidavit, "meaning that my confession was not true in that Tony Thrash was not with me." In 2008 the Arkansas Board of Pardons and Parole considered Thrash's petition for clemency, and voted in his favor. Thrash was elated but ultimately this was not enough: the governor denied his appeal, as did the Arkansas Supreme Court and US Supreme Court.

I was shocked to learn the details of these two murder convictions, about the potential miscarriages of justice, and the prison break. The stories seemed impossible to understand without context. Jorell's uncle and great-uncle may have made terrible mistakes, but they were also raised in crippling poverty and caught up in a justice system that was often racist, dysfunctional, and corrupt.

Jorell was so young that he likely didn't understand these complexities, however. I can't imagine what he believed his uncles' imprisonment said about himself and his family.

When I spoke to Joe about the cases in 2021, he said he'd visited his brother Bennie frequently for years, but that the COVID-19 pandemic had stopped him.

"I'm sure it's been hard on your family," I said.

Joe nodded when I said this, but then pivoted toward dark humor.

"Not knowing the whole details, folks look at me, like, 'Yeah, you one of them!'" Joe said with a laugh. "Whatever. It wasn't me!"

"Jorell has been through more than I could have imagined," I wrote in my journal, as our time together in New Jersey in 2010 wound down. On our last day we ventured two and a half hours by train to Coney Island, where we rode the wooden Cyclone roller coaster and the bumper cars. We watched a carnival-style sideshow, where the ringmaster pounded a nail into his nose, a sexy woman swallowed a sword, and a victim of thalidomide—the now-banned drug given to women with morning sickness—came onstage in an overcoat and prosthetic limbs, before removing them to reveal his nubs for arms. Jorell was impressed that the man wasn't ashamed.

"Best day ever," Jorell said as we headed back. I beamed. The next day, over brunch, Anna told him how glad we'd been to have him, and how great things lay ahead in his future. Returning home after putting him on a plane, the house felt too quiet.

CHAPTER FIVE

Though the work didn't pay me much, *Dirty South* was a chance to dive deep into a rich music scene and culture. My love for this hip-hop strain was informed partly by my wife's southern roots, and partly by Jorell, who turned me on to subjects like the wildly entertaining but highly combustible rappers Gucci Mane and Lil Boosie. Jorell was thrilled to hear the audio file after Lil Boosie called me from prison.

Though the lyrics often concerned wild parties and displays of wealth, Southern rap reminded me of the blues. Deep pain sat just beneath the surface, and despite my subjects' success they couldn't seem to get ahead in their personal lives. I spoke with the legendary rapper Scarface, who grew up in Houston's South Acres neighborhood and had been thrown into a mental institution after attempting suicide as a teenager. He later went to jail for missing child support payments. In New Orleans I visited Hollygrove, the neighborhood devastated by Hurricane Katrina where Lil Wayne was raised, though he was locked up on a gun charge.

Upon *Dirty South*'s release, in early 2011, I embarked upon my first book tour, beginning in St. Louis. I took a shot of whisky to calm my nerves before addressing the crowd at Left Bank Books, which included Jorell, his friend Jordan, and Jorell's father, Joe. The next morning I drove out to Ferguson to pick up Jorell, whom I was bringing to my reading in Memphis. Even more people were now living with the family since I'd last visited, including Jorell's twenty-year-old adopted sister Chaz and her seven-year-old son. Chaz and I chatted in the kitchen while I waited for Jorell to get ready. She couldn't work, she told me, because of her diabetes.

Soon Jorell bounded downstairs with his bags, and we loaded up my rental car. "This is gonna be a great vacation," he said.

"I think you're excited to miss a day of school," I said.

That night we stayed at a Candlewood Suites in Cape Girardeau, dipping in the pool before retiring to our queen beds. The next morning I let him sleep in—he didn't seem to get much sleep at home—before we decamped for Memphis. The approaching highways were lined with pumps and sandbags, to fight flooding from the rising Mississippi. In town, Riverside Drive was washed out and tourists were snapping pictures. "When else will we be able to say we went swimming on Beale Street?" a man quipped.

The book reading was similarly a wash out, though I couldn't blame the flooding. Wearing a ballcap and a wrinkled thrift store shirt, I spoke before maybe five people, with Jorell videotaping the proceedings on my phone. I sold about two books. It didn't bother me, though, since Jorell and I had such a good time. I'd been to Memphis before, but Jorell hadn't, and it was thrilling to see it fresh through his eyes. Though he hardly knew who Elvis was, he pored over every inch of Graceland, from the Jungle Room to the pink Cadillac to the queen-size bed on the *Lisa Marie* plane, complete with gold-plated safety belts.

We ate barbeque on Beale Street, where he dumped sugar packets into his already sickly sweet tea. Afterward we visited the Memphis Music Foundation so I could do a little book-related networking, and when we exited Jorell saw and identified—from two blocks away—the Lorraine Motel, where Martin Luther King Jr. was murdered. (His killer, James Earl Ray, lived in St. Louis for much of his life, and King's killing was precipitated by Ray's 1967 escape from the Missouri State Penitentiary.)

We walked over to the motel. It had been transformed into a civil rights museum, and it was under renovation. Even though it was closed, Jorell was thrilled just to see it, to be standing in its space.

On the way back to our Memphis hotel, we passed through a poor neighborhood.

"This is the ghetto," he said.

"Yeah," I said, looking out the window, trying to figure out what to say. "I mean, it's not fair that white people get to live in the better areas and Black people in the worse ones."

"Yeah," he responded. "But they used to be nice areas and the Blacks made them bad by putting trash everywhere."

This comment fairly shocked me. I muttered something about redlining and racist housing practices, but ultimately trailed off. They didn't tell you how to handle conversations like this in the Big Brothers Big Sisters manual. At the historic downtown Marriott on Monroe Avenue, we spent more time in the pool. At the breakfast buffet he served himself eggs, sausage, and French toast, drenching the entire plate in syrup.

"You can't always eat stuff like this!" I castigated him, insisting he would be headed for diabetes if he kept it up, like his sister Chaz.

"That's just what people eat for breakfast," he said, sulking, before dumping the food in the trash and grabbing a banana instead.

I felt terrible. Throughout the trip I was torn between simply enjoying my time with him and trying to change his behavior. There was a part of me that just couldn't leave him alone, that felt a dubious responsibility to try to fix everything. After learning he was failing pre-algebra, I quizzed him on math problems as we drove back to St. Louis in the dark. He was fourteen, but he had never been taught the concept of "x." I tried to break it down for him, until he was correctly solving for "x" in problems like 4x-1=15.

"I didn't realize it could be so easy," he said.

"It makes me think he just needs personal attention in school," I wrote in my diary. "He reminds me of myself in a lot of ways, all energy and enthusiasm."

My talk with Jorell's sister Chaz in their family's kitchen was the last time I would see her. She died not long after we returned from our Memphis trip, on June 12, 2011, from liver and kidney issues, leaving behind a young son. I learned about it over the phone when I was back in New Jersey. "She was a very young mother, daughter, sister, and mentor," said her sister Iesha.

Jorell didn't have a lot to say, other than that he missed her. I tried to find the words to console him, and also his brother Jovan, who was hit especially hard. Though Jorell and Chaz weren't related by blood, Chaz and Jovan had the same mother, a woman from Arkansas named Kim Jones, who later died when her diabetes got so out of hand that she developed kidney failure and gangrene, which required one of her legs to be cut off. "I feel lost and numb," said Jovan.

In the midst of all this I got a new job, as *L.A. Weekly*'s music editor. Anna and I moved across the country, finding an apartment on a bright street near the Los Angeles County Museum of Art. Anna telecommuted to her office in New Jersey. I joined a heavyweight staff that featured a pair of Pulitzer Prize winners, including Jonathan Gold, the famed food critic who mentored me in his previous discipline—gangsta rap. When I was still in elementary school, Gold wrote the first cover story about the pioneering group N.W.A.

My next book, *Original Gangstas*, would focus on the West Coast sound, and during my time at the *L.A. Weekly* I got to interview my childhood favorites. I met Dr. Dre and label executive Jimmy Iovine at a charity gathering, hung out with Ice Cube at a Coors Light–sponsored event, and talked with Snoop Dogg while he was smoking a joint and modeling Swedish socks (true story). Visiting Eazy-E's former house in Compton, I was shaking as I stepped out of the car. In the movies and music of my adolescence Compton had been portrayed as the scariest place on Earth, and I worried people would mistake me for a narc. Eazy's son Eric Wright Jr. just laughed when he answered the door, however, noting that if anyone paid me any attention at all they'd just assume I was a Mormon missionary.

In the meantime…Anna and I had a baby. Two, actually, boys born two and a half years apart at UCLA hospital. These were natural births heroically delivered by Anna, who made it look easy, and overseen by our doula Dawn, who in her spare time starred in music videos and hostessed at the Chateau Marmont. Anna and I moved into a house on a Culver City cul de sac, and tried to withstand the roller coaster of life as two working parents caring for two babies, a cat, and a dog, with no family nearby. We should have had Jorell out there to visit, but we never did.

I missed him, and I missed St. Louis. In a land of perpetual sunshine with extraordinary live music and cultural offerings, it might sound crazy that Anna and I were contemplating moving back to the Midwest, but the cost of living in Los Angeles was making us anxious. We wanted space to spread out, and to be closer to our families.

Jorell called me now and then, but he wasn't much for chitchat. In the fall of 2013, he casually mentioned that his dad had been nonfatally shot—by one of Jorell's former best friends.

"What?" I exclaimed. "What happened?"

The guy went by Lil Glen, Jorell said, and he lived just up the street from the Clevelands. Jorell was reluctant to tell me the whole story, but I managed to make sense of it all after consulting other family members and reading the police report.

Lil Glen and Jorell had been very tight in junior high, it turns out. Best friends, practically. Glen frequently spent nights at the Cleveland house. He was a bit slow—Glen's mom later told police he had a "mental disability"—but Jorell stood up for him. "He always had Glen's back," said Jorell's sister Rece. "He'd protect Glen if anyone had a problem with him."

One night in early July 2013, while the Clevelands were out of town, Lil Glen broke into their house and stole a number of items. It's not clear why he did this (Rece suggested peer pressure), but his intimate knowledge of their home helped him execute the crime.

Upon the Clevelands' return it quickly became clear that Glen was the guilty party. He tried to sell some of the stolen items—specifically, Joe's guns—to a woman who lived nearby. She immediately recognized them as Joe's, and she told him. Joe and Jorell went over to Glen's house to confront him, but before they could reach the front door, Glen came out and began shooting at them. Joe was hit, but they escaped in Joe's truck.

Thankfully Jorell was unharmed, but his dad had to be taken to the hospital, where his wound was dressed.

The police were called. Glen was taken to the St. Louis County Jail, his bail set at $100,000. "[Joe] Cleveland had a small bullet wound on the right side of his lower back, just under his pant line," reads the Ferguson police report. "His truck... had been hit with some bullets also."

I was stunned by this, but Jorell didn't want to talk about it. He seemed embarrassed, somehow, or didn't think it mattered as much as I did. Eventually Glen pled guilty to second-degree felony assault. In September 2014 he received five years in prison, though he'd serve less.

Joe's wounds never really healed; he still limps today.

Receiving this news shook me up. It was so casual, this violence, seemingly born out of poverty, loose gun control laws, and the lack of access to proper disability and psychological care. I was also disturbed that Jorell hadn't told me about it until months after the fact. He almost acted like it was no big deal.

I began to feel worried for Jorell's safety. From two thousand miles away, his life seemed to be chaotic and perilous. It was only upon moving back to St. Louis, however, that I got to see it up close. Unfortunately, that's when I realized things were even worse than I'd imagined.

CHAPTER SIX

Visitors to St. Louis will look for the city's landmarks: the Arch, Busch Stadium, the Old Courthouse, or the City Museum. But the St. Louis experienced daily by most of the region's population is the expansive county, which is separate from the city and has more than three times as many residents.

Containing nearly ninety municipalities, St. Louis County cups the city like the letter C. Many of these towns have less than a thousand residents, operating as tiny fiefdoms that award patronage jobs and rely on speed traps and petty fines to make payroll. The county is a bureaucratic mess, and it siphons off the city's tax revenue. Plans to combine the city and county (as they were before 1877) are perpetually floated and then shot down.

The segregation that has plagued St. Louis for so long has simply mirrored itself out in the suburbs. South County is white and middle class, West County is white and wealthy, North County—where Ferguson is located—is Black and poor.

Yet there are many exceptions to these generalizations. In fact, North County's demographics have been in flux for decades, and I find the place uniquely fascinating. Old traditions do battle with new ones. Superfund sites give way to strip malls and historic buildings. Subsidized housing surrounds a fancy golf club. Vestiges of the area's once-great wealth include abandoned pools and ornate mansions selling for pennies on the dollar.

In the late 1950s, an interstate was built directly through the county's most important African American cemetery, Washington Park, displacing thousands of bodies. Since then giant billboards and a cell phone tower have been erected on the cemetery grounds, yet it somehow remains an oasis of serene calm. My favorite North County micromunicipality is Champ, with a population of thirteen. It was founded by a former shot put champion who envisioned building a sports stadium there that never materialized. Now it houses a landfill.

Bounded on three sides by the snaking Missouri River, North County sprawls from unincorporated Earth City—home to the St. Louis Rams's practice facility, before the team left for Los Angeles—to the breathtaking confluence where the Missouri River joins with the Mississippi River, a marshland-surrounded habitat for wintering trumpeter swans and ospreys hunting for fish. Elsewhere, North County is home to both dense woods and rolling native grasslands, as the deciduous forest of the eastern US meets the western prairie.

North County's dozens of municipalities have vivid monikers like Cool Valley, Black Jack, and the deceptively named, poverty-stricken Country Club Hills. They can be difficult to differentiate, like the adjacent, twin municipalities of Vinita Park and Vinita Terrace, which recently voted to merge.

Historically significant North County burghs include the small city of Pine Lawn, still the countryside in the early nineteenth century when William Clark moved there following his westward voyage with Meriwether Lewis. He picked snacks from his fruit trees, hunted with his grandson, and, in his capacity running the region's Indian affairs, signed treaties stripping the native Osage of their land.

Prominent North County municipality Jennings was named for Virginia farmer James Jennings, who purchased three thousand acres with $15 in gold in 1839, and whose dozens of enslaved people built his twenty-three-room mansion. In fact, more enslaved people lived in North County than any one part of the city, likely because wealthy city founders owned land there. "My ancestors were property and were as much a part of the mechanism as the horse, and the wagon and the saw mill. We were people, but we were a hammer. We were a saw," KMOX radio journalist Carol Daniel told the *St. Louis Post-Dispatch*. Daniel also wrote the foreword to Andrew J. Theising's book *In the Walnut Grove*, whose title refers to the stunning Taille de Noyer antebellum mansion in Florissant, which ran on slave labor and was home to the area's last "aristocracy." Now available for tours, Taille de Noyer just so happens to be located on the grounds of Jorell's high school, McCluer.

In the century following the Civil War, North County was almost entirely white, until, all of a sudden, it wasn't. The demographic flip took place partly because African Americans were kicked out of their St. Louis homes. In 1959, as part of a "slum clearance" project, the city began razing Mill Creek Valley, an African American neighborhood and business district that housed some twenty thousand residents, not to mention hundreds of Black-owned businesses.

Many moved to the famous Pruitt-Igoe housing projects, a series of St. Louis high-rise buildings that opened in 1955, designed by famed architect Minoru Yamasaki, who went on to design the World Trade Center. Pruitt-Igoe was initially hailed for its attractive, modern apartments and layout meant to encourage communal activity. Resident Robert Ellis remembered jumping from building to building via the rooftops with his playmates, and riding atop elevators from inside the shafts. Soon, however, the neglected facilities descended into squalor. Crime began to accelerate; firemen demanded police escorts to enter the buildings, and residents felt like prisoners in their own homes. The towers were condemned, and their 1972 demolition was televised.

The housing projects model gave way to the Section 8 housing program. Established in 1974, Section 8 is a voucher system that theoretically gives low-income people the choice of where to live. In practice, however, choices are limited. Ferguson was one of only a few better-off suburbs that began permitting multifamily dwellings. Many of its landlords accepted the vouchers, and as a result Ferguson began drawing low-income Black families from the city.

This played out against the controversy of school desegregation and civil rights protests. Many Black residents looking to buy homes faced racial "steering," with realtors pointing them toward more run-down areas. Meanwhile, some real estate speculators attempted "blockbusting," seeking to create panic by moving Black families into blue-collar white neighborhoods, in an attempt to scare white neighbors into selling quickly. According to *The American Prospect*:

> Sometimes, agents hired black youth to drive around blasting music, placed fictitious sale advertisements in African American newspapers (and showed copies to white homeowners), or hired black women to push baby carriages around.

Of course, many African Americans moved to Ferguson for the same reason white families did—safe schools and clean streets. The Black population in Ferguson reached 14 percent by 1980 and 25 percent by 1990. "There was an influx of Black residents," remembered Dorothy Seiter, publisher of the *Ferguson Times*, in a documentary about this era called *Where the Pavement Ends*. "Prior to that time we seldom saw a Black person, even though our neighboring community is [the primarily African American city of] Kinloch. Many people moved out, the white people, because they were afraid Ferguson was going to become a ghetto."

These white families decamped to exurban areas like St. Charles County, where they could get a big house and spacious yard for cheap. By 2000 Ferguson was 53 percent Black, and today the African American population accounts for over two-thirds of the residents. It and other North County towns have become what Samuel Kye, a sociologist who studies residential segregation, calls "ethnoburbs."

People have long moved away from urban centers for a better life, but that model has been turned on its head. American suburbs now have more poverty than the cities, and in places like Ferguson the public school systems have eroded while crime has accelerated.

By the early 2000s North County was a nexus for cocaine trafficking, by way of a notorious crew called the Black Mafia Family (BMF). Run by a pair of brothers from Detroit named Demetrius "Big Meech" Flenory and Terry "Southwest T" Flenory, BMF gained fame for its lavish parties featuring zebras and lions, and even rented billboards reading, "The World is BMF's." Much quieter was their operation running hundreds of kilos per week through Florissant-area homes, according to the book *Black Mafia Family, St. Louis: The Untold Story*.

With quick access to interstates heading in every direction, North County made for an ideal distribution center. BMF opened restaurants around town, purchased exotic cars, "made it rain" on strippers they flew in from around the country, provided dancers for a Nelly video, and joined traditionally white golf clubs. But the end came quickly. On October 25, 2005, Terry Flenory's going-away party in North County was raided, and he was arrested. He and Big Meech received thirty-year prison sentences for their crimes.

North County's danger makes daily life for some citizens nearly unbearable. In 2020 the wife of Jorell's dad, Ashleigh Selmon, was the victim of an attempted carjacking during a trip to Walmart for groceries. One of the perpetrators—only sixteen years old—pulled out a gun, a threat to which Ashleigh responded by removing the firearm she wears in her bra. She shot at him; when he put up his arm to cover his face, the bullet struck his hand. The assailants tried to escape, but a citizen who'd witnessed the attempted robbery blocked them in with his own vehicle, and they were arrested by police. Ashleigh was shaken up, and shocked to learn the sixteen-year-old had been armed only with a BB gun.

Joe Cleveland laments that, in an area that once felt safe, he's now sometimes reluctant to leave his own house. "It's crazy enough out here just pulling up to the service station to get gas," he says.

The Cleveland family thought they were leaving the high crime rate of St. Louis behind when they moved to North County in 2006. But Ferguson's reputation as a safe, quiet community quickly became a thing of the past.

I was excited to return to the Midwest, upon moving back to St. Louis in 2014 with my family. We initially considered living in the city, and we saw some gorgeous houses online. But it became clear that wasn't going to happen, since the city schools were a mess. In 2007, the state of Missouri took over the system, stripping the district of its accreditation for the next ten years. There were good schools here and there, but they often involved a lottery, and we didn't want to take chances with our boys' educations. So we chose a midcounty suburb I'll call Ashwood.

Though our wealthy neighboring municipality is almost entirely white and doesn't permit multifamily dwellings, Ashwood is more diverse, particularly our neighborhood, which has maybe one-third white families, one-third African American families, and one-third immigrants from countries such as China, India, and Ethiopia.

But when it comes to zoning, Ashwood has been part of the problem. While jogging across the railroad tracks, I noticed subsidized housing sandwiched in by a cab company, a metal works company, and other loud, dirty businesses. This withering residential area is a historic African American community, one of the few parts of St. Louis County where free Black people were allowed to settle after the Civil War. Lots there were sold for as little as $25 in the 1890s, writes Colin Gordon in *Citizen Brown: Race, Democracy, and Inequality in the St. Louis Suburbs*:

> Many of the first lots went to former slaves or their children.... The occupational mix included day laborers, farm workers, clay- and brickyard workers, and servants.

But the expansions of Ashwood and an adjacent town squeezed this community. These two traditionally white suburbs "protected" themselves through a combination of annexations and zoning decisions, ensuring that the African American community would remain "an 'isolated pocket' of unincorporated land." Today, this area barely registers. One of its only recent mentions I could find was a *St. Louis Post-Dispatch* article from 2012 about concerns over a metal-shaping company's chemical spill decades earlier, which contaminated the local groundwater. One resident of the community said she was worried the chemicals had caused heart problems in her now twenty-five-year-old child. "I wouldn't have purchased a home in this area if I would have known about the contamination," she said.

My issues with the area were much more mundane. When we arrived to Ashwood I was used to city living, and was disappointed that we couldn't walk to a coffee shop or any decent restaurants. White people problems, you might call them. On the other hand, the city was only a ten-minute drive, and our neighborhood was perfect for kids. Young families lived all around us. Our backyards ran together, mostly without fences, creating a huge field of grass for the kids to play. As they got older, our boys rode their scooters and bikes to the park, and they played soccer at the recreation center just up the hill. Anna found a great job managing investments for a health system, and I worked on my gangsta rap book from my office in the basement.

Jorell was thrilled that we'd moved back, and I went out to Ferguson to see him soon after our arrival. The backyard of the Cleveland house was now filled with barbeque equipment and rusting cars, and the garage was cluttered with tools and lawn-maintenance equipment. When I pulled up Jorell was out front, shirtless, holding a wrench in his hand and working on an old Buick. I was struck by how handsome and strong he looked. "How are you doing?" I said, parking in one of the two driveways that bookended the lot.

"Good," he said, giving me a sleepy hug.

"*What* are you doing?" I asked.

"Fixing the brakes," he said.

Many of the Cleveland men were jacks-of-all-trades who could roof, do electrical work, light plumbing, and oil changes, but I wasn't aware that Jorell knew anything about automobiles. As for this car, his dad got it for him.

"But you don't have your license."

"I have my learner's permit, though," he said.

"Were the brakes out when he gave it to you?"

"No."

"Then, how did you learn they didn't work?"

"I crashed into a tree."

"Seriously?"

"Just softly, though," he added. "I wasn't going fast."

"Are you okay?"

"Yeah, I'm fine. But I have to fix these brakes."

In such moments I felt awash in conflicting feelings. I was glad he was learning about cars, but would have preferred he didn't have to be a crash test dummy. It was the kind of thing that made me more eager than ever to provide positive guidance in his life.

Since I knew nothing about cars, I tried to help him in other ways. A few weeks later we opened an account at US Bank. He'd begun doing odd jobs around the neighborhood for cash, and he was worried about people around him stealing. I cosigned so he would be approved, and he got a debit card and learned how to balance a checkbook. I opened an email address for him on Yahoo with the password "Littlebrother1." I told him to use a condom with his girlfriend, and tried to convince him of the merits of higher education.

Anna and I put money into an account to help him pay for a trade school or college. Even though he said he wanted to go into the military, it never occurred to me that he wouldn't eventually continue his education. That's just what you *did*, at least where I came from. I assumed he understood that life's doors closed to those lacking education.

Jorell appreciated the bank account, but now that I was back in St. Louis, I noticed he hardly ever asked me for anything anymore. As a kid he'd sometimes hit me up for candy, and when we shopped at Kmart he'd ask for toys. But now, when I asked if he needed money, he just shook his head.

He no longer wanted to rely on anyone else. He wanted independence.

Some teens are like this. Not me—I used to hit my parents up for everything from new tennis rackets to prom tuxedo rentals to magazine subscriptions. My brother Alex, on the other hand, was like Jorell. He always had jobs and work-study positions growing up, and he never asked our parents to support him, even when he moved out at age sixteen to enroll in college classes early. Over time I began to understand why.

Life is simpler if you're paying your own way. It's more dependable and regular, and gives you a sense of pride.

In the spring and summer Jorell cut grass, in the fall he raked leaves, and in the winter he shoveled snow, carting his shovel from door to door to solicit neighbors. He did roofing for his dad, he delivered phone books; he'd literally take on any task offered. Having money became a big part of Jorell's identity. He had a girlfriend now, Danielle, who lived in the nearby town of Berkeley and also came from poverty. He wanted to be able to take her to dinner and a movie. He also had other financial responsibilities at home, beyond what I could have imagined at that age. "He would make money, bring home a loaf of bread, a gallon of milk," Joe told me. "He knew that I was a single parent."

The problem was that Jorell couldn't often land a regular job. He was seventeen now, and applied everywhere he could, within walking distance and beyond, from the Schnucks grocery store to Subway to McDonald's to nearby auto body shops.

I helped him fill out applications, and was stumped by the constant rejection. The economy was rebounding, and Jorell was a hard worker who'd never been to jail. It was difficult to understand why he wasn't getting offers. I sometimes worried that a scar across his face—courtesy of a fingernail of an ex-girlfriend, who believed he was cheating—held him back. Just as likely it was his face itself. But he didn't blame racism, at least not to me. He just figured he'd have to hustle harder.

Jorell was never very verbal. My attempts to engage him in philosophical conversations usually petered out pretty quickly. Sometimes I felt like I didn't know him at all, especially after we became Facebook friends. I was disturbed to see him blanket his page with taunts against unnamed adversaries, featuring swearing and threats of violence.

When I brought this up he unfurled difficult-to-untangle accounts about misunderstandings involving former friends, denying any culpability, which left me with even more questions. On a more practical level, I had a hard time understanding why he was presenting himself this way. Couldn't potential employers see these posts and get spooked? What I couldn't decide was if they represented a legitimate threat or not. Anna speculated it was mostly a calculated facade, the product of having grown up in a tough area and not wanting to be taken advantage of. Jorell insisted these disputes wouldn't spill over into his real life.

I accepted this. But what I failed to realize was that Jorell's world was changing rapidly, and he was having a difficult time keeping up. In addition to his daily personal drama, a revolution was rising in the very city where he lived. Change was afoot, and Ferguson was about to go up in flames.

Some of our family thought we were crazy to move back to St. Louis when we did, just two months after Michael Brown was killed by a white police officer. The resulting unrest continued to reverberate throughout the St. Louis area.

Jorell wasn't friends with Brown, but he knew him casually. Brown was an eighteen-year-old recent high school graduate, who on August 9, 2014, stole cigars from a bodega called Ferguson Market & Liquor, which doubled as a mini grocery store in an area that didn't have many. When confronted by a clerk, Brown shoved him into a display rack of chips and then walked off with his friend Dorian Johnson. Moving toward Brown's grandmother's house, they were flagged by a police officer named Darren Wilson. Though accounts differ about what happened next, Brown and Wilson scuffled, and Brown was fatally shot, struck by six bullets. His body was left in the sun for hours, with his blood slowly trickling down the hill. Grieving and increasingly agitated onlookers posted about it on social media. The story quickly became national news.

"It was something about the way they let him lay there," wrote Ferguson resident and Washington University student Nia Plump. "I was usually unphased by the anonymous people who had been killed in Saint Louis, but this was almost literally in our backyard."

People placed teddy bears and flowers on a makeshift memorial to Brown, while protesters carried handmade signs paying tribute to "Mike Mike." After Dorian Johnson said Brown—who was unarmed—had raised his hands and begged Wilson not to fire, the phrase "Hands up, don't shoot" became a rallying cry. Peaceful protestors walked along West Florissant Avenue, through land once owned by wealthy slave owner and physician Bernard Gaines Farrar in the early nineteenth century. They chanted the Kendrick Lamar lyric "We gon be alright!"

The demonstrations turned violent after night fell, with local businesses set ablaze. Rioters destroyed eighteen buildings, from locally owned braiding supply stores and a chop suey restaurant to chain auto parts and cell phone stores, mostly along West Florissant Avenue. Stolen hair and other goods were posted for sale on Facebook. Heavily armed vigilante defense crews guarded businesses that included a gas station and a tattoo studio.

Cops fired rubber bullets at protesters and arrested journalists. The St. Louis County Police eventually ceded to the Missouri State Highway Patrol, and then the National Guard was called in. "They had choppers, they had smoke bombs, they was macing everybody, they had beanbag shots," remembered Jorell's sister Rece, who, along with their sister Iesha, was pregnant at the time. Helicopters circled overhead so loudly that kids couldn't do their homework, with police armed with military-grade Humvees, night vision sights, and Kevlar helmets. "I remember seeing tanks," said Jayson Tatum, then a standout St. Louis high school basketball player and now a Boston Celtics star, adding: "The National Guard brought in tanks being driven down the highway." Activist Cornel West, sixty-one at the time, was knocked over while demonstrating at the police department and was then arrested.

Clad in an American flag T-shirt, a protester named Edward Crawford Jr. picked up a burning tear gas container and, sparks flying, heaved it back toward the police. This image was captured in an iconic *St. Louis Post-Dispatch* photo, helping the paper win a Pulitzer Prize. The police claimed the canister hit an officer, and assault charges were filed against Crawford, which were still pending when he killed himself in 2017.

Some fifty students from Jorell's high school, McCluer—though not Jorell himself—walked out during a lunch hour, marching all the way to the Ferguson police station, where they met students from McCluer

North High School. Their chants of "Hands up, don't shoot" gave way to "Fist up, fight back," said a student named Marcus Stewart, noting that they didn't want to be portrayed as victims in need of mercy.

Jorell and I talked during this time, but I couldn't tell how he really felt about all of this. "I don't think he took no big offense to the Mike Brown thing, not that I could tell," said Jorell's dad Joe. But he was undoubtedly curious about the protests, and walked the couple miles to the center of the action with his friends and brothers.

"We wasn't even really necessarily protesting, we were just standing out looking at what was going on," said Jorell's brother Jermaine.

"Everybody was chanting, 'No justice, no peace,'" said Jorell's friend Big Ant. "They shot at us with tear gas, all types of stuff. We ran!"

Jorell and his group made their way into the QuikTrip gas station on West Florissant Avenue, which was engulfed in chaos. One member of their party grabbed beers and scratch-offs, while Jermaine and Jorell took rolling papers and cigarillos. A group of five or six men they didn't know pulled the ATM off the wall and dragged it past the store's front door. An alarm sounded. Someone pulled a car around. They lifted the ATM into the trunk, but couldn't close it, and the ATM fell out onto the ground. At this point the group abandoned the heist and sped off.

The QuikTrip itself was soon burned to the ground, reportedly following a false rumor that a store employee called 911 to report Michael Brown had robbed the store. Its smoldering remains became the protesters' primary staging ground, "their Tahrir Square, their Tiananmen Square," in the words of the *Washington Post's* Wesley Lowery.

Georgia-based rapper Young Jeezy found himself in St. Louis performing at a nearby casino on the evening of August 12, 2014, three days after Brown's killing, at the height of these protests. "That was the worst show in the tour, because you could tell people was on edge," Jeezy told me. "Should they enjoy the show, or should they protest?" After the concert he made his way to West Florissant Avenue, posing in front of the burned-down QuikTrip for an Instagram post that became one of the protest's most indelible images. "I had to see it for myself!" he captioned the photo. "The answer is not tearing down our own neighborhoods and communities, the answer is goin to the source of the problem in numbers. So many numbers that they know they don't have a chance."

Brown's funeral two weeks after his death drew more than four thousand people, including Jesse Jackson and Al Sharpton. But the protests weren't over; they were just getting started. The fatal shooting by police of another St. Louis man, Kajieme Powell, on August 19, incited further unrest. And the dam burst on November 24. That evening St. Louis County prosecutor Bob McCulloch announced that Darren Wilson, the police officer who had killed Michael Brown, would not be indicted on criminal charges.

Protesters surrounded the Ferguson police station before setting squad cars on fire and throwing bricks. Police said they sustained "heavy" automatic gunfire, and the National Guard returned. "[Before] it was more or less more females," Jamie "JC" Dennis of the Ferguson Community Empowerment Center told me. "Guys in their forties, my age, didn't really get out here until the verdict hit the fan and chaos ensued." Some sixty people were arrested that first night, and more stores were burned. St. Louis County Police Chief Jon Belmar said there was basically "nothing left" along a commercial stretch of West Florissant Avenue.

That same evening, freshly arrived to St. Louis, I covered a hip-hop concert doubling as a rally against police injustice, just blocks from where Jorell had grown up in Forest Park Southeast. Performers included local activist Tef Poe and a duo called Run the Jewels, the latter led by the rotund, bombastic rapper Killer Mike. He offered "thoughts and prayers for the people who could not hold their anger in, because riots are only the language of the unheard." My fears for Jorell were distilled further when he added, "I have a twenty-year-old son, and I have a twelve-year-old son, and I'm so afraid for them." Afterward I wove home on side streets, as the interstate was blocked by protesters.

The protests in Ferguson ignited despite the fact that, unlike Rodney King's beating in 1991 or, later, George Floyd's killing in 2020, there was no video of Michael Brown's killing. And once the facts came out, it was clear that Brown's death was no murder. The US Justice Department's investigation supported Darren Wilson's account, contradicting Brown's friend Dorian Johnson's claim that Brown had his hands up and told Wilson not to shoot. According to eyewitnesses, Brown attacked Wilson through the window of his squad car, punching him and trying to take his gun. Wilson shot at Brown, hitting his hand, and then he followed Brown away from the car as Brown retreated, before Brown changed course and began moving sharply toward him. This is when the fatal shots were fired. Neither the Justice Department nor Wesley Bell, the reform-minded St. Louis County prosecuting attorney who later replaced Bob McCulloch, charged Wilson with any crime.

The anger that inspired the unrest, however, went far beyond the treatment of just one person. It was about the institutionalized persecution of African Americans, which was explored in the Department of Justice's hundred-page investigation of the Ferguson police department and city government, published in March 2015. Despite its Black majority, Ferguson's power brokers remained overwhelmingly white, and the DOJ uncovered racist emails sent among officials, including one that "depicted President Barack Obama as a chimpanzee." The report also showed how extensively the local police department made everyday life miserable for taxpaying citizens.

The police weren't conducting quality of life enforcements that had the community's best interests in mind, or even just "driving while Black"–style offenses, like broken tail lights. Ferguson police made arrests and issued citations concerning nearly every aspect of daily life, from housing violations like "high grass and weeds" to "barking dog and dog running at large" ordinances to "manner of walking in the roadway." (Missouri State Senator Jamilah Nasheed was arrested and charged with the latter during the protests.)

Like other municipal departments in North County, Ferguson police, under the authority of city officials attempting to balance the budget, aggressively extracted wealth from Ferguson's poorest citizens. Those who couldn't pay the fines often spent time in jail. Ironically, Ferguson needed this revenue largely because of failed corporate welfare projects, like using municipal bond issuances to attract big box retailers.

The Ferguson unrest launched a long national conversation about race that continues as of this writing. Increasingly the conversation is not just about garden-variety racism—racial epithets, the Ku Klux Klan—but about institutional racism tipping the scales in everyday lives. Like many others, I engaged in heated conversations about white privilege with friends, family, and random people on the internet. The truth is, most of us were doing more talking than listening. My ultimate takeaway was that poverty and racism are inextricably linked, especially in St. Louis.

The activists Patrisse Cullors, Alicia Garza, and Opal Tometi founded Black Lives Matter in 2013, following the death of Trayvon Martin, the hoodie-clad seventeen-year-old fatally shot in Miami Gardens, Florida, by neighborhood watch volunteer George Zimmerman. Ferguson mobilized the movement. All around St. Louis, Black Lives Matter lawn signs began popping up. Young people dropped out of school and quit jobs to join the fight. Protests spread around the country and the globe, eventually touching more than 170 cities worldwide, including my hometown of St. Paul in July 2016. At a traffic stop less than two miles from where I grew up, a motorist named Philando Castile was killed by a police officer, with his girlfriend and her daughter in the car. (The officer claimed Castile was reaching for a gun.) Born in St. Louis, Castile was a beloved cafeteria supervisor at a St. Paul magnet school where some of my friends sent their children.

The name Black Lives Matter—as a sentence, as a fact—rang true, and in 2020 the cause became ubiquitous following the killing of George Floyd and the release of a video showing Minneapolis police officer Derek Chauvin kneeling on his neck. Former Republican presidential candidate Mitt Romney endorsed the movement, as did multinational brands like Microsoft, Uber, and Netflix, the latter going on to promote a "Black Lives Matter" collection of titles.

The cause had gone mainstream. Mike Mike's death had ignited the biggest protest movement of our time, and it coalesced right in Jorell's backyard. No longer could Americans ignore how we shunted people like Jorell into the dark recesses of society. The days of walking around like nothing was wrong were over.

CHAPTER SEVEN

In Ferguson the fires eventually died down, and as winter fell in late 2014 the plywood-covered storefronts on West Florissant Avenue were painted with colorful murals portraying themes of hope.

Powerful businesspeople and politicians from around the country arrived to survey the damage and pledge assistance, such as Howard Schultz, who green-lit the opening of a Ferguson Starbucks. Local health-care giant Centene rolled out a $25 million call center. St. Louis County Executive Steve Stenger hyped a massive revitalization project on West Florissant Avenue.

These were nice gestures, but this goodwill didn't amount to much. Very little of the revitalization project funding materialized, and Stenger later resigned in 2019 amidst corruption charges. A closer look at Ferguson's dysfunction showed that just throwing cash at the problem wasn't a viable solution. Rather, by the very nature of its design, the city had been rigged against poor people from the beginning.

To better understand the underlying issues at work, I talked to the renowned, Minnesota-based urban planner Charles Marohn. Marohn observed that Ferguson, like many American suburbs that came of age following World War II, was doomed to fail. In these suburbs' early days, state and federal governments subsidized their roads, sewer systems, and other infrastructure, leading to rapid growth. But this same infrastructure now weighs them down, as these suburbs can't generate the money they need to maintain their infrastructure. Marohn calls this phenomenon the "suburban Ponzi scheme," in which places like Ferguson require "ever-increasing rates of growth necessary to sustain long-term liabilities."

Ferguson tried to capture this growth through mechanisms like tax increment financing (TIF), in which municipal bond money is used to improve "blighted" areas and entice new business. This helped bring a Home Depot, Walmart, and Sam's Club to the north end of Ferguson in 1997. But Ferguson's TIFs have been a disaster. In 2018, $2 million from the city's budget was used for debt service, which includes TIFs, out of a total budget of only $21 million. (This Walmart, incidentally, was the site of the attempted carjacking of Joe Cleveland's wife.)

Who ultimately pays for this debt service? Ferguson's poorest. "TIF bonds are serviced by regressive taxes and fines levied on black motorists," according to a 2015 analysis of Ferguson by Walter Johnson in *The Atlantic*. (Since then, the use of fines as a means of public revenue has eased, only to be replaced by rising sales tax—another regressive tax on the poor.)

When the Clevelands arrived to Ferguson, the funds to maintain the city's aging infrastructure were running out. That was partly owing to a Missouri law designed to keep local taxes low, as well as other misguided tax incentive schemes. As a result, Ferguson received only a pittance in taxes from the Fortune 500 company within its city limits, Emerson Electric, whose lush two-hundred-acre campus on West Florissant Avenue (very near the protests) is wrapped by high fences and barbed wire. The company paid only an estimated $68,000 in property taxes annually as of 2013, though it did contribute more than $16 million toward revitalizing Ferguson in the aftermath of the Michael Brown unrest.

The urban planner Marohn believes Ferguson should tap the entre-preneurial spirit of its residents, rather than squandering more money on TIFs. This spirit can be seen all over Ferguson, often by people operating on the fringes of the law, working at in-home tattoo parlors or selling essential goods like toilet paper and socks out of the trunks of their cars. Many dream of opening businesses but are impeded by red tape and lack of capital.

"For some reason we believe that market principles means that Starbucks needs to come in," Marohn told me. "But someone with a dream needs to have a path to starting their own coffee shop. That's how you build wealth, that's how you create prosperity that you can pass on to the family. That's how poor people become powerful."

The post–Michael Brown era was nonetheless a hopeful time for many Ferguson residents. On the site of the burned-down QuikTrip rose a community center, where I took Jorell's brother Jovan to sign up for a job training program. In the coming years, Black representation on the Ferguson City Council grew, and the city's first Black police chief and first Black mayor took charge. The latter, Ella Jones, a former Mary Kay cosmetics sales director, was also Ferguson's first female mayor.

As Christmas 2014 approached, normal life returned. In early December, Jorell accompanied Anna, me, and the boys across the Mississippi River to get a Christmas tree. At a seasonal market in Illinois called Eckert's Farm we rode a tractor out onto a field of blue firs. While Anna huddled with the boys, Jorell and I surveyed the choices. I'm never quite sure how to pick a Christmas tree; is it most important for it to be tall? Thick? Symmetrical?

"What about this one?" Jorell asked, shivering in the cold.

"Looks good," I said.

After he chopped it down we went inside to drink hot apple cider and take pictures with an inflatable Santa. Jorell bent over at the waist to pose with our almost-three-year-old, which made me smile; not long ago, Jorell had been the short guy himself. Eckert's Farm employees strapped the tree to our roof and we scooted back across the river feeling like a cozy little family, just as when Jorell stayed with us in New Jersey.

But reality dawned as we crossed back into Missouri, driving Jorell home along the decimated West Florissant Avenue strip. As our baby slept in the back seat, Jorell showed us areas that hadn't made the news, including a Ferguson house near his whose front lawn was torn up, the dirt turned violently and left exposed.

"My friend's brother was driving his truck when it hit a car," Jorell explained, "and it flipped the car onto the curb and killed one of the passengers." The truck's driver—Jorell's friend's brother—got out to try to help, but someone from the flipped car emerged and started shooting at him, apparently believing him to be an adversary.

Jorell didn't know any more details about the incident, and I didn't see news reports about it. But the story shook me. It spoke to extreme situations happening off camera during the protests, and made me wonder just what else hadn't made the news.

Another time when I was driving Jorell home he took control of the car's music, plugging in his MP3 player and putting on a hip-hop group called 3 Problems. I sat up straighter in my seat. Who was *this*? They'd developed a huge following in North County, Jorell explained, and I later learned they had been signing autographs at the Michael Brown protests. Though none of my friends had heard of them, I was mesmerized by their stark depiction of street life and mournful hooks, and soon had them on repeat.

On Valentine's Day 2015, Jorell, his friend Jordan, and I went to see 3 Problems perform at a Jennings club called The Ambassador. We waited in line for hours before finally being let into the venue, but it was worth the trouble. The show was great. Afterward I met the two group members, whom Jorell knew casually. They were eighteen-year-old first cousins with movie star looks—Swagg Huncho, from Ferguson, intimidating but charismatic, and his groupmate Lil Tay, from Jennings, more shy but an incredible songwriter. We got back together a couple of weeks later at a downtown restaurant, where I interviewed them for a *Rolling Stone* profile and they talked about the group's journey.

Their mothers were sisters and they'd started off as a boy band performing PG rhymes, before moving into darker material. Their music didn't just showcase gratuitous violence, it documented, in autobiographical fashion, how poverty informs criminality. In fact the group's other member—the third "Problem"—was in jail awaiting trial. His name was

Relle Rell, and he was accused of providing the gun and driving the getaway car in a South St. Louis killing, following a heroin transaction gone wrong. (He'd later be convicted of second-degree murder.)

After the interview Swagg Huncho and Lil Tay got in my car and directed me to an abandoned loading dock where the body of their friend Geno had been dumped, following his recent murder. The guys lamented his passing, and they showed me their new tattoos of his name, across their jugulars. Then we drove to the poor North County city of Spanish Lake, while Swagg smoked a cigarette, the window open, his ashes flying everywhere. Along the way he asked to stop at a bodega, where he purchased, and then swallowed, a couple of loose pills. We soon arrived at the apartment studio of an up-and-coming producer named Playboy, where everyone except me smoked weed and drank Muscato out of Styrofoam cups. I watched the guys record some new tracks, and the artistic energy in the room was palpable. It was exciting.

Jorell and I had more fun times together that spring. In May 2015 he and his girlfriend Danielle came to a surprise party for my birthday thrown by my wife, Anna, at a Central West End restaurant called Brasserie. My friends and I had champagne and whisky; Jorell and Danielle had mocktails. Everyone got along great. By about midnight I was out of gas, but Jorell looked like he could have stayed out all night.

Jorell's life looked to be on track during this time, at least from the outside. For one thing, he'd gotten his first job—frying chicken at Popeyes. His sister Iesha helped him land the gig, and he was ecstatic.

He didn't mind the greasy work, but soon lost the job after getting into a dispute with a customer. The patron asked for extra sauces with her meal, and he said he'd have to charge her. Apparently he was joking, but she didn't think it was funny. She threw her chicken at him, and he responded by tossing a drink at her. "I had to fire him," remembered Iesha, who was his manager. But it all worked out, as he simply walked across the street to a fast food spot called St. Louis Fish & Chicken Grill and started working there the next day.

What made the new job even better was that he got to work with his girlfriend, Danielle. He was over the moon for her, and they practically lived together at Jorell's house.

But was he making time for schoolwork? I became increasingly concerned that studies ranked low on his priority list.

I had long suspected his schools were poor learning environments. His junior high, Ferguson Middle School, scored a 1 out of 10 GreatSchools rating, and his high school, McCluer, maintained a 2 out of 10. "This school is far below the state average in key measures of college and career readiness," summarized a report.

It wasn't always this way. During Ferguson's post–World War II population boom many families moved there specifically for its top-tier academic institutions. "We chose Ferguson for the good school system," remembered long-time city resident Roberta Clevenger, whose family arrived to town in 1953, as mentioned in *Ferguson: A City Remembered*. A local named Peggy Tucker McDonald remembered winning a championship medal from an NRA shooting club in 1950; the firing range was in Ferguson High School's basement. "[They] named me 'Ferguson's own Annie Oakley,'" she said.

Of course, the system really only worked for white children. In the early twentieth century Ferguson had an elementary school for Black students, but it lacked a Black high school, which meant that once African American students reached ninth grade they had to commute to the southern St. Louis suburb of Webster Groves. There was no busing, so Ferguson students either took the 6:00 a.m. train or rode the streetcar. It was an hour and a half trip, each way.

Following the *Brown v. Board of Education* decision in 1954, St. Louis–area schools were forced to integrate. Twenty-one years later a court order required the Ferguson-Florissant School District to accept students from the neighboring, mostly Black, towns of Berkeley and Kinloch. This, combined with factors like the influx of Black families following the closing of the Pruitt-Igoe housing projects, led to changing demographics in the school district—and exacerbated the cycle of white flight that led to falling real estate prices, incomes, and tax receivables.

Now funded by a smaller tax base, the schools began to deteriorate. By the time the Clevelands arrived in Ferguson in 2006, the school district feared losing its accreditation. Though the Ferguson-Florissant School District was over 80 percent Black, its school board remained almost entirely white. This inspired a 2014 lawsuit from the ACLU, which led to a voting process change favoring racial equity.

I knew Jorell wasn't an honor student. At our house he sometimes read bedtime stories to our boys, tripping over words I'd expect a high school junior to know. But I still believed he was progressing normally toward graduation. We had the same conversation every time: How's school? I asked. Good, he said. When pressed, he said he was passing his classes with mostly C's. I'd ask for specifics about certain subjects—science or English or math—and he'd say he recently aced a quiz, or completed a difficult homework assignment. "Nice!" I'd say, and pretty much leave it at that.

As his senior year began in August 2015, though, I became increasingly confused. One night when Anna and the boys were gone Jorell and I had dinner at our house, just the two of us. We were finishing up when he said his fall schedule had been completely revamped. Instead of the typical load of a half dozen classes, he now only took three, and his school day ended at noon. After that he would go home and sleep.

This made no sense to me. Seniors taking a lighter load is a time-honored tradition, but Jorell was no university-bound overachiever who could afford a little breather. He had no plans to go to college, and so this could represent his last shot at formal education.

Then, the conversation got really strange.

"Actually, it looks like I'm going to graduate early," he said.

"What? Why?"

"I'm going to take the TABE test, and if I do well I'll graduate a semester early."

I looked at him askance. This was absurd. I had no idea what the TABE test was, but why would someone with subpar reading skills graduate early? "That's just what they told me," he said.

As I took him back home to Ferguson, I wondered: Was this some weird cost-cutting measure by the Ferguson-Florissant School District, to wean students off the rolls early? Was Jorell exploiting some loophole? I couldn't tell if he was pulling one over on McCluer High School, or if McCluer was pulling one over on him.

Soon afterward I talked to Jorell's father Joe, who was similarly confused about what was going on. He agreed to call McCluer and give permission for me to talk to the principal, Jane Crawford, to try to get to the bottom of things. Crawford and I finally connected in early October 2015. She was very pleasant, answering my barrage of questions: Why was Jorell taking so few classes? What was the TABE test? Why in the world was he going to graduate early?

"Jorell isn't on pace to graduate early," she said. "In fact, he's not on pace to graduate with his class at all." She explained that students needed to earn seven credits per year, but Jorell had accumulated only 10.5 credits total in his first three years. Though he called himself a senior, technically he was still a sophomore. "He's less than halfway there."

Because he was so far behind he'd been enrolled in an alternative curriculum, which could potentially put him back on track. It required him to take three classes, while also working or volunteering for thirty hours a week. Further, to graduate, he also needed to pass a test called the HiSET, which was similar to the GED. "The HiSET test is very hard," Crawford went on. "Sometimes we have kids who really struggle to pass it." In preparation, Jorell had taken the TABE test, which is designed to show which areas of study a student needs to improve upon for the HiSET.

Before I could process all of this, Crawford dropped a bombshell: Jorell was no longer attending McCluer.

"What? He's not?"

"No, he's at the Mark Twain Student Support Center," she went on, referencing the alternative school in Florissant for kids with behavioral and academic issues.

"Was he transferred there because he was behind on credits?"

She consulted her files. "No, that was following an incident that took place when he was getting off the bus at the bus stop by his house in January," she said. "It involved Jorell and some outside people who were in an altercation. A weapon was used, some shots were fired. As a safety precaution, he was transferred, so as to not have trouble at the bus stop."

She might as well have been speaking a foreign language. I had no idea what she was talking about, and her use of the bureaucratic passive voice only made me more confused. "Wait, Jorell shot at someone, or someone shot at him?"

"It's not clear. There was a lack of statements from witnesses. He denied being the shooter."

"But I don't understand. If he wasn't the shooter, why was he kicked out of McCluer?"

"There were other students at the bus stop who were in harm's way, when this all went down. He was obviously the target for these outside people, so we needed to remove him."

I felt completely out of the loop. Here I was, Jorell's big brother, and I had no idea that, ten months earlier, he'd been shot at. "So, you don't have any more details about this? Was there a police report?"

"It's unclear. I do know there's a lot of violent gun situations going on relating to that household. I don't know the level of his involvement."

"Okay," I stammered. "Thanks for telling me."

We hung up. I sat stunned, letting the information sink in. Jorell had been shot at. How awful. But I was as confused as I was saddened, unclear if I believed everything Crawford told me. Gun situations at the Cleveland house? I'd never heard anything about that, other than when Jorell's former friend Lil Glen had stolen Joe's guns, and then shot him.

Further, I was annoyed by how the school had handled this problem. Someone who was attacked, as Jorell was, needed stability in his life to process and recover from the trauma. He shouldn't be kicked out of school. This would likely only compound his academic problems.

Jorell didn't have a phone, so I called Joe to have him patch me through. But Joe was out of town for a couple weeks, so the next day I went over to Oak Avenue unannounced. Jorell was working on his car again, and we spoke in the front yard.

"I talked to Principal Crawford," I said. "I couldn't believe what she told me. You were *shot at* while getting off the bus?"

"Yeah," he said. "That was a while ago." He broke eye contact and turned back to the car. I couldn't read his emotions.

"Why didn't you tell me about it? That's an incredibly scary thing to happen. You could have been killed."

"Yeah," he said, not looking up. "I don't know. My dad said not to tell you. We didn't think you'd take it well."

I wanted to throw my hands up. "Me? Who cares how well I'd take it? I'm your big brother. It's my responsibility to help you with things like this." He shrugged his shoulders. It occurred to me that he likely didn't tell me because he thought I'd be mad at *him*. "But anyway, forget all that. What happened? Who shot at you?"

Again, he was uncomfortable sharing the details, and only unfolded the story in fits and starts. The perpetrator was a neighborhood guy called Poncho, who was a few years older than Jorell and lived across the street from Oak Park, which was near the Cleveland house. The conflict with Poncho started the day before the bus stop shooting, when Jorell and his friend Dezzy had been hanging out at the park. For some reason they began arguing with Poncho; Jorell said he didn't remember exactly what they were bickering about. The confrontation became heated, with threats tossed in both directions.

"The next day when I got off the bus, Poncho started shooting at me," Jorell said. Twelve shots were fired, he estimated, some of which he saw whizzing past his head. "I moved a girl from the bus out of the way, hid her behind a pole until he left. Then I walked her home." He made the whole thing sound cinematic.

"Did you go to the police?"

"Yeah, but they didn't really do anything." A school administrator soon came by the house, though, he added, which led to his transfer to the Mark Twain school.

I mulled on this. What kind of terrifying world did Jorell inhabit, where he was in danger of being killed while *getting off the school bus*?

"Were you freaked out? I know I would have been."

"Yeah. I was scared every time I left the house for a week."

His eyes caught mine for a moment before he looked at the ground. It wasn't often that Jorell was so vulnerable, and while I was horrified by his description of events, my heart leaped that he'd opened himself to me. I wrapped my arms around him and brought him close. Later we went to get pizza at Imo's. We didn't talk further about the shooting that day; he clearly didn't want to rehash it. Nor did we discuss the fact that, unless he got his act together, he wouldn't graduate that spring. I just didn't have the heart to press him. Considering that his life had nearly been ended and he hadn't felt comfortable telling me about it until ten months later—and then only after I brought it up—I wanted to be his friend right now, not an authority figure.

After we said goodbye that night, I considered Jorell's account. Something didn't quite add up. Nagging questions remained. Like, was Jorell a truly innocent bystander in all of this, as he made it sound? It seemed odd that he couldn't even remember what he and Poncho argued about. Then again, perhaps Oak Avenue was simply a war zone. If that was the case, did he still remain in danger?

Thinking about these questions made me weary. I was out of my depths. In my heart I didn't believe he would be killed, because I didn't personally know anyone who'd been murdered. I'd written articles and books that featured violence and killings, but I never imagined my work would overlap with my personal life. How could it? Those people were part of history. Jorell was flesh and blood.

I had to be honest with myself: I wanted to understand Jorell's paranoia, but...I couldn't. Or maybe I just didn't try hard enough. It wasn't until a few years later, when I read Shaka Senghor's *Writing My Wrongs*—an account of the author's near-death experiences and murder conviction in 1990s Detroit—that I began to get a sense of it all. "I knew that it was only a matter of time before I would have to kill or be killed," Senghor wrote. "If I was quick on the draw, it would be the former. But, if not, I would join the hundreds of young men and women who were lost in the war that rages through our community. How can a child expect to exist like this and not go insane?"

CHAPTER EIGHT

In the coming weeks I wrestled with how to help Jorell. It became clear that I couldn't do anything about the violence on Oak Avenue. The area had clearly grown more dangerous since the Clevelands arrived in 2006. Hoping for their own slice of the American dream, they thought the suburbs would be safer than the city, but it hadn't turned out that way. "Out here in the county I didn't think it was nothing like it was," lamented Joe. "It fooled me."

One thing I could do, however, was help Jorell with his schoolwork. Maybe it sounded hokey, but if Jorell could graduate high school and get on a career path, he could get off the block and stay off.

I come from a long line of academics, and I had experience tutoring. Aiding him in this quest was something I could do. And so Anna and I set to work. I'd already been working with him informally, but we put together a plan to help him improve academically.

The first step was to get a sense of where he stood in school. And so, after coordinating with Joe, on a Tuesday night in mid-October 2015, while Anna gave the boys supper, I picked Jorell up and we drove to his new school, the Mark Twain Student Support Center, for parent-teacher conferences. On the drive Jorell sat listless in the front seat, uncommunicative. I couldn't tell if he was tired, or if he was just irritated to be a part of this. Maybe he feared a poor evaluation. Maybe he was just being a moody eighteen-year-old.

Unlike the monolithic design of many high schools, Mark Twain instead resembled a community college, with four separate buildings decorated in colorful tile patterns separated by neatly trimmed lawns. There was something calming about the place.

Arriving from an appointment, Joe pulled up alongside us in the parking lot. He was driving a GMC Sierra truck with a mismatched door, a vehicle I hadn't seen before. "How are you doing?" I said, shaking Joe's hand. "Good looking truck."

"Thanks," he said. "I'm having trouble getting it to pass inspection."

Inside, Joe and I talked to a counselor from an organization that offered free therapy to Ferguson-Florissant students. Though Joe seemed reluctant to hear him out, I strongly suggested it could be a good idea for Jorell, considering he'd been shot at not long ago. Joe came around to my perspective, and after signing him up we entered Jorell's science classroom. The teacher, middle aged and elegantly dressed, greeted us warmly and invited us to sit down in the kids' desks. Joe and I sat in the front row, with Jorell behind us. The teacher handed us worksheets from the curriculum, a hodgepodge of biology, chemistry, and physics. I'd helped Jorell with some of these worksheets before, and I knew he didn't have a good handle on the material.

"How's Jorell doing?" Joe asked.

"He's doing very well," the teacher said. She paused. I thought she was going to say more but she just smiled.

I turned around to face Jorell. "How are your quizzes going?" I asked. He gave me a nervous glance and muttered something under his breath. His teacher interrupted to say he needed to make up one or two of them, but he was well on his way.

"He's a great student," she said. "He just sits quietly in class and doesn't say anything."

So that was it. Jorell was in the teacher's favor not because he was excelling, but because he wasn't disturbing anybody. He wasn't likely learning anything, but because he wasn't causing trouble she was going to pass him.

His social studies teacher noted Jorell's oft-poor test scores, but gave him the benefit of the doubt, noting how difficult things can be for a young Black man in an era when police were killing them. I was sympathetic to this argument, but still thought it critical for Jorell to improve his academic performance, especially after we spoke next with his English teacher. "Jorell reads at a sixth or seventh grade level," she said. And there was more bad news: he'd done very poorly on the TABE test, and therefore had been withdrawn from the special track program that might have allowed him to graduate on time. "To get his credits to graduate he'll just need to keep plugging forward," she said. That meant he'd be in high school for a fifth year (at least), and likely wouldn't graduate until he was twenty. That's about as far as he could push it, since students "aged out" of Ferguson-Florissant public schools at twenty-one.

This was news to Joe and me, and may have been news to Jorell as well. Sitting at the back of the classroom, he was stone silent. I appreciated his English teacher's candidness, however, and she ended on a bit of good news: he could earn extra credits by reading books in his spare time like *To Kill a Mockingbird* and *The Great Gatsby*.

"I have these books at home," I told Jorell as we exited the building. "I'll let you borrow them, and you can get closer to graduating, just by reading. I'll tutor you. It'll be fun."

He kept his head down, and didn't answer. Joe began to get annoyed. "Answer him when he's talking to you," he said sternly. We were out in the parking lot now, and it was the first time I'd ever heard Joe raise his voice. "He's trying to help you get your education!"

"Okay," Jorell muttered, still not raising his head. He turned around and got into his dad's truck. Joe shook his head.

"Thank you for coming," he told me, sticking out his hand.

"You're welcome," I said.

On the ride home I felt discouraged, though it was hard to put my finger on exactly why. Certainly I was disappointed in Jorell, who wasn't being proactive with his studies, to say the least. For some time now he'd given me half-truths about his performance, and now he felt exposed.

But I was equally disappointed with some of his teachers, who didn't seem to care if he learned anything at all, so long as he didn't cause disruptions. There was also blame, I thought, for the district, which had shuttled him off to this new school after the bus stop shooting, which had taken place apparently through no fault of his own. Then there were the larger factors oppressing kids like him since birth, which were so numerous they made my brain hurt.

Jorell was at the edge of a precipice. The only thing I could think was: How can I help him? It didn't occur to me that I might not be the person best suited for this task, or that I couldn't understand the bigger picture. He was basically my family, and the impulse to help him consumed me.

The tutoring was a good start, but Jorell needed more. His academic and safety issues couldn't be so easily separated. If he was in danger every time he walked out of his house, he certainly wouldn't visit the library, for example. His potential enemies seemed vague and varied; his adversaries included his own former friends, like Lil Glen. How could one be expected to succeed academically in an environment like that?

I came up with an idea: Jorell should come live with us, at least for a while. He could stay in our basement, which was finished, and where he'd have some privacy, and I could drive him to school every day.

I raised the idea with Anna when I got home that evening. She agreed it was worth considering. "I'm scared for his life," she said, adding that, beyond just basic protection, he could also benefit simply by getting more sleep every night. I wasn't sure why he was always so tired, but perhaps it was because he slept in the room with the house's main TV, which people used at all hours of the day and night, watching shows and playing video games.

Who knew if Jorell would be interested in staying with us, however, considering how irritated he was with me right now. There were also Joe's feelings to consider. Joe had always been supportive of the activities Jorell and I did together, from swimming lessons to road trips to hosting him over the summer. But this would be literally removing him from his home environment. We needed to handle this delicately. Anna and I didn't want to offend him.

"Let's do a trial run," I suggested. "We'll have Jorell over for some weekends, and see how it goes. If he's game, we'll start thinking about a more long-term arrangement."

Anna agreed to the plan as something of an intervention for Jorell, a way to get him off the streets for a few days at a time, to test the waters for a more permanent move.

"Would you want to stay over here on the weekends a couple times?" I asked him, when he finally called me back on his dad's phone.

"Okay," he said. He didn't sound very excited, but it was hard to tell.

"It'll be fun, like it was when we used to do this," I said. "Like when you used to chase my cat around the apartment."

"Sounds good," he said with a laugh.

I lingered on the line for a few more seconds, unsure what to say. I didn't have the heart to express how much Anna and I feared for his safety, and I didn't want to scare him by laying out our grand plan. So I just said we'd see him soon.

In the meantime Jorell started therapy. After his first appointment I spoke with his therapist, who said Jorell was having a hard time opening up about the traumatic incidents in his life. "He says that other people have it much worse than he does," the therapist said. Apparently Jorell thought his own troubles were no big deal, as if it were commonplace for bullets to whiz past your ear when you stepped off the school bus.

Jorell didn't realize—or perhaps didn't want to admit—that his environment was uniquely troubled. And that fall and winter brought a string of tragedies, which would make his situation even worse. The first was on October 28, 2015, when the boyfriend of Jorell's younger sister Peaches died, though the manner of death wasn't clear. His name was Amonderez Green, and he was eighteen. According to the police report, his family believed he was suicidal and called the cops, who arrived to find Green walking along the border between Ferguson and the neighboring town of Normandy in an agitated state. Unwilling to be consoled, Green suddenly "produced a silver revolver and began firing shots at the officers present," read the account. After unsuccessfully attempting to taser him, the police began firing. Their shots missed, the report says, and Green fled through residential backyards, again firing at the officers. Once he was out of their sight, officers heard one more shot and then found him on the ground, "suffering from what appeared to be a self-inflicted gunshot wound located under the chin." He was taken to the hospital, where he died.

Others disputed this account, including Green's father, who claimed the officers shot his son. "The police officers was not even six, seven feet away, and stood over him and shot him dead in his face," said a woman who said she was an eyewitness. This statement appears in a video taken at the scene by an activist named Darren Seals, with the sound of a helicopter in the background. None of the body camera footage from police captured any gunfire. The St. Louis County medical examiner concluded that the death was a suicide, but considering that this was only a year after Michael Brown's death, distrust of this finding ran high. Curiously, the following September, Seals himself was found dead in a burning car. Seals was one of six local activists connected to the Ferguson protests who died under suspicious circumstances. Were these activists killed in unrelated homicides—the victims of everyday life in dangerous St. Louis—or was this an orchestrated effort to squelch dissent?

Jorell didn't think to mention Green's death to me when it happened. I only found out later in an unrelated conversation, when I randomly asked him how his sister Peaches was doing. "Her boyfriend was killed by police," he said nonchalantly, as if speaking about the weather. I immediately went online, reading a news account saying Green had tested positive for HIV. Thankfully, Peaches had since gotten tested, Jorell said, and she was negative.

On a Friday night in early November I picked up Jorell for a weekend together. He threw a plastic Hefty trash bag of his clothes into the back of my car and climbed into the front seat. A green Lacoste bag was slung over his shoulder. It reminded me of the stylish yet often mocked man purses I'd seen before, and it had a small lock on the zipper. I looked at it curiously, wondering what he kept in there.

We picked up Chinese food for dinner. Jorell grabbed extra sweet and sour packets, which he used to saturate his plate of chicken fried rice, before asking if we had any more. I'd often scolded him about his diet, but this time I didn't say anything and instead just retrieved a bottle of sweet and sour sauce from the fridge. My goal was to make him feel comfortable, to make our house feel like his. So what if he ate what he wanted? Right now, we needed to focus on the bigger picture. Here he was, surrounded by people who cared about him, in a safe neighborhood, with four walls around him and a sturdy roof above his head. He was in no danger. I intended to keep things this way.

After dinner we put on a kids' movie and Jorell fell asleep on the couch. The next night he babysat while Anna and I went out to a restaurant with friends. The boys loved him as a sitter, and I paid him with three twenties.

In the morning, hungover, I looked out the front window.

"You raked the yard?"

"Yep," Jorell said. "It looked like it needed it."

"Thanks," I said, and gave him a couple more twenties. "Raking was about the last thing I wanted to do today."

I could get used to having him around the house, I thought to myself.

That afternoon I took him and our elder son to Forest Park to visit the Missouri History Museum, which I love for its indulgence of St. Louis's obsession with its past, particularly the 1904 World's Fair. Even in 2015, when we visited, locals still talked about it like a recent event. The Fair, which drew twenty million people and inspired the classic 1944 Judy Garland film *Meet Me in St. Louis*, is still regarded as the high water mark in the city's history. The museum's exhibit describes the herculean efforts taken to put it on, the technology that debuted there, and numerous troubling oddities. Premature babies were displayed at the Incubator Exhibit, while foreign countries showcased their country's "savages" going about their days in what were called "living exhibits"—basically like a zoo but full of people. More than a thousand Filipinos lived on the grounds for months, tilling the land while white audiences observed them. Before settling in at the fairgrounds, a Native American tribe from Oklahoma camped next to a Ferguson farm, capturing the imagination of Ferguson students. "The first high school yearbook, *Miaketa*, was named for the

Chief of 'Ferguson's Indians,'" recalls *Ferguson: A City Remembered.* "The *Miaketa* was published from 1924 to 1926. Residents who bought the yearbook were entitled to vote for the Miaketa Queen."

My son romped around in the kids' play area, where children dressed up like French fur traders. After that we strolled through an exhibit called St. Louis in Your Cup, which told the story of the city's once-significant coffee industry, largely forgotten in the era of Starbucks. A series of 1960s- and 1970s-era commercials for St. Louis–based Safari Coffee played on a loop. The ads featured its eccentric owner Dana Brown going on safari in various far-flung locations around the globe. Brown is something of a St. Louis legend, a white guy in camo gear who went to Africa and Asia to buy coffee beans, and then stuck around to film the Indigenous people and animals. Generations of St. Louisans grew up watching these commercials. In one, a rhino gores Brown's Jeep. In another, an elephant digs a water hole. They barely mention the coffee. I asked Jorell what he thought. "Funny," he said, cracking up as one set in Rhodesia featured baby baboons riding bush pigs in Kentucky Derby–style races.

After the museum we had lunch in Clayton, and then dropped in on our family friends Doug and Inna, who lived nearby. They were watching the Rams game. The family, who had teenage kids we hadn't seen in a while, admired my three-year-old. "So cute," said their daughter. "He looks just like you!"

When we got back Jorell took a nap on the couch. Anna meanwhile washed his clothes. They stunk of marijuana. I wasn't sure if Jorell himself smoked weed; I knew others did in his household, and perhaps their smoke clung to his clothes. Marijuana was still contraband in Missouri, though decriminalization would soon come to St. Louis County. Jorell had friends and family members who sold it. They called it gas and posted photos on Facebook—of buds, or even just a gas station—to advertise their wares.

I was the last person to judge Jorell for smoking pot. When I was nineteen I spent a night in jail after getting caught returning from Amsterdam with weed and hash in my rucksack. My dad paid a lawyer $1,000 to get it knocked down to a "disturbing the peace" misdemeanor. That little marijuana charge hadn't derailed my future, but Jorell wasn't so lucky to have a father who could write a sizable check.

Smoking it was one thing, but I didn't want Jorell showing up to job interviews smelling like Cheech and Chong. I wondered if he kept marijuana in his little Lacoste man purse. My curiosity got the better of me, and as Jorell snored I crept into the guest room and tried opening the bag. It was locked. I immediately felt sheepish for violating his privacy. He was in my house to feel safe, not to be judged. Still, the situation felt complicated. I wanted to help him, but how could I best do that? By staying out of his way, or by getting into his business, even if it meant potentially breaking his trust?

I didn't know, but I was now more curious than ever about the bag's contents.

That night a married couple in town from Seattle came over for dinner, including my friend Mike, who'd known Jorell since we were colleagues at the *Riverfront Times* back in 2005. (In fact, Mike had written my original recommendation letter for Big Brothers Big Sisters.) For the occasion Anna baked a cake and prepared made-from-scratch mac and cheese. We ate well and the conversation ran late. I wondered if Jorell thought it was strange that I frequently brought him to dinners with a bunch of white people, but whatever the case, he fit right into our little party.

It felt to me like a successful weekend. He'd caught up on his sleep, earned spending money, and made progress on a book called *A Long Way Gone*, a memoir of a boy soldier from Sierra Leone, which would help him earn credits toward graduation. The next night Anna and I discussed the possibility of inviting Jorell to move in. There were barriers. He didn't have his driver's license, so one of us would have to drive him to the Mark Twain school and back every day, a long commute. Another possibility was having him transfer to our local school district. It was top tier, which would have been great if he was starting as a freshman. But he was already an upperclassman, and the other students his age would be more advanced than he was. This raised another question: Would the culture shock of being surrounded by privileged, college-bound kids just make things worse for him? Further, we'd be taking him away from his family, his support system. Even if the environment we provided was ostensibly safer, there was bound to be a psychological toll. Most people struggle in new places, at least initially, and the last thing he needed was more stress.

We grappled with what we *should* do versus what was the *right* thing to do. We pledged to mull on it more.

I talked to Jorell a couple more times in the coming days, and he continued insisting things in his life were fine. But on December 2, 2015, I logged on to Facebook and came across an alarming post. "And whoever want it man its comming out that 16 16 shot berreta 16 shot whatever riden with yo mans take 16 shots together," Jorell had written, the message followed by emojis meant to look like a gun firing bullets.

✴✴✴✴✴✴✴✴✴✴✴✴✴✴✴✴🔫

I didn't know what to make of this post—the threats, the use of the unsettling squirt gun emoji. Reading it, I saw a Jorell different from the one I'd just spent a pleasant weekend with. I saw a young man expressing rage, fear, and desperation. I was disturbed for safety reasons and practical ones, considering that law enforcement, potential employers, and everyone else could see this post.

The next weekend, when I pulled up to his house to pick him up, I raised the issue. He'd just finished a long work day in the rural town of Troy, Missouri, dropping off phone books on people's stoops. He was clearly tired, and as we drove he sat slumped in his seat.

"What was that Facebook post about?" I asked. "Who do you have this beef with?"

He looked at me for a moment like he didn't know what I was talking about. "Oh that, that's nothing," he said.

"It looked pretty serious to me."

He stayed silent in the front seat, his eyes drooping. After a moment I wondered if he'd fallen asleep.

"Couldn't something like that spill over into your real life?"

Jorell opened his eyes and shook his head, as if it were the dumbest question he'd ever heard. "It won't," he said. He had nothing more to say on the matter, so I let it go.

At our house I set up the living room so he could study. But when he sat down on the sofa he immediately spaced out, as if he'd forgotten what he'd come to do.

"Where are the textbooks I asked you to bring?" I said.

"Oh." He went through his backpack. "I forgot them, except science."

I sat down next to him, annoyed. "All right, then, what are you working on in science?"

He opened his book and flipped through the pages. He showed me the week's assignment, and we spent a few moments reading it over together. I tried to explain what he should do, but none of it seemed to sink in. Granted, I'm not the world's most inspiring teacher, but learning this material didn't seem like a priority to him.

"He says it's his third time going through these concepts, but has no clue about stuff like Density = Mass/Volume," I wrote in my diary. "He clearly has bigger things to worry about."

Jorell was dull and sullen all weekend, hardly speaking. He barely choked down any of the food we made for him. He showed off his new tattoos, which I hadn't seen before. They included one that said "JMC"— for Jorell Marsay Cleveland—as well as one of a pit bull, and one of a handgun. I couldn't decide if that last one was a harbinger of doom, or just another everyday aspect of his life I wasn't equipped to understand.

CHAPTER NINE

J orell and I didn't make a deeper connection that weekend; I tried to get closer, but he kept me at bay. Even so, it was a good thing he stayed with us, because during that time someone we knew was murdered—Swagg Huncho, the member of the rap group 3 Problems, whom I'd profiled for *Rolling Stone*.

He was shot very early Sunday morning, in midtown St. Louis; dead at only nineteen.

Jorell had already received the news when I called him.

"Do you know why he was killed?"

"It might have had something to do with drugs," Jorell said, before trailing off. I couldn't tell if he knew more than he was letting on.

Jorell didn't seem shaken up, perhaps because he heard about murders like this regularly, but the news sent me into a tailspin. Swagg's burgeoning rap career was supposed to represent a way out for him; 3 Problems had started making good money doing shows and appearing on others' songs. I knew that escaping dangerous circumstances in St. Louis wasn't easy, even for those who came into money. But it depressed me that the city refused to spare even its most talented.

Later that week I attended his funeral, in the once-affluent municipality of Country Club Hills. A crowd of five hundred people arrived, many in custom-designed memorial T-shirts, blasting 3 Problems songs from their cars. Though he had been shot in the head, it was an open casket.

Swagg's face had been reconfigured into something that resembled a grotesque stop-motion animation version of himself. It was the first time I'd ever seen a dead body. At the service his groupmate Lil Tay rapped a few verses, and a homicide division liaison pleaded for attendees to tell police what they knew about the murder. Afterward Swagg's casket was taken to the cemetery by horse-drawn carriage.

The event was peaceful, though on Facebook Swagg's rivals had threatened violence against anyone who attended. Afterward I traced the threats to the page of a clique residing in the same midtown neighborhood where Swagg had been killed. The guys on the page were practically taking credit for his murder. I figured the police would be interested in this information, and phoned in a tip. I chatted with a detective, but hung up feeling unsatisfied. He couldn't access Facebook in his office, for some reason, and so the detective jotted down by hand the URL of the page as I read it aloud, a long string of random letters and numbers.

It undercut my faith in St. Louis County PD. To fans around St. Louis and beyond, Swagg Huncho was a talented star, someone poised to break out nationally. But to the cops he seemed to be just another anonymous murder victim.

Following Swagg Huncho's murder, a change of scenery for Jorell seemed more urgent than ever. Though he'd practically sleepwalked through our latest weekend together, I resolved to broach the subject of him moving in with us.

As I scrolled Facebook shortly after he went home, I changed my mind. Jorell's recent update recounted how bored he'd been with us, how he missed his girlfriend and his friends. I'm sure he didn't intend for me to see it, but he was clearly unimpressed with our suburban lifestyle.

I tried not to take it personally. Teenagers will be teenagers, and I wasn't trying to win any cool points. But Anna and I hoped our home would be a beacon of calm for him, a refuge of sorts. Clean and quiet, it was a place he could relax without worrying about someone gunning for him. I struggled to understand his urgency to get back to Oak Avenue. The truth was simpler than I let myself believe.

That's where his family was. That was home. To think that we offered something preferable didn't make sense. We could provide all the material comforts in the world, but nothing could replace the intimacy of kin.

If he didn't enjoy a weekend with us, he probably wouldn't want to move in permanently. I talked to Anna and she agreed; it wasn't the right time. Maybe it could still happen someday, but it would have to be further down the line.

When I think back to this moment, I wish I'd pushed harder. Maybe I could have overcome these barriers. I could have enlisted his dad's support to sell him on the move. I could have carved an hour and a half out of my days to drive him to school, and figured out ways for him to see his girlfriend Danielle regularly. Maybe it would have been inconvenient, but it would have been doable.

At the time, having Jorell move in didn't feel realistic. But the reality was that his daily life had become the worst-case scenario.

On January 27, 2016, we received more awful news: Jorell's oldest sibling, Joseph Cleveland Jr., had died in a freak accident. I'd only met JoJo, as he was known, once or twice. He'd stayed in Arkansas for most of his life and died near his home in Dumas, where he lived in a trailer. He passed after having a seizure and falling into a ditch while strolling along a highway.

"He was walking in the country," Joe told me, "and the ditch had water in it. Because of the seizure he couldn't get out of that water, and he got hypothermia." JoJo was thirty-five. Jorell was absolutely devastated. Despite the distance, he felt very close to his brother, and after the funeral wore a shirt with his photo on it. They had different mothers, but I was struck by just how much they looked alike. But for the age difference, they could have been twins.

This was Jorell's second sibling to die, following his sister Chaz in 2011. I wanted to be there for him, but he was growing increasingly difficult to reach. I left lots of unreturned messages with Joe, Iesha, and Danielle. They all assured me that Jorell wanted to speak with me, but he was just busy. I assumed his work schedule was hectic, but there was more to it than that. Occasionally I caught glimpses of his life through cryptic and increasingly caustic Facebook updates.

"Jumping out with 223s shooting at everybody," he wrote on March 30, 2016.

A week later he posted: "I'm out sliding with my squad tinted sliding with them 9s like tony hawk I'm trinna glide like la read I'm in my prime they kno I'm bout that papa ill send shots at his neck drop the tint no regrets."

Were these rap lyrics or actual threats? Maybe it was dark poetry helping him get through the recent tragedies? The previous months had seen Amonderez Green's suicide (or perhaps killing by police), Swagg Huncho's murder, and JoJo's accidental death. Jorell's relationships with each were quite different. But they were all young Black men he knew, taken down in senseless, often violent ways. It had to weigh on him.

He likely didn't have time to dwell. More pressing concerns, things he hadn't revealed to me, had begun dominating his moment-to-moment thoughts. As I would come to learn, his paranoia had peaked. As his dad told me later, Jorell no longer answered the door without his gun.

Jorell's life was spiraling out of control, but in the spring and summer of 2016 I was consumed by events in my own life. My first book for a major publisher, *Original Gangstas*, was publishing in September. I spent the months beforehand treating its publicity like a full-time job, soliciting endorsements and preparing excerpts.

The book focused on West Coast gangsta rap, and I'd interviewed many ex–gang members for the book, burly fifty-year-old guys who could still out-bench-press me. The era culminated in the murders of Tupac Shakur and Biggie Smalls, who were friends before a dispute sent their relationship into a deadly tailspin. Their war forced hip-hop community members to choose sides—the West Coast or the East Coast. Decades after their still-unsolved deaths, they remained arguably hip-hop's two most famous personalities.

Because of their celebrity, I never thought to compare their lives with Jorell's. Perhaps I should have seen the connection. Jorell and his adversaries (whoever they were) weren't famous, but they too were young, engaged in heated rhetoric, and had easy access to firearms. A difference was that, rather than lashing out on diss tracks, their taunts were levied over social media.

In the summer of 2016 Jorell and I barely communicated at all. There was no dramatic falling out, but we'd had a tough time understanding each other's perspectives in recent months. When we did speak, he expressed excitement about my new book, pledging to attend my reading at Left Bank Books in September.

Jorell said he wanted to take Anna and me out for a meal and a movie some time. He had his own money now, and wanted to do the treating. I looked forward to it. But more importantly, I looked forward to our lives intertwining again. It seemed inevitable that we would come back together. I was determined to make this friendship last, and I knew he was too.

We would never be given the chance.

On August 27, I got the call from Danielle's mother. I climbed into my car shaking, and entered onto I-170. Only then did I consider where I was headed: Kinloch. Just the word filled me with dread. Ferguson has its rough areas, but they are nothing compared to Kinloch, the municipality just to its west. Kinloch is barely a town. Scattered with trash, and full of burned-out apartment buildings, it's a largely lawless patch of land.

What the hell was Jorell doing in Kinloch?

The afternoon was sticky and still. The sky grew dark as I exited the interstate and approached Kinloch's residential streets. I struggled to find the intersection Danielle's mother gave me, Jefferson and Courtney Avenues, roads that aren't marked with street signs.

Then I saw the police cars and the crime scene tape. The gathered crowd. I parked and dashed out of my car, somehow imagining I might still be able to help him. I pushed to the edge of the tape and that's where I saw him, maybe thirty feet away, his body on the ground, lifeless. He lay on his back with his eyes closed, in a strange, unnatural position. He was alone, no medics attending to him, no family surrounding him. The police kept everyone back. His breath had stopped.

"Ben?" said an older white woman, whom I quickly surmised was Danielle's mom.

"Thank you for calling me," I said, giving her a hug. "Where's Danielle?" I asked, fearing the worst.

She pointed to a petite high school girl with her hands on top of her head, standing near Jorell's family on the other side of the police barrier.

We stood and watched as a pair of first responders in dark uniforms, a man and a woman, picked up Jorell's body off the ground. One grabbed his wrists, the other his ankles. They put him in an ambulance, which quickly departed. Soon a fire engine pulled up. Firefighters got off the truck and unwound a giant hose, connected it to a fire hydrant, and sprayed the concrete. I stared at the water splashing onto the asphalt. It took me a moment to realize what they were doing. They were washing away Jorell's blood.

I stood, sweating. If I had only been here an hour earlier, I thought, I could have stopped this. But I wasn't entirely filled with despair. "Believe it or not, I was glad to see him one last time, even in this way," I wrote in my diary.

Soon I got back in my car and drove around the police barricade. I embraced Jorell's sisters Rece and Iesha, the latter of whom just happened to be wearing a commemorative T-shirt for their brother JoJo. I made eye contact with Jorell's father.

"Joe, I'm so sorry," I said.

"Thank you," he said, strangely calm.

There was a long pause.

"Does anybody know what happened?" I asked. Everyone shook their heads. All they knew was that Jorell had been shot and killed at point-blank range.

A St. Louis County police detective named Dennis Cook soon came by taking statements. I volunteered to tell him what little I knew, and he ushered me into his squad car, where we retreated from the heat into the air conditioning. We were two of only a few white people on the scene. I looked around at the surrounding crowd, which had grown to encompass seemingly half the town of Kinloch. It was an entire community I knew little about.

"What was your relationship to the victim?" the detective asked.

"I was his Big Brother in the Big Brothers Big Sisters program," I said, horrified to hear myself using the past tense. I gave all the information I could and then offered to stay in touch as I learned more. "I'm actually a reporter," I went on, adding that I sometimes wrote about criminal cases like this one, and further that I maintained close contact with Jorell's family and friends. I would be happy to share any information I came across.

"Someone will call you," he said.

And then...that was it. I got out of the car, and I walked back over to where Joe was standing. We shook hands.

"I'll call you about the funeral," he said.

I thanked him and said goodbye. There was nothing more to do. I saw that I was an hour late for a dinner at the home of our friends Doug and Inna in Clayton, the affluent nearby suburb. I got into my car and wound through Kinloch back to I-170.

As I drove south a rainstorm sprang up, followed by a sudden, breathtakingly loud thunder clap, and then a flash of lightning. I looked out the window and saw a rainbow, back in the direction from where I'd just come.

PART II

CHAPTER TEN

In the days following Jorell's death, I sorted through hundreds of photos of him, including school pictures, prints from my wedding, and the one I loved so much of him at the Museum of Natural History in New York, pretending to cower before the tiger in the glass cage. It warmed me to look at these photos, until I considered that there would be no more of them to catalog the life he would have lived. No more mile markers, no high school graduation, no wedding of his own.

At Joe's request, Anna designed the funeral program, and we printed up a couple hundred copies at Kinko's.

Anna's mother watched our children during the service. It was held at a North St. Louis chapel that, from what I could tell, specialized in services for young Black men. It was stuffy and elegant, in that somehow-comforting way of funeral homes. Anna and I sat near the back. It was a hot September day and the air-conditioning never really kicked in. I shifted in my seat, sweating in my suit. Jorell's sisters spoke, as did Anna, who said that when she met me she knew Jorell and I were a "package deal." After Anna finished the pastor looked in my direction.

"Come on up," he said, gesturing.

I stood and walked to the lectern. I hadn't prepared anything. Perhaps I was still in denial. But I knew it was important to honor Jorell's memory.

"Jorell never wanted anything from anybody," I began, my pulse quickening. I had a lot of public speaking experience, but immediately all of that went out the window. I tried to just speak from the heart. I talked about Jorell's unconditional love for his friends and his family, as well as his struggles to find work and his desire for financial independence. "He just wanted to be self-sufficient."

Spooked by the memory of Swagg Huncho's distorted, reconfigured face, I decided not to line up for the viewing. Jorell had also been shot from point-blank range, and there was no telling how the mortician had put him back together. What was the point of open caskets, anyway?

After the service we milled around with Jorell's friends and family. The older generation wore collared shirts, the younger ones freshly screen-printed t-shirts commemorating Jorell in vivid color, blown-up pictures from Facebook of them hanging out together. "Rest In Peace Relly World," said one, referencing a nickname I didn't realize his friends had for him. "Relle Gang," said another.

I approached his girlfriend, Danielle, and we hugged.

"Are you doing okay?" I asked her.

"Yeah," she said, bleary.

"He was such a great guy."

"He was," she said. "His dream was to buy a car that the two of us could use."

We stood for a few seconds without saying anything further. I thought about this dream. It was so simple. It should have been obtainable.

Beforehand I'd notified Big Brothers Big Sisters about the death, and to my surprise the CEO of the regional chapter was there, Becky J. Hatter, a Louisiana native and a Big Sister herself. She said the organization would contribute to funeral costs.

A white hearse drove his body northwest, toward the cemetery in the North County municipality of Pagedale where he'd be buried. A procession of vehicles followed, including a car with a group of Jorell's friends, which whipped back and forth. A boy of about sixteen sat in the windowsill, his body hanging out, clowning around, and I stared at him with an incredulous annoyance. How could he think this day was so normal?

The large blue sun shield canopy set up for the funeral could barely hold everyone. Joe sat in the front row, unshaven and in a white bowler hat, next to Jorell's sisters Iesha, Peaches, and Rece, the latter wearing heart-shaped sunglasses. She was howling. People took camera phone pictures of the casket, which was two shades of blue and topped by a bouquet of red and white carnations. I noticed a boy, maybe eleven, in slacks and penny loafers. He stood apart from the main group on the edge of the canopy, observing the service from behind the pastor. He was maybe a nephew; I didn't recognize him. I wondered what he made of this. Did he feel despair? Was it just another funeral to him? Did he fear for his own future?

We went back to Oak Avenue for the repast, where Anna and I prepared trays of barbeque, coleslaw, and vegetables. I drove to Shop 'n Save to buy utensils with the wife of one of Jorell's brothers. We'd never spoken before, but perhaps because of the circumstances, she immediately began opening up to me. She told me that her eight-year-old daughter was recently sent to the hospital after saying at school that she was going to kill herself.

"Jeez," I said. "That's awful." I tried to understand the difficulties of parenting such a distressed child, but I just couldn't wrap my mind around it, and was left speechless.

Back at the house I saw that Jorell's mother, Dianne Robinson, had arrived. We'd never met, and I was struck by just how young she was—around my age—and how much she looked like Jorell. She had the same smile, the same eyes, the same way of cocking her head slightly to the right when she spoke.

"Wonderful to meet you, Ben," she said, putting her arms around me.

"I'm so sorry," I said.

She continued hugging me, and when she let go she looked me right in the eyes. "He was lucky to have a person like you in his life," she said, and hugged me again. Dianne was warm and charming throughout the evening, though eventually the veneer cracked as she drank too much and began hanging on people's shoulders, crying hysterically.

I wasn't sure how to carry myself. I'd mourned grandparents whose times had come, and as a journalist I'd spoken with many grieving mothers. I'd felt their tears. But I'd never been close to someone who was murdered. I'd never cried my own tears of grief. In fact, in the first days after Jorell's death, I still didn't cry. I felt like I should be crying—that if I truly cared about Jorell, I would be crying—but I couldn't process everything. One minute I wanted to probe my despair, the next minute I wanted to suppress it.

Part of the problem was that I didn't know why he'd been killed. Could it somehow be related to Swagg Huncho's death, or that of Amonderez Green? What about the people who apparently shot at him before, like Lil Glen, his former friend from high school, or Poncho, from the bus stop? No one I spoke to thought any of these situations were linked to Jorell's death, so I concluded it must have been random.

In my darker moments, Jorell's passing made me mad. It made me want vengeance. Other times it made me feel lethargic, like I didn't want to leave the bed. The world became dull, drained of color and sharpness. I imagined Jorell living to eighty. All the glories and transcendent moments he would have experienced. Now they were only theoretical. I thought about the kids he would never have, and the kids they would never have. Full generations, lost.

I began losing confidence in the everyday tasks of raising my own boys. If I couldn't take care of Jorell, what made me so sure I could take care of them?

Only one thing was clear: I was a failure.

"When I signed up for Big Brothers Big Sisters, my job was to look out for my Little," I explained to Anna. It was a Saturday morning not long after the funeral, and we were weeding in the garden. "That was my one job."

"It's not your fault he was killed," she said.

I grabbed a weed that was taller than I was, trying to pull it out, and, when that didn't work, grabbed a handsaw and went after its roots in the dirt.

"I'm not trying to make this a pity party," I said. "It's just a fact."

She pulled a scrum of weedy vines off the fence without looking up.

"Do you really think that? You brought so much into his life. Nobody blames you. He certainly wouldn't have."

I put my head down. I appreciated what Anna was trying to do, and I would have said the same to someone else in my position. But that didn't change the truth. Jorell had been my Little Brother. I was tasked with preparing him for adulthood and helping him navigate safely through the world.

And at that I'd come up short. Undoubtedly, unequivocally.

In the meantime I coped with Jorell's death the best way I knew—I wrote. I pored through my old diaries to research my obituary for Jorell, which was published in the *Riverfront Times*. "Every time we talked, he ended with, 'I love you,'" I wrote in the piece. "It took me aback; 'I love you' wasn't even something I said to my parents much. But I said it too, and it became less awkward. It was only just. He was a guy I loved, a guy so many people loved."

The article went viral on social media, with seemingly everyone I knew sharing it, as well as celebrities including the actress Mira Sorvino. All of this spurred thousands of dollars in donations toward a site set up for Jorell's funeral expenses. A group called the Crime Victim Advocacy Center wrote to offer free counseling services to the Cleveland family.

A pair of local television stations contacted me for interviews. News trucks arrived at our house and overly made-up newscasters and lighting techs set up in our living room. We had our boys play in the basement while this was going on, because we still hadn't told them about Jorell.

In quick soundbites I tried to explain what made Jorell special, his kindness, his loyalty. It all felt very strange: so many young Black men are murdered every day, and their deaths go virtually unnoticed in the media. Simply by virtue of being a white journalist, I was able to bring attention to Jorell's life. I wanted to take advantage of this opportunity on his behalf, but the disparity of the situation came into focus.

My tribute and these news segments were widely seen, inspiring people I'd never met, or hadn't heard from in years, to reach out offering their condolences. "The beautiful piece you wrote about your Little Brother

Jorell had me in tears. I cannot tell you how sorry I am for your loss," wrote a college friend.

"Jorell was a former student of mine," wrote his fifth grade teacher. "This is the first student I've lost. Jorell did struggle in school, but I swear he had more street-smarts and common sense than any other student I've had."

"I hope the memories you have of Jorell, of his life, of your time together can bring you peace," wrote an ex-girlfriend. "As they say in Judaism—may his memory be for a blessing."

Most of the comments to my *Riverfront Times* obituary expressed similar sentiments. But not all of them. At the very bottom I found a comment from a young woman whose name I didn't recognize, Lacey Plumb. She wrote: "Lived by the street, got his ass killed by the streets! Karma MF'r!"

Others in the comments section did not appreciate this, demanding she explain herself. "I use to live with them," she responded, referring to the Cleveland family. "His brother and I were together for some time."

I didn't know if this woman was telling the truth, or if she was just some random internet troll. I wasn't in any hurry to find out. Jorell was a well-meaning kid whose life was stolen in some horrible, random accident, I believed. There was little reason to think otherwise. So I pushed this woman's comment to the back of my mind, chalking it up to the vagaries of the internet.

In the months following Jorell's death I drove up to Ferguson with increasing regularity. I would find reasons to come by the Cleveland house—say, to drop off a box of diapers that my kids had outgrown—but really, it was to talk about Jorell with family members like his dad, Joe; his sister Iesha; and his brother Jermaine.

I wonder what they thought of me, interrupting their days, lurking around and asking strange questions. I was like some weird uncle who just kept inviting myself over. No one ever questioned my being there, though; I'm sure they understood I was working through my loss, just as they were working through theirs. I went to their Fourth of July party and did a shot of vodka with Joe from a two-foot-tall bottle of Grey Goose. I declined food from the grill by explaining my conversion to veganism, and I watched a Cardinals game with Jorell's grandmother and her boyfriend.

My grieving process manifested itself in strange ways. I kept Jorell's senior photo on our fridge for years—never putting it in a frame—I guess so I'd see it morning, noon, and night. Anna and I got into a form of yoga called Kundalini, which focused largely on meditation. I tried to meditate on Jorell, what his life had been like, what was motivating him. I tried to feel his energy, to put myself into his shoes.

Sometimes I'd go to North County for no reason, other than to drive around Ferguson, Kinloch, Jennings, or Berkeley, meandering down back roads I'd never traveled before. I attended random street fairs, visited the sites of abandoned factories. I was driven by an inexplicable compulsion to be there, to understand the place, to unlock its mysteries. I couldn't have told anyone what I was looking for. Maybe I was trying to find Jorell, or rather trying to see the world in which he lived, in order to understand it more. Anna said I started to seem like a ghost. Any time I had a few free hours I left my family and was gone.

It became clear that I was looking for ways to atone for failing to keep Jorell safe. I considered taking on a new Little Brother in the Big Brothers Big Sisters program. I could help someone else who might be in harm's way, and do a better job this time.

But it occurred to me that I already knew plenty of young people who needed help. Jorell's friends and siblings came from the same disadvantaged background he did, and they were suffering from grief to boot. I began spending time with some of them in an informal mentorship role.

I went out to lunch with Jovan Cleveland, who was four years older than his brother Jorell. We'd spoken sporadically over the years. He'd wanted to come along on some of my early outings with Jorell, but I'd said no, something for which I still harbored guilt. "It occurs to me that maybe I should be Jovan's big brother now," I wrote in my diary. "He's probably super neglected."

My heart went out to Jovan. In recent years he'd lost close family members almost annually, starting with his sister Chaz in 2011, followed by his grandmother, his uncle, and his big brother JoJo. After Jorell died in 2016, Jovan went down to Little Rock, Arkansas, to be with his mother, who underwent a leg amputation and died soon afterward. "I took too many losses," Jovan lamented, one day when we were walking around Ferguson.

Anna and I invited him to house-sit and watch our dog when we left town. When I picked him up he played Bob Marley on his phone and spun conspiracy theories about the Illuminati. He had sleepy eyes and a resigned posture. I sometimes wondered how he was going to get ahead. His Southern accent was so thick that I often asked him to repeat himself. He'd attended even less school than Jorell.

While Jorell was alive the two of them did odd jobs around the neighborhood together, alongside their friend Shawn'trell. "We made legal money together," Jovan said. "I tried to keep Jorell away from the streets." Following Jorell's death Jovan took a job assembling cardboard pizza boxes—taking a bus into the city, since he had no car—and then later worked at a used tire place, which required another long bus ride. There were plenty of low-wage jobs to be had. It's just…who wants those jobs? Day in and day out, it's hard enough working a job that's fulfilling. But low-wage work, with long commutes and poor conditions? No wonder he changed jobs frequently.

Jovan had big ideas: he wanted to start an auto body store, with perhaps a day care attached "to help take care of the people in the community," he said. But he didn't have the capital, and I worried he'd fall through the cracks. He also said he wanted to be a welder, and I encouraged him to go to trade school. Anna and I could pay for it, I told him. We had saved money for Jorell's college fund, and it might as well go to a good cause. He hemmed and hawed. One hitch was that he'd need to get his GED before trade schools would accept him, something he was reluctant to try for reasons that were unclear.

Another time I took Jorell's pregnant younger sister Peaches and her boyfriend CJ out to breakfast in a trendy neighborhood called the Loop.

The restaurant, called Moonrise, was bougie, and neither of them liked their food. CJ found the grapefruit juice too bitter. Peaches wondered why they gave her ketchup with her hash browns, and she asked the waiter if she could take home the small glass jar of jelly on the table. "It doesn't belong to me," he responded cryptically. Afterward I drove them to a social services agency so she could sign up for WIC, the supplemental food and nutrition program for pregnant women, infants, and children. On the ride they asked me if signing up for WIC would automatically make CJ responsible for paying child support. I said that no, I didn't think that would happen.

I was concerned for them. They were very young, living in Iesha's cramped apartment near the Loop. They didn't have a car, and though they both worked at a restaurant they could walk to, they were soon laid off. Not long afterward I drove CJ out to West County for a meeting at a temp agency, where the recruiter chewed him out because he smelled strongly of marijuana. He said others in the apartment smoked, not him. He didn't get the job.

I also spent time with two of Jorell's closest friends, Jordan and Dezzy. I'd known them casually while Jorell was alive, and after his funeral I told them how much I liked their memorial tribute T-shirts. Jordan helped me acquire one of my own—black, oversized, and off-gassing—which read "Relle World" and featured photos from different eras of Jorell's life, including one from elementary school, around the time I first met him. In it, he's oddly dressed in a newsboy cap, polka dot vest, and bow tie, with a baseball glove, wearing a tremendous smile. The shirt still hangs in my closet, virtually untouched; I'm never sure the right time to wear it.

I took Jordan and Dezzy to Imo's Pizza in the Central West End. We ate St. Louis–style pizza, the wafer-thin crust—almost like a Saltine cracker—coated with Provel, a white, processed cheese that is ubiquitous throughout St. Louis. We remembered Jorell, his subtle sense of humor, his earnestness. Based on his first name, they called him "Relle Rell"— a moniker he just so happened to share with the member of the rap group 3 Problems who was sent to prison for second-degree murder.

Dezzy was the cool kid, reserved but confident, while Jordan was easygoing and loquacious, with swinging dreadlocks and a tall, athletic figure. Unlike Jorell, they'd both graduated high school, and now had big plans. Jordan wanted to enter the military, or open a gun store, which he and Jorell had dreamed of doing.

They reminisced about high school, speaking candidly.

"We was well known around McCluer, the three of us," Jordan said.

"Well known for what?" I asked.

"Well known for getting girls and always having money," he said. "And always having weed."

"Really?" I said. "I didn't know about that."

"Yeah, sometimes he and I would be smoking out in front of his house when you were coming," Jordan went on. "And then when you pulled up he'd hide the weed and rub his eyes and try to get rid of the smell." To demonstrate, Jordan frantically swatted away an imaginary cloud of smoke.

Dezzy laughed uproariously. I gave a small chuckle and shook my head. It was a funny image, but the conversation made me slightly uncomfortable. It didn't bother me that Jorell smoked weed. But was he selling it too? That's what Jordan seemed to be implying. Sure, weed was on the verge of legality, but it nonetheless remained a dangerous black-market business to be in.

There was more to my discomfort. The Jorell they described ran counter to the Jorell I remembered. I'd always thought of him as a kid who wanted to do kid things—eat junk food, goof around with his friends. This was the Jorell I knew best. But they described an older-than-his-years, alpha dog type, who had the respect of his peers and rebelled against authority figures. This was certainly not unusual for a teenager, but it just didn't jibe with the Jorell I knew. How could I have missed that?

Jordan and I continued getting together. I took him to the DMV to take his driver's license exam, which he passed on his first try. Another time he called me in severe stomach pain, and I drove him to the emergency room. It wasn't clear what the issue was, but after being hooked up to an IV and receiving fluids he felt better. Every few weeks we got Mexican food and discussed his life and job prospects.

Jordan reminded me of Jorell, and his trajectory perhaps resembled what Jorell's might have been if he had lived. One difference was that Jordan had incredible people skills, and didn't have trouble landing jobs—be it at Walmart or in fast food. Keeping them, however, was more difficult. I began mentoring him through a program called Mission: St. Louis, which focused on job training. I believed that what he needed was an actual career, something he was passionate about and that would maintain his interest. The stars appeared to align when he was offered, and accepted, an internship at a CrossFit gym in the suburbs. The manager loved him, offering to fund his training for permanent job placement within the organization.

But on the very last day of his internship Jordan didn't show up for work. Without warning he dropped out of the program entirely, citing the internship's low pay and the long commute. Anna and I put him to work doing odd jobs around the house. He soon lost interest in those as well. At one point he was selling plasma for cash. Before long, Jordan and I fell out of touch. I later tried to track him down, but he no longer had a phone. A mutual friend saw him nodding off in the park. I heard he was descending into drug abuse. Even his own father couldn't find him.

I found myself thinking of him whenever I was in his old neighborhood, North Grand, one of the most dangerous parts of the city, which I've heard called the "heroin mile." I went there for research for my new book about the fentanyl epidemic, and I witnessed street dealers selling fentanyl in front of hourly motels. I remembered a story Jordan told me, about a wino posted up by the liquor store near his house, who sometimes bothered Jordan and his sister when they walked past. One time the wino took things too far—I believe he said something obscene to Jordan's underage sister—and Jordan told his father. His father immediately went down to the liquor store and punched the wino's lights out.

Jordan told me the story with pride. It showed how much his dad cared about him and his sister, he said. And yet, the more I drew him out, the more I realized those weren't his true feelings. Really, he admitted, his dad's actions filled him with guilt and self-loathing. This wino had suffered a brutal payback, one that may have permanently diminished him, because Jordan had tattled. Sure, the guy was a creep, but he was also just an old, feeble drunk. And Jordan was only a kid. A grown man's beating shouldn't have been on his conscience.

I couldn't help but wonder if Jorell's life might have eventually taken a downward trajectory like Jordan's. Particularly since, as was becoming clear, Jorell was not the person I thought he was. Compared to what I'd previously believed, he was bolder, more headstrong, and more willing to engage in risky behavior.

This was difficult to accept. And it made me wonder what other secrets he might have been keeping from me.

CHAPTER ELEVEN

In the first years of my journalism career I was a hip-hop-obsessed music writer who'd never made a Freedom of Information Act request. But while doing research for *Fentanyl, Inc.* I not only uncovered government documents, but met with dark-web traffickers and traveled to China, where I impersonated a drug dealer. I got in a car with the owner of a fentanyl operation, who took me to his *Breaking Bad*–style lab outside of Shanghai. This was risky behavior, but the trip helped me develop my investigative reporting skills, and in the years following Jorell's death I shifted from cultural stories toward those involving narcotics and criminality. I interviewed convicted killers, wore a bulletproof vest to drug sites, and pored over crime statistics.

In the process I learned something that surprised me. Most murder victims, it turns out, have some connection to the person who killed them.

I had assumed a large percentage of murders were random, but in reality most happen among acquaintances. In cases where the perpetrator doesn't know the victim, a robbery or burglary is often involved. Jorell was killed outdoors, in broad daylight. As far as I knew he wasn't being robbed, and he wasn't trying to rob anyone. And since he'd been shot at point-blank range, he was clearly the intended target.

A troubling thought started to develop within me: What if Jorell knew his killer?

Two years had passed since his death, and the wounds were no longer so raw. I began examining it more dispassionately, with fresh eyes. I had allowed myself, or perhaps even forced myself, to accept a story that fit my worldview. But speaking with Jorell's friends helped open me up to truths I'd previously ignored. I no longer wanted to tell myself a story that made me feel comfortable. I wanted the truth.

One thing that kept nagging at me was the comment in my *Riverfront Times* obituary from the woman named Lacey Plumb. She wrote that Jorell "lived by the street." For the first time since his death, this thought began to nag at me. I reread her words. And the more I read, the more I realized I could no longer shut them out.

Soon afterward I sent a Facebook message to Joe. "Do you know someone named Lacey Plumb? She said she dated one of Jorell's brothers and lived at your house."

"Yes," responded Joe. "She was with Jermaine."

I thanked him and called Jermaine, who recalled their time together. "We met in 2013 in a city in Arkansas called Mountain Home," he began. "She stayed in the same trailer park as one of my previous ex-girlfriends." He and Lacey began a relationship, and she followed him back to Ferguson, moving in with the Cleveland family. She and Jorell didn't get along, and before long her relationship with Jermaine descended into bitterness as well. Finally they broke up and she moved back to Arkansas. "She got very disrespectful, calling me all sorts of things," Jermaine said.

It sounded like the rough outlines of her story as presented in the *Riverfront Times* comments section checked out, and I'd eventually contact her personally. But in the meantime, my thinking about Jorell and his murder case began to shift. It wasn't something that happened all at once, but I began thinking about his case less from the perspective of a friend and mentor, and more from the perspective of a reporter.

I stopped assuming his killing had been random. I started talking to people about the details of his final months, the time when he stopped returning my phone calls.

I spoke with Jorell's family and close friends, who told me that Jorell had been engaging in self-destructive behavior. He'd been associating with people with criminal records, some of whom sold drugs and illegal guns.

Jorell never told me about any of this, but maybe I shouldn't have been surprised. When he was alive, Jorell looked up to me. He wanted me to be proud of him.

"How are things in school?" I'd ask.

"Fine," he'd say.

"Is there anything bothering you?" I'd ask.

"Nope," he'd say.

Looking back on these conversations, I realize that Jorell was going through some of the most trying times of his life. But rather than discuss them with me, he went out of his way to make me think everything was okay.

It became clear that there was a Jorell I never knew. He wasn't the carefree kid I'd naively imagined him to be. He was deeply paranoid and often consumed by anger. His violent temper regularly took him to the edge of danger.

The first person I spoke to about the intricate details of Jorell's case was his father, Joe Cleveland. In November 2018, more than two years after Jorell was killed, I gave him a call.

"Hey Joe, how are you doing?"

"I'm fine, Ben. How's the family?"

Normally for a story like this I'd interview the source in person, but this time I felt nervous. I didn't know if Joe wanted to revisit all of this. I worried I'd be dredging up painful memories he'd prefer stay buried. But he appreciated my interest, and had a lot to get off his chest. Some of the broader strokes he'd already told me: shortly after Jorell's death police had arrested a suspect, a guy who lived near the Clevelands and was at least a decade older than Jorell. The detectives wouldn't tell Joe his name, but it didn't seem to be anyone Joe knew. This suspect didn't stay behind bars very long though. Although police had requested cell phone records attempting to place him at the scene, apparently they couldn't gather enough evidence to prosecute him. So they let him go.

This had all happened more than a year ago. Joe had received no updates since.

"The longer it went, the more sour it got," Joe told me. "I really don't think the detectives are putting forth the effort into the case that they should. That's my opinion. They could do a lot more than they're doing."

This nearly broke my heart. It seemed to confirm the worst stereotypes about police detectives assigned to Black cases. I wanted to believe differently. When I thought of heroic detectives on the homicide beat, I pictured Bunk and McNulty from *The Wire*, hard-drinking cops who may have been louses, but they nonetheless worked hard to pursue the truth.

But the police assigned to Jorell's case didn't seem invested. When I tried to get in touch with the lead detective, Jason Rodesiler, he didn't call me back for days. When we finally talked he was curt.

"Can you tell me the name of the suspect who was held in custody?" I asked.

"I cannot," he said.

"Would you mind telling me why?"

"We can't reveal information about an ongoing investigation," he said. He gave this same response to most of my other questions.

I learned what I could about this detective. He was from Michigan originally and served in the Navy. In 2003 he received the Medal of Valor, presented to police officers who perform "a conspicuous act of bravery exceeding the normal demands of police service." I'd imagine that he meant well, and, at the time Jorell was killed, was likely hamstrung by a heavy caseload. The St. Louis County Police Department says its detectives each handle six to eight homicide cases per year, which is better than in the city, where officers handle an average of thirteen, but still more than ideal. A Department of Justice study recommended detectives be assigned only three per year.

The inability of the St. Louis County PD to prosecute anyone for Jorell's death brought to mind a 2018 *Washington Post* investigation, which showed that only about half of murders in the nation's biggest cities get solved. The rate in St. Louis was a dismal 36 percent in 2020, though the numbers were better in St. Louis County. Both nationally and in St. Louis, conviction rates were lower when it came to murdered Black men.

The Cleveland family has a complicated relationship with the police. Jorell's brother Jovan told me about times he'd been harassed for jaywalking, or simply "walking while Black." But following the Ferguson unrest of 2014, including the appointment of the city's first Black police chief, Jovan believed the situation had improved. "I think they're trying to be more friendly," he said. "I think the police actually learned a lesson."

Rece was not so optimistic, maintaining the violence had gotten worse. "After Mike Brown it got really grimy," she said. "Not just in Ferguson, but in St. Louis everywhere—city, county—with the deaths." She blamed police indifference for Jorell's unsolved killing. "Nobody trust the police to do nothing. So [nothing] get solved. They have to actually be caught, at the crime scene, with the weapon in their hand, for them to find out who did anything."

Some observers also cite the so-called Ferguson Effect, which claims the antipolice protests following Michael Brown's killing led to more homicides due to a decline in "proactive" policing, because some cops didn't want to be considered racist or put themselves into hostile situations.

Travis Campbell, an economics PhD student at the University of Massachusetts Amherst, found that, post–Michael Brown, police killings declined while other homicides rose. Campbell studied 1,600 Black Lives Matter protests around the country from 2014 to 2019, finding "a 15 to 20 percent reduction in lethal use of force by police officers— roughly 300 fewer police homicides—in census places that saw BLM protests," according to an analysis by *Vox*. At the same time, there were "somewhere between 1,000 and 6,000 more homicides than would have been expected if places with protests were on the same trend as places that did not have protests."

We'll never know if the Ferguson Effect led to Jorell's killing or affected his case. Another potential factor was witness collaboration with police.

While Jorell's family spoke with detectives, some eyewitnesses and people with relevant information did not. This dovetailed with historic distrust of police in many African American neighborhoods.

In this regard, I believed I could be helpful. As I told Detective Rodesiler, many of Jorell's friends who were unwilling to speak with authorities would talk to me—even with the knowledge that I would bring their information to the police. Rodesiler declined my help.

"We're professionals," he said.

I kept bugging him for updates, until a year or so later a different detective with a hard to pronounce surname took over the case, Ryan Wojciuch. He was friendlier, but also tight-lipped. Everyone kept telling me the same thing—that they couldn't share information about Jorell's case until it was solved.

This was doubly frustrating because, by the looks of things, they would never solve it.

"That's my only son, and I'm still fuckin' mad," Jorell's mother Dianne Robinson told me, when we talked on the phone three years after Jorell's death, her voice rising. "Cause they haven't caught the fucking killer."

I understood this feeling. When I sat in that cop car on the humid afternoon of Jorell's killing, I told them everything I knew. I wanted desperately to help them solve this case.

When they declined my help, at first I hoped this meant they knew what they were doing—that they really didn't need me. But as the weeks turned to months, and as the months turned to years, I began to understand why so many people in Black communities were cynical about the police, how the seeds of their distrust had been sown. The cops were up in everyone's faces giving tickets all day long, yet when it came to something this heartrending, they had nothing to say. Jorell's loved ones were walking around with holes in their hearts, and this killer believed he'd gotten away scot free.

Meanwhile, the Cleveland family's grief and desperation mounted.

Frustrated by the St. Louis County detectives' silence, they sought information from alternative sources. Jorell's older brother Jermaine told me he was considering hiring a "psychic detective," similar to a program he saw on TV. "I need some type of closure with this," he said. "If not who it was, then what was the meaning behind it. What my brother do so bad to piss somebody off to take him to that level?"

"I wish I could have a dream with Jorell in it," his sister Iesha told me, "so he could just tell me who did it so that I could be at ease."

Tonya Walker had been a surrogate mother to Jorell while dating Joe in the 2000s, when she lived with the Cleveland family. Even after she and Joe broke up, and she moved back to her native Arkansas, she maintained a maternal bond with Jorell and called him her son. She was wrecked by his killing, even enlisting a fortune-teller for answers. "Don't worry too much, because the person that did that to your baby is no longer here," she was told.

I felt particularly bad for Joe, who had now lost three children, including two in 2016 alone. "I think about it all the time," Joe said of Jorell's death. "I'd like to know who did it, and what was the reason: Why? That would make me feel a lot better. My son being gone, I don't want it to affect my health, me worrying about it. I try not to let it take me out too."

Hearing this was devastating. A murder conviction in a court of law wasn't necessarily important for him, he stressed, but he wanted to know who killed Jorell, and why. It was clear that the St. Louis County police were not going to provide this information.

I wasn't a detective, of course, but I'd grown increasingly confident in my investigative reporting skills. The work wasn't really so different. It similarly involved a lot of "shoe leather" reporting: interviewing, gathering clues, assessing motives, and pulling public records.

The sad truth was that if I didn't do this, no one else was going to.

I had no idea if I had the skills or courage to pull it off. But at the very least I wanted to understand the unjust world that took Jorell down, how the socioeconomic injustices that shaped his life came to be. I wanted to know the particulars of his last months, and to understand the *real* Jorell, the person he kept from me. How had his life reached the breaking point?

One woman I talked to, named Nett, was particularly thoughtful. Nett, the sister of Jorell's ex-girlfriend Khrys, was frustrated that no headway had been made in his case. She'd heard all the neighborhood theories about who might have done it, but wasn't satisfied. "Nobody really knows who killed Jorell, it's just all talk. It's all speculation," she said.

But when I insisted that the truth had to be out there somewhere, she softened.

"Yes," she said. "Somebody has to know something."

CHAPTER TWELVE

I started my investigation with the hours leading up to his death. What brought Jorell to the intersection of Courtney and Jefferson Avenues, where he was killed? This was just over a mile from Jorell's house, but it wasn't in Ferguson—it was in the adjacent municipality of Kinloch. Really, it was a world apart, considering, as I learned, there was a gang rivalry between the two areas. I had no idea why Jorell would have been there.

His family painted a picture for me: The early hours of August 27, 2016, were hot and muggy. Unfortunately for the Cleveland boys, Joe had promised their next door neighbor they would reshingle his roof. And so that morning they climbed up with their gear. "I was doing siding and hatching tar," Jorell's brother Jermaine told me. "It was plenty hot." As for Jorell, after doing this punishing work for a time, he decided he'd had enough.

He climbed down, went inside his house, showered, and put on his outfit for the day: a black T-shirt, jean shorts, and black Nike basketball shoes, complemented by a pair of square gold earrings and a large gold chain necklace.

The evening before, Jermaine had admired the chain. "I want one," he told Jorell, to which Jorell smiled coyly. "Damn, big bro trying to be like me," he said. They laughed. The necklace, featuring the Freemason symbol with a square and compass, cost about $25. Neither of them were

Freemasons, but the chain looked cool, how it evoked images of rich and powerful men plotting in secret corridors of power. Jermaine gave him the cash to buy one, and Jorell told his girlfriend Danielle he'd buy a necklace for her as well.

He planned to make the purchases at a bodega called Airport Market, located about two miles away from the Cleveland house, in the town of Berkeley. It was a low-rent operation that was part head shop and part junk food convenience store, and that also had a locked case of inexpensive jewelry.

As Jorell prepared to depart the house that morning, he asked his father if he could borrow his GMC Sierra truck.

"Where are you going?" Joe asked him.

"I'll be right back," Jorell responded.

"But where are you going?"

"Why do I always have to tell you where I'm going? You let Iesha take the truck anytime she wants it!" Jorell responded angrily.

Jorell's anger seemed misplaced; he didn't even have his license, after all. Since he couldn't procure the truck, he stormed out of the house on foot. He took with him his black 1911 semiautomatic pistol, which, I'd later learn, he kept on him almost all the time.

It was maybe 1:45 p.m. when Jorell departed. He headed north along Oak Avenue until he cut over to his friend Malon's house. He wanted Malon to come with him to the store, but his girlfriend said he wasn't there. So Jorell went back to Oak Avenue, heading north to Carson Road, where he took a left into Kinloch.

This was a shortcut to the bodega, but an ill-advised one. At the Kinloch city limits, Carson Road becomes Martin Luther King Boulevard. It is a desolate, rural-feeling street, and the few houses along it were populated with drug and gun dealers. Jorell passed these homes and nearly made it to the western edge of Kinloch before he was gunned down at Courtney and Jefferson Avenues.

His family learned of his shooting when three young men from Kinloch pulled up in front of the Cleveland home.

"Hey, aren't you Jorell's brother?" one of them said to Jermaine, seeing him up on the roof. Jermaine didn't know the guy, but he noticed he had a prominent neck tattoo and that he pronounced Jorell's name in an odd way.

"Yeah," responded Jermaine.

"He's been shot," the guy said. "He's laying in the street."

"Bullshit," said Jermaine, wondering who these guys were. "Stop playing."

"Naw bro, for real. It's him."

Jermaine hurried down the ladder to tell Joe. In the meantime, the three guys rang the front doorbell, breaking the news to Jorell's sister Iesha and her boyfriend Mike.

"Is y'all Jorell family?" asked the guy with the neck tattoo.

"What you mean?" said Iesha.

"Because he in the street right now in Kinloch, dead," he said. The three guys claimed they'd seen Jorell just moments before the shooting, walking in the opposite direction. They'd said hello before continuing on their way, but soon heard a gunshot. They ran back to find Jorell lying in the road, with no one else around.

Iesha grabbed the keys to her father's truck from between her bosoms. She and Mike hightailed it over to the scene.

Joe and Jermaine came quickly too. When they arrived, Jorell was still breathing. The police had formed a barricade around him. Jermaine begged to be allowed to employ his Marines paramedic training and administer CPR. They wouldn't let him. Jorell died minutes later.

There were clues to be found in this timeline of events, I believed. In an attempt to flesh out the details, I began conducting interviews. I wanted to identify Jorell's enemies, and who might have had a motive to kill him.

Starting in 2018, I spent increasing amounts of time in Ferguson and Kinloch, at the Cleveland house, on Oak Avenue, on Martin Luther King Boulevard, and throughout North County. Now I wasn't just wandering aimlessly, but visiting sites relevant to Jorell's case and conducting interviews, some with people who knew Jorell closely, and some with people who didn't, both on and off the record. I also spoke with numerous in-carcerated people, sometimes using coded language so my sources would not incriminate themselves over recorded lines.

These sources answered thousands of my questions. They described Jorell's character, his strengths and his flaws, and their memories of him. They conveyed the depth of their heartbreak, and gave their theories about who might have killed him. They helped me understand his daily life and the ins and outs of life on the margins. They described what it was like for him to live without a safety net, to attend failing schools, and to maintain a peer group that included convicted felons.

I compiled our conversations into an outline.

Patterns emerged. Certain names kept coming up, people who'd pissed Jorell off or been pissed off by him. It was shocking how quickly he'd escalated small disagreements into major beefs.

He'd even managed to get into it with a guy in a wheelchair, a man a few years older who apparently lived by Jorell's girlfriend, Danielle, in nearby Berkeley. Jorell's friend Big Ant said this guy was paralyzed, to the extent that he needed someone to hold a cigarette up to his mouth so he could smoke. One source told me that Jorell took offense when he flirted with Danielle, and that Jorell had perhaps brandished a weapon against him. "He came to Jorell like, 'This is how I got into this wheelchair, because of beefing with people like you,'" Jorell's sister Peaches told me.

I eventually eliminated this man as a suspect. But I continued gathering information on a half dozen others, all of them men from Ferguson or Kinloch. I compiled dossiers on this group of six, including information about their backgrounds, motivations, and allegiances. I tracked down their real names—not always easy, considering many were known only by nicknames—and investigated their criminal records. I read about the charges against them on Missouri CaseNet, the website of the state courts. I viewed their photos on their Facebook pages.

I was struck by the similarity of their postures, the way they brandished their pistols, intended as boasts or warnings. They were sometimes smiling and defiant, other times nonchalant. What they had in common was that they all came from poor North County families, plagued by generations of societal indifference to their plight. American poverty these days isn't just dusty trailer parks and food stamps; it's equally likely to be young men holding semiautomatic rifles in YouTube videos.

I began making regular visits to the Ferguson police station and the St. Louis County Police Department in Clayton to pull police records and court documents, departing with reams of printouts. For federal cases I visited the Thomas F. Eagleton US Courthouse, named for 1972 Democratic presidential candidate George McGovern's original choice for vice president. A Missouri senator at the time, Eagleton was forced to drop off the ticket after revelations surfaced that he'd received electroshock therapy for depression.

My suspects had long rap sheets, including crimes from before and after Jorell's killing. None had murder charges, just drug and gun violations, with some accusations of robbery and violence. Not all the charges were prosecuted, and I took any unsubstantiated police allegations with a grain of salt.

Much of what I learned made me squirm. While looking into the January 2015 bus stop shooting on Oak Avenue—in which Jorell said he'd been targeted while stepping off the bus, through no fault of his own—I found the files of Poncho, the alleged perpetrator. The Ferguson Police Department's report deviated sharply from Jorell's account.

According to the report, an officer named Michael White responded to the scene at the bus stop. He talked to a few people and didn't learn much. But he soon received word that a black Cadillac SUV was "driving through the area and flourishing weapons." The vehicle was stopped by Ferguson police sergeant Harry Dilworth, who spoke with Poncho.

"It was then learned from Sgt. Dilworth that Poncho was actually the victim of the earlier shots fired," reads the report. "Poncho was in the area [when the] bus stopped and let out some students. Poncho stated that a subject he identified as Jorell Cleveland approached him. According to Poncho Jorell fired multiple shots at him as he fled for safety. Instead of calling the police it was learned that Poncho called his cousin who had in his possession two firearms and they were circling the area prior to being stopped."

That was all the report said. Poncho declined to pursue criminal charges against Jorell.

I wasn't entirely sure what to believe. Poncho clearly had his own incentives to lie. But it appeared likely that Jorell hadn't told me the whole story. Even if he had been shot at (which wasn't clear), he wasn't an entirely innocent party. Perhaps his transfer away from his high school made sense.

That's not to say Poncho was an angel. Since the bus stop incident he had been arrested on a number of low-level charges relating to drugs, weapons, theft, and resisting arrest. There were no indications he was involved in Jorell's death, however. The bus stop shooting took place some nineteen months before Jorell was killed, and Poncho had moved away from Ferguson in the interim.

Still, it made me question the narratives Jorell had told me, and made me wonder how many enemies he had out there. I continued pulling files and conducting interviews, and eventually was able to eliminate more suspects. One was Lil Glen, Jorell's former friend who used to sleep over at the Cleveland house, who stole Joe Cleveland's guns and then later shot at him and Jorell, hitting Joe in the back. He seemed to have been incarcerated at the time of the shooting.

Ultimately I settled on three suspects. Each had serious issues with Jorell. Each seemed equally plausible as a suspect. From there, however, things got murky.

CHAPTER THIRTEEN

Iesha Cleveland was one of my favorite members of the Cleveland family. About four years older than Jorell, she had style and panache, apt to change hairstyles or fly off to Vegas to party with girlfriends at a moment's notice. But she was also grounded, and something of the Cleveland matriarch. The eldest of Jorell's four living sisters, she was the family glue, planning get-togethers, organizing remembrances of the three deceased siblings (Chaz, Joseph Jr., and Jorell), and making herself available to look after her nieces and nephews. Like Jorell, Iesha was a hard worker, always holding a job. She mopped up bathrooms, cleaned airplanes at St. Louis Lambert airport, or worked the drive-thru dispensing fried chicken. She shared an apartment with her boyfriend, Mike Fuller, and their baby near the Loop. Various members of the family stayed with them at different points.

Following Jorell's death I also became close with Mike. Though he was about six years older than Jorell, the two had been best friends. Before Mike and his clan moved to the Loop, they lived in the Cleveland house, staying in a room just down the hall from Jorell. Mike and Jorell spent a lot of time together, playing zombie video games, smoking weed, and just rolling around the neighborhood.

When I had questions about Jorell's secret life—the stuff he kept from me—people often referred me to Mike, who knew him better than almost anyone.

Mike was happy to chat. Verbose and outgoing, he was the opposite of Jorell, who tended to be inward and quiet. Mike was always trying to do right. He earned his Occupational Safety and Health Administration license and for a stint drove a forklift at the Schnucks warehouse in Kinloch. Sometimes he stayed home full time to care for his daughter.

I'd begun speaking with Mike at Jorell's funeral repast. He is short with bright hazel eyes, and has a way of quickly drawing you into his confidence. He talked to me like we were longtime friends.

"I heard a lot about you from Jorell," he said. "I feel like I already know you."

He was clearly suffering. He got Jorell's name tattooed on his left arm in the weeks following Jorell's death, with a crown above it. "Me and Iesha never got married but me and Jorell still called each other brothers," he tearfully reminisced one time, adding that he'd been having dreams about him. "Him straight talking to me. I loved him."

Mike added that I too had been a very special person in Jorell's life. "You don't know how much influence you had, Ben," he said. "He used to watch the porch for you, when you came to pick him up on the weekends. Your opinion of him mattered."

This surprised me to hear. I thought Jorell considered me a nag, in his later years, since I was always hounding him about his schoolwork and eating habits. Plus, he hadn't trusted me enough to tell me the truth about the stickier aspects of his life.

"He felt like he had to put on a fake persona for you because he didn't want to ever let you down," Mike explained.

His words nearly brought me to tears. I hated the idea that Jorell couldn't show me who he really was, but Mike's insight seemed to positively affirm our relationship.

Mike spoke in a thick St. Louis accent. The local grocery store chain Schnucks became "Snooks," errands were "urrends," "I don't care" was "I don't curr." He used "scary" to mean "scared," as in, so-and-so was "too scary" to have killed Jorell.

He spent a lot of time with his identical twin brother Montrel. Both were light-skinned with tufts of chin hair, except that Montrel wore long dreadlocks and packed on a few extra pounds.

They were both charming, but I quickly learned they were complicated people who'd had troubles with the law. In August 2017 they were both arrested and charged with second-degree robbery. Feeling remorseful, neither wanted to discuss the details of their crime; they knew they had made mistakes that could cost them years of their lives, and they were both fighting substance abuse issues simultaneously. Though I don't have any legal training, I tried to help them navigate a legal system that was historically stacked against African Americans. In late 2018 I began meeting up with them at the St. Louis County Courthouse on days when they had hearings, and sitting in on meetings with their lawyers.

The courthouse is in downtown Clayton, a rare part of that wealthy suburb where the rich and the poor comingle, where people on different sides of the law keep company. On a typical weekday you get down-and-outers, young mothers pushing strollers, quick-walking prosecutors, and eager assistants. Sartorial styles range from long synthetic braids and baseball caps to polished leather shoes and bow ties. The courthouse is a windowless environment lit by dull fluorescents, with the smell of stale marijuana hanging in the air. Some defendants are white, though more are Black, and most of the legal professionals are white.

Attached to the courthouse is the county jail, part of the Buzz Westfall Justice Center, named for the late St. Louis County executive, a doughy white guy who grew up in St. Louis public housing. After Mike and Montrel's arrests they spent about five months in the jail while their mother put up the deed to their house as collateral to secure their bond. Now, as their cases unfolded, they returned frequently to the courthouse.

The days featured long stretches of boredom while we waited for the wheels of justice to turn, interspersed with chaotic spurts of activity when a lawyer or judge called them to attention. During the periods of downtime we had wide-ranging conversations about Jorell. Mostly I spoke with Mike. I wanted to know everything—good and bad—even if it was sometimes difficult to hear. When it came to Jorell's case, Mike was something of an amateur investigator himself. He badly wanted to know the shooter's identity, and he kept his ear to the streets.

As my efforts ramped up he was willing to share his theories, and I was glad to hear them. I needed grassroots help with my investigation, since working official channels had failed. Mike described to me the movers and shakers in the world Jorell inhabited.

I first wanted to know about the man St. Louis County police arrested as a suspect. Though he was never formally charged and they let him go, I figured there must have been *some* reason they apprehended him in the first place.

Though I'd later learn his name was Chauncey James, at the time I had no information about him. The detectives told Joe Cleveland he was a married man who lived near the Cleveland home in Ferguson. One of my sources told me where she believed he lived, so I scoped out the location and ran the address through databases. But it turned out to be the wrong house.

Mike Fuller, however, had more accurate information about Chauncey James. He didn't know him, but he knew about Jorell's interactions with him. To my shock, Mike said Jorell had been involved in violent incidents with both this man and his wife, Marsha James. Mike told me the details one winter morning in early 2019, in the courthouse's fourth floor waiting area.

The first altercation happened a couple of months before Jorell's death. It was an ugly incident that occurred at a time when Jorell was behaving particularly recklessly, Mike said. He had stopped listening to reason.

It was a late evening in June or early July 2016. That night Mike and Jorell were in the market for Swisher Sweets cigars; they planned to empty out the tobacco and fill them with weed. To make the purchase, they drove to a convenience store called R&R Mini Mart & Liquor.

Located just across the street from an Imo's Pizza franchise, R&R was a stand-alone, nondescript bodega selling snacks, cigarettes, and booze. It's the kind of establishment that dots Ferguson, North County, and low-income neighborhoods all over the country. In November 2017 a man was shot and killed in front of it. Surveillance footage captured the presumed shooter, a woman in a red, white, and blue stocking cap who ambushed the man in his car. In her retreat she dropped the cap, which later tested positive for her DNA.

All was quiet on the night Jorell and Mike arrived. They'd come in Montrel's car, and brought Mike's young daughter with them. They purchased their items, and in the parking lot encountered a guy Jorell knew, who was passing through on his bike. He and Jorell embraced; Mike had no idea they knew each other. The guy said he wanted to buy some weed and Jorell said he'd be happy to supply him, back at the Cleveland house. "We'll give you a ride," Jorell insisted. "You can throw your bike in the back." The guy nodded in agreement and Mike popped the trunk.

Just then Marsha James—the wife of the man police would arrest as a suspect in Jorell's murder—showed up. She was also the older sister of the boy who wanted weed from Jorell. She was African American, in her early thirties.

It's unclear why she had come. In Mike's recollection, she was drinking from a plastic cup filled with a purple-colored drink. She stopped when she saw the assembled group. She did not like the idea of her brother getting a ride from Jorell and Mike. Although she didn't know them personally, she knew them by reputation.

"Don't get in the car with them," Marsha told her brother loudly. "They be having guns!" She also derisively noted that they didn't have Mike's daughter in a proper car seat.

Jorell did not take kindly to this. He began to get heated. "Calm down," Mike said to him quietly. But it was no use. Jorell told her to shut up, and he and Marsha began to argue. She gave as good as she got. She was "talking crazy," Mike said. "She was getting all in his face."

As her argument with Jorell escalated and reached a breaking point, she threw the purple beverage from her cup in his face, Mike recalled. Jorell responded by punching her in the mouth.

"I couldn't believe he would hit a woman that hard," Mike told me.

My eyes bulged. I couldn't believe it either.

Marsha's brother tried to intercede. "That's my sister!" he said. Then Jorell punched him too, Mike said. He and Jorell quickly got into the car and peeled out.

Mike couldn't remember any more specifics about the incident, which had taken place almost three years ago. It all happened in a flash. The police weren't called, but one thing was clear: Jorell had made an enemy that night. In fact, he'd made a whole family of enemies.

I didn't have to pry these details out of Mike; it seemed almost cathartic for him to share memories of a violent incident that unfolded right before his eyes.

"I couldn't believe it, Ben," he said. "Jorell just lost it."

I didn't know what to think. Playing the scene in my mind's eye was almost like watching a movie, except the part of Jorell was played by someone altogether different. Punching a woman just didn't align with the Jorell I knew.

Jorell never revealed his temper to me. Not once did I see him lose control, or even so much as swear loudly.

But following his death, many people spoke to me of his volatility. When he was only nine or ten, Joe said, he threatened his mother when they had a disagreement. "I'll pick up a brick, and I'll bust your head," he told her, in Joe's recollection. Jorell's friend Nett called him a "ticking time bomb" who "fought everyone in the family." Apparently he didn't hesitate to pull out his gun at the smallest provocation—his friend Big Ant said he suffered from a Napoleon complex. Once, Jorell had a dispute with an associate while they were riding in a car, which culminated in Jorell spitting on him. The guy's nickname? Killa.

You have to be pretty brazen to antagonize someone named Killa.

Another person who testified to Jorell's menace was Lacey Plumb, the woman responsible for the disparaging comment on my *Riverfront Times* obituary. "Lived by the street, got his ass killed by the streets!" she wrote. Eventually, I got ahold of her. She was living in Arkansas, where she'd originally met Jorell's older brother Jermaine, before moving in with him in the Cleveland house. Their relationship didn't last; each had ugly accusations against the other. But when I wrote to Lacey, she accused Jorell of assaulting her.

"I had a very traumatic experience," she wrote back. "I was assaulted while living there on 2 occasions once being by Jorell."

Lacey didn't go into further details. She still needed more time to reflect on the incidents, she said.

She sounded credible. I tended to believe her account, especially considering that at the Ferguson bodega Jorell had apparently assaulted another woman, Marsha James, the wife of the man who would become a suspect in his murder. As much as I didn't want to believe Jorell was capable of such horrific behavior, it was becoming apparent that he was.

Back at the courthouse on that winter morning in 2019, as we waited to hear from Mike's lawyer, Mike described the fallout from the incident at R&R Mini Mart & Liquor.

Mike wasn't with Jorell on the Fourth of July in 2016 when Jorell next saw Marsha James, only a few days after he'd punched her at R&R. But Jorell told Mike about it afterward.

Jorell was again headed to R&R, but this time on foot. He was accompanied by his girlfriend, Danielle, and another of his friends. Jorell had purchased fireworks for the occasion, and they started the Independence Day celebration early. "They were walking up and down the street shooting fireworks," said Mike.

I could imagine the scene. People go all out for the Fourth of July in St. Louis. Even though lighting fireworks is illegal in both the city and the county, that doesn't stop many from detonating elaborate works right in the middle of streets. The madness begins well before nightfall, and liquor and marijuana inevitably get involved. By the time it's over, scores of adults and children have landed in emergency rooms with fireworks-related injuries.

Jorell and his group soon passed in front of Marsha James's home, Mike explained to me. I later visited the area. The modest, pale bungalows on the block are spaced about twenty feet apart, with oversize backyards of thick grass and weedy vines. Kids play outside, and people arrive on Sundays for church nearby. The short distance between the Cleveland home and the James household explained how Marsha could know Jorell and Mike by reputation, and be wary of her brother hanging out with them, as she'd said at the bodega.

On this night it wasn't yet dark when Marsha, who was either out in front of her home or looking out the front window, recognized Jorell passing by. She told her husband, Chauncey James, the murder suspect, who proceeded to address Jorell and walk toward him.

"Hey bro, come and let me holler at you," Chauncey said, acting as if he were interested in making a weed purchase.

Jorell had his Lacoste manpurse with him—the one I'd tried to open when he stayed with us. It likely contained marijuana he had for sale. Even though Jorell didn't know this man, Jorell was nonetheless prepared to transact right there. He asked Chauncey specifically what he wanted.

"As he started to pull his weed out, dude just punched Jorell dead in his mouth," Mike said.

Jorell immediately dropped his bag, pulled out his gun, and began firing. Chauncey James went running back behind the couple's house.

"You wanna play with guns? Okay, I'ma kill you!" Chauncey yelled, in Mike's telling.

"I should kill you right now, then!" Jorell responded.

By now Marsha James was screaming for mercy. Danielle also desperately urged Jorell to leave the premises. "You'll go to jail," she wailed.

Jorell relented, and they hustled back to the Cleveland house, where Jorell described to Mike what had transpired. But Jorell hadn't calmed down; he wanted to turn around and go right back, "to whoop him," Mike said. Danielle intervened, however, and convinced him to stay put.

I could barely make sense of what I was hearing. This story sounded incredible to me. During Jorell's life I had no idea that he regularly kept a gun on him, or that he sold weed.

These turned out to be two more aspects of Jorell's life that he kept from me. And though the Ferguson Police Department had no record of this incident, Jorell's sister Peaches would confirm much of Mike's account.

Yet there remained many things I couldn't understand. Why would neither Chauncey James nor his wife Marsha—nor any of the neighbors—have reported this shooting? Could the gunshots have been mistaken for Fourth of July fireworks?

Had Jorell really become so unhinged that he would shoot at someone?

And then, finally, there was the most important question of all: Had Chauncey James retaliated for these incidents by killing Jorell?

I chewed on the possibility that this man murdered Jorell. I considered the idea that something so small, so silly—a dispute in a liquor store parking lot—might have led to his undoing. It depressed me profoundly.

I got to work learning everything I could about Chauncey James. Born in 1983, he was raised in Pagedale, the inner-ring North County suburb where, coincidentally, Jorell is now buried. He was fourteen years older than Jorell, and married with, I believe, two daughters. Having previously served as a security officer, he now cut hair. Sometimes wearing a tuft of chin hair and diamond earrings, he had silver grills on his teeth and tattoos all over his neck, chest, and arms.

I'd never met him in person, but he left a large internet footprint, posting photos of haircuts and beard touch-ups he'd given, pictures of his family, and occasionally unnerving Instagram posts. In one he wears a bulletproof vest; in another, posted four years after Jorell's killing, he almost seems to take credit for it: "mfs crossed me," it reads, "ain't even cross em back, I crossed em out."

He'd also uploaded dozens of YouTube videos, some intended to be humorous, like one where he torments his aunt by not providing her access to a restroom when she badly needs to go number two. In others he shows off assault rifles and looks intimidating. But mostly he posted rap videos. Though he hadn't achieved a significant following, he clearly dreamed of hip-hop stardom, photographing himself in front of the famous Capitol Records building in LA, and in front of a mural of deceased rap icon Nipsey Hussle.

Chauncey James carried himself a bit like Wu-Tang Clan's Ghostface Killah (they have the same smile), but he lacked the lyrical acumen of the famous performer, as he delivered standard boasts about money, jewelry, women, and the violence he'd enact upon his foes. Sure, impersonating a nihilistic killer was common in St. Louis hip-hop. Yet some of his videos were genuinely frightening, with guys in ski masks and laser-sighted guns robbing people and taking them hostage.

The lyrics to one of his songs in particular really got to me. The track derides men who talk tough until a gun is in their face.

> *Then they call for God*
> *"Please don't take me out"*

But James shows no mercy in the song, gunning his adversary down.

Performing alternately before a red brick wall and sitting on a set of frayed interior steps, an AK displayed behind him, he seemed to summon the words from deep within, mocking his victim and putting his hands together like a desperate man in prayer.

Why would someone boast about such a lack of humanity, even under the guise of a rap persona? I had to turn the video off. Unlike most of his lyrics, these didn't seem like idle boasts. Something about the track sounded way too real.

Did it come from a true experience?

Could "Please don't take me out" have been Jorell's last words?

I was still processing this when I heard a related rumor that caught my attention. According to one of my sources, Chauncey James—whom Jorell allegedly shot at on the Fourth of July—was related to another one of Jorell's enemies: the guy in the wheelchair who apparently bothered Jorell by flirting with Danielle.

It was unclear how they were related. But my source said James's vehicle could regularly be seen parked in front of the house where the wheelchair man lived.

Further, my source heard rumors of a conversation in this house, which happened only a few days before Jorell died. In this conversation, someone said "something was about to happen" to Jorell.

It's unclear who said this. It was a vague rumor, one that would be difficult to verify. Particularly because, as I soon learned, the man in the wheelchair had been killed sometime after Jorell's death.

Details were sparse. But I was intrigued by the possibility that two people with strong grudges against Jorell were related—and that they may have been plotting together.

I spoke again with Joe Cleveland. He'd also learned about the drink-throwing incident and the Fourth of July altercation from Mike, and he had recognized the moody behavior in his son. "He should have been humble," Joe told me. "Sure, she threw a drink on him, she might have made a mistake, but he shouldn't have to retaliate every time somebody's out there being stupid."

As for Chauncey James, Joe couldn't decide if he should take him seriously as a suspect. "I don't know what to think, what to believe," he said. After all, he had an incomplete picture. If Jorell encountered Chauncey or his wife, Marsha, again before his death, he didn't mention it to anyone.

I was frustrated by the lack of available information. If only the detectives would collaborate with me, I believed, we could solve this case together.

More questions: How did Marsha James and her brother—both of whom Jorell had punched at R&R, according to Mike—play into all of this? Remember, Jorell and the brother knew each other; his asking Jorell for weed had set this chain of events in motion.

Further, Jorell had been shot in broad daylight. Had there been any witnesses? Had any of them identified Chauncey James as the shooter? There were signs pointing toward his potential guilt. He seemed to have a clear motive: anger at Jorell's treatment of his wife, and fear for their lives. So why had the police let him go?

To me, Chauncey James seemed a clear person of interest in Jorell's murder. In my investigation, I considered him suspect #1. But not everyone felt he was guilty. In fact, many of Jorell's friends and family believed a different man was responsible for his death, someone to whom the police never spoke.

This young man was named Leron White. He lived in the neighboring municipality of Kinloch, where Jorell was killed. I began considering him suspect #2. Leron was about a year younger than Jorell, and was a particularly complicated figure in Jorell's life.

For starters, Jorell considered him a friend.

CHAPTER FOURTEEN

For all of Jorell's troubles in his final months, he had one bright spot in his life: he was in love.

His girlfriend, Danielle, was a junior at McCluer, one year younger than he. She was soft-spoken and super sweet, a pale, red-haired girl with a chin piercing, who was also raised in poverty. She'd come to my surprise party in May 2015, and I'd chat with her when I visited Jorell. We stayed in touch after his death, though she didn't want to be interviewed for my investigation. I suspect she feared retaliation.

In his final year, they were eager to share their love with the world. One of their Facebook photos was framed by emojis blowing kisses. In another picture, her pastel-green nails match her jacket, and he looks sharp in a hoodie and designer jeans. They're hugging so tightly it's like they're holding on for dear life.

Jorell was proud of this relationship. He'd officially graduated from being the short, broke, runt on the block to manhood, and had the beautiful girlfriend to prove it. They would have spent every moment together, but she lived more than a mile and a half away, in the nearby municipality of Berkeley, and he had no driver's license. Though he sometimes convinced family members to lend him their vehicles, he often found himself making the long slog on foot.

To get to her house he would cut through Kinloch—the same shortcut he took the day he was killed. In an effort to understand what this route was like, I traced it one autumn afternoon, leaving the Cleveland family's Ferguson house and going north along Oak Avenue. I passed cars and trucks parked up on the curb, and the occasional passing bus. I kept going past an urban farm and turned left at a church.

From there it got quiet. I continued down blocks of declining property value into Kinloch, where the quality of the road deteriorated and the grass was no longer mowed.

Much of the landscape smells fresh and undisturbed in Kinloch, like you're in the woods. Vines wrap around tree trunks. Birds sing. Though Kinloch was a bustling place until fairly recently, it's now turning back into what it was in the nineteenth century—the country.

The town was named for a horse farm owned by James Lucas Turner, a Virginia-born West Point alum who, following the Civil War, was briefly jailed for his Southern sympathies. He brought his farm to the area around 1883 and, when he died of typhoid five years later, the land was sold off for residential development. City residents were lured by clean water and a rail line that had been established from downtown St. Louis, twelve miles to the southeast. Kinloch's airfield made international news in 1910 when Teddy Roosevelt, recently out of office, became the first president to fly in an airplane, a three-minute flight on one of those boxy contraptions with bicycle wheels. That same year, a man who was believed to be the country's only African American pilot at the time, J. Arthur Headon, gave a flight exhibition. The airfield also hosted the country's first control tower, its first parachute jump, and its first animal—a cow—to be airlifted by plane.

By the early twentieth century Kinloch was a quickly developing suburb, with white commuters bringing their Black servants with them. Some Black people had already moved to the area; historians believe Kinloch may have been a pre–Civil War Underground Railroad site, where escaped enslaved people built farms. During the Great Migration it became a refuge for African Americans fleeing persecution in the South. Others arrived as a result of the East St. Louis massacre of 1917, which included lynchings and the burning of Black homes while residents were still inside. Plots of land in Kinloch were sold to both races, although in some cases African Americans were charged twice the price. Despite these obstacles, dozens of Black families moved into the southeast section of Kinloch, and before long the area's population included more Black people than whites. This majority elected an African American school board member for the first time in Missouri history.

This was too much for Kinloch's whites, who in 1937 broke away and incorporated the northern part of Kinloch as an independent city— Berkeley. There, they could have their own school district, one entirely free of Black people. Yet once again, Kinloch persevered. It opened its own high school, saving students the hour and a half commute to the only other Black high school in the county. Kinloch elected Missouri's first Black school superintendent, and, in 1948, became the state's first municipality to be incorporated by African Americans.

It went on to become the largest all-Black city in the country, and completely self-sustaining. Kinloch had its own grocery stores, appliance store, drug store, YMCA, and library, as well as a chapter of Marcus Garvey's Universal Negro Improvement Association. You could even see good live music; B. B. King once played a club in town, called 12 Oaks. The town's population peaked in 1960, with about 6,500 residents.

Actress Jenifer Lewis's hundreds of television, movie, and theater roles have included Anthony Anderson's straight-talking mother on *Black-ish*, Will Smith's Aunt Helen in *The Fresh Prince of Bel-Air*, and Tupac's mother in *Poetic Justice*. She is among Kinloch's most famous alums, and she discusses her childhood in her memoir *The Mother of Black Hollywood* :

> The Kinloch of my childhood consisted of little wood houses, some not more than shacks, outhouses, and rocky roads. Most residents were so damn poor they couldn't afford to go to the doctor unless they were damn near dead. It seemed that people were always dying just walking down the street or coming out

of the Threaded Needle, the only legal bar in town (there were many underground juke joints that sold moonshine).

When Lewis was a toddler, she, her mother, and her six siblings were forced to take refuge in a windowless room in the basement of an abandoned Baptist church to avoid homelessness. Even when they found permanent housing they still had to use an outhouse—or, if it was too cold, a bucket. Growing up, she would sneak out to see movies in Ferguson, despite warnings that it wasn't safe for Black folk. But not everything about her childhood was bad.

> The people in authority came from our community and were part of our culture.... When Mama was really struggling and our refrigerator was empty, I could stop by the house of any of my play mamas: Miss Barnes, Miss Clark, or Miss Benson. When I got real lucky, someone had made a tub of greens or cornbread in a skillet or a pot of neck bones.

As a young girl she held one-woman talent shows in the Catholic school basement. She posted handmade signs all over town for these Saturday night performances, for which she charged thirty-five cents, performing songs by Aretha Franklin and Gladys Knight. "The talent shows became so popular," Lewis writes, "folks would barbecue outside in the parking lot and sell rib tip sandwiches, pigs' feet, and hot dogs, with orange and cream sodas. It was *the* Saturday night event in Kinloch."

Just as they are today, protests against law enforcement were common in the Kinloch of Lewis's childhood. In 1962, hundreds protested and rioted for days following the killing of a teenager by a Kinloch police officer. (Both were Black.) It's unclear exactly what happened; officer Israel Mason was apparently trying to serve nineteen-year-old Darnell Dortch with a traffic court summons following a drag race. Mason contended the young man wrestled for his pistol, which then discharged by accident, though others said Mason pulled the youth from his car and fired on him. Mason doesn't appear to have been criminally charged.

In the aftermath three policemen were shot and fires were set around town, including at the home of Kinloch's police chief. St. Louis County police reinforcements patrolled the streets with machine guns, and they rounded up people they thought had set the fires.

Neighboring Ferguson, meanwhile, had developed into a mostly white bedroom community. Some residents chafed at the all-Black city next door, and around the 1960s Ferguson installed a barricade on a main thoroughfare, Suburban Avenue, which blocked traffic between the two towns. These types of roadblocks can be found all over the St. Louis region. In the city, giant concrete planters filled with dirt and scraggly plants block traffic at many intersections. They're known as Schoemehl pots, after Vince Schoemehl, a three-term mayor of St. Louis from the early 1980s to the early '90s. Though they were imagined as crime deterrents and intended to slow traffic, many believe they have racist intent. A Saint Louis University study showed they don't actually reduce crime.

Following Martin Luther King Jr.'s assassination in April 1968, Kinloch citizens marched to the site of the barricade with Ferguson and demanded it be removed. Ferguson leaders complied, though another version of the roadblock sprang back up. In 1975 a Ferguson city councilman proposed erecting a ten-foot fence running for thousands of feet along the border with Kinloch. The measure failed, and Ferguson's mayor permanently opened up Suburban Avenue. Today, cars can pass freely, and the Ferguson side of Suburban Avenue has been improved by attractive medians with manicured shrubs and flowers. At the Kinloch border, however, the quality of the road diminishes.

For Jenifer Lewis, show business called. She departed for New York City following her graduation from St. Louis's Webster University in 1979. She didn't know it at the time, but Kinloch would never be the same.

The construction of I-170—which cut right through Kinloch—had already displaced many. But the death knell rang in the 1980s, when

TWA moved its hub to St. Louis and the airport began expansion plans. It bought up more than a thousand properties in Kinloch as part of a noise abatement program. Kinloch drew up an elaborate relocation and renovation plan, but most of it was never realized, and pretty much anyone who could afford to leave town, did.

Meanwhile the airport's plans fizzled. American Airlines' acquisition of TWA in 2001 was followed shortly by 9/11, and local air traffic withered. No expansion was needed after all.

This doomed program, combined with the easing of racist housing restrictions around the region, led to Kinloch's unraveling. "We got what we wanted, which was the freedom and the ability to go places and buy homes," said former Kinloch resident Dorothy Squires in the documentary *Where the Pavement Ends*, "but we lost what we had."

Tax revenue declined and public facilities fell into disrepair. Rent-paying residents were replaced by squatters, whom corrupt politicians began bribing for their votes. In the early 2000s, St. Louis County Executive Buzz Westfall asked Kinloch's mayor to consider disincorporating, but he refused. Ten years later the town sued a different mayor for buying a house with city funds. Her replacement was charged with spending money stolen from the volunteer fire department on liquor, cigarettes, and a family member's funeral. City Hall was sold to a man who had once been convicted of cocaine dealing.

In 2015 I profiled Kinloch for *Vice*. I saw vagrants burning fires in shells of homes, and I photographed a hand-painted cement wall, trumpeting town accomplishments like "First Black-Owned Theater" and "First Black School District," that had become overgrown with weeds. Kinloch had a postapocalyptic beauty, with trees growing inside abandoned apartment complexes and whole blocks gone back to nature.

But just getting around was a challenge. The city's Google Maps grid included many unnamed and grayed-out thoroughfares, making navigation difficult, and some roads had dining room table–sized potholes. People from all over the county came to Kinloch to dump trash. Giant heaps of it have been known to obstruct emergency vehicles. Sometimes bodies were even dumped there, such as a murder victim named Darrius Marks in 2017.

My *Vice* story was published not long after Michael Brown's killing, when news reports were portraying Ferguson as a racist police state. But locals at a Kinloch salvage yard—one of the town's only remaining consumer businesses—told me Kinloch was worse. "They're crazy-ass motherfuckers," a former Kinloch resident named Gene Lee said of the cops, adding he'd been unjustly arrested the previous evening for allegedly depositing trash.

"They lock you up and tow your car for running a stop sign," said Lee's friend CJ Jones. "Kinloch stopped me more times than Ferguson. Once you get to Ferguson, it's smooth sailing! Ferguson, they have to see you doing something wrong. Here, you just have to come through."

It seemed strange that a place as small as Kinloch—with a population below three hundred—needed its own police force at all. Its three police cars were uninsured around the time of my article (making them illegal to drive), and when a TV news reporter tried to report on this in 2016, he was handcuffed and shackled to a holding bench. Meanwhile Kinloch's violent crime rate was much worse than Ferguson's, reaching almost three incidents per one hundred people by the mid-2010s, four times the rate in St. Louis—which was, and is, the most dangerous big city in the country.

Today Kinloch's unemployment rate is a staggering 55 percent. Of the eighty-eight municipalities that comprise St. Louis County, Kinloch is probably the poorest. The town's violence and ubiquitous drug dealing have driven almost all the residents away.

Still, those whose families called it home for generations retain nostalgia for the city and its history. "Take the name Kinloch and stop with the first three letters: Kin," Gene Lee told me. "We all kin, or close to it."

"We don't say we're from St. Louis, we say we're from Kinloch," said Justine Blue, the Kinloch city manager. "We're all proud to be from here. We're not proud of what's happening, but we are proud to be from here."

CHAPTER FIFTEEN

In my efforts to walk where Jorell walked, I continued tracing his path toward Danielle's house, going west on Martin Luther King Boulevard, a Kinloch street that resembles a rural country road with its prairie grass, towering ash trees, and invasive honeysuckle bushes.

Before long I encountered a tidy-looking ranch house, which Jorell's friends call the Gutter Crew House, named for the local gang that hangs out there. A bit farther along I passed a shotgun home with brown siding known as the Horse House. Its curious name came from the horses the inhabitants kept on the property, including, in Jorell's time, a white mare.

This fascinated me. How whimsical, to keep a horse in the suburbs! "They just let it roam free," Jorell's brother Jovan told me. "It always went back home."

But, as I would learn, the Horse House was a sinister place where illegal guns and drugs were sold. Jorell was killed not far from the Horse House, and in fact he stopped there to talk to someone just minutes before his death, apparently about a gun.

As I continued investigating it became clear that the Gutter Crew House, the Horse House, and Kinloch itself were integral to Jorell's case. And so in 2019 I visited the town's brand-new city hall building. There I spoke with Justine Blue, the city manager of Kinloch.

Kinloch City Hall was quiet. The modest, new construction facility had no other visitors, and Blue agreed to meet with me even without an appointment. She was in her fifties and wore a bouffant-style hairdo. As a native of Kinloch, Blue knows the town and its plight as well as anyone; she lost her childhood home when her mother took an airport buyout in the late 1980s. Blue's task nowadays? Saving the town from obsolescence.

She laughed when I mentioned the Horse House, noting that Kinloch didn't technically permit equestrian animals. "But the gentleman who owned the horse was friends with the chief of police, so there you have it," she said. The horse was nonetheless beloved by people in Kinloch. "She would just go to and fro, and everyone would feed and water her. She'd come by City Hall and we'd give her some carrots and apples."

I asked if Blue might be willing to go back to the Horse House with me, and show me some other local sites. "Why don't we take the whole city tour?" she suggested. We got in our cars and drove a few blocks south, to a warehouse serving the local Schnucks grocery store chain. Mike Fuller had worked there. A sprawling complex surrounded by barbed wire, it had opened not long before and brought hundreds of new jobs to the area. It was part of an office park called NorthPark, built to take advantage of the proximity to the airport, and which has brought more than $2 million to Kinloch. This money funded the new city hall, as well as an ambitiously imagined historic district featuring a history museum and the Kinloch Walk of Fame honoring notable town residents, including Jenifer Lewis, comedian and civil rights activist Dick Gregory, singer Ann Peebles, US Congresswoman Maxine Waters, and *Star Trek* actor John Cothran Jr.

However, Blue lamented that over $1 million of the NorthPark money could not be accounted for; it was siphoned off during the tenure of a former mayor, Keith Conway. In 2011 Conway was sentenced to twenty-one months in federal prison for allegedly using city funds to buy Caribbean cruises, a Palm Beach time share, and to pay his own taxes. News Corp's erstwhile tablet-based newspaper *The Daily* reported in 2011 that Conway "doled out city property to his inner circle, created a secret city account to which only he had access and allegedly blocked police from arresting his shady associates and took kickbacks from a chop shop operating behind City Hall and the Police Department." He also managed to get himself added to the Kinloch Walk of Fame.

In 2018, Kinloch disbanded its police department, contracting with St. Louis County for law enforcement services. (The town did not disclose its reasons for the change.) Kinloch retained its own fire department, however. One day I drove past a huge brush fire that was burning behind the fire station, smoking up the town. Presumably it was being used for a training drill.

Blue and I continued down Scott Avenue, Kinloch's main drag, such as it is. Abutting the Kinloch Walk of Fame was the former site of the Holy Angels Parish, for decades a refuge for Black Catholics across the region. An order of Black nuns—known as the Oblate Sisters of Providence—ran a school here, and in the 1960s civil rights era the church sanctuary featured a seven-foot-tall statue of the Black Virgin Mary. The parish closed in 2002. The Archdiocese of St. Louis later donated the church to the city of Kinloch. It was promptly turned into a nightclub, called the Cotton Club, which violated the wishes of the archdiocese. Prostitution was trafficked inside the Cotton Club, lamented Blue. It soon closed as well.

"Want to go inside?" she asked, pushing past the unlocked door of the church-cum-nightclub. I nodded tentatively, worried there might be squatters lurking inside, trying to keep warm. There weren't, but the place was in shambles. A chandelier lay smashed on the ground. Some walls were splattered with graffiti, while others featured fine portraits commissioned for the club, of musicians like Louis Armstrong and East St. Louis native Miles Davis.

Next door was the rectory, where the nuns who taught at the school lived. More recently it had been reimagined as Kinloch's history museum, but that too was shuttered. We continued on, pushing past thick overgrowth behind the former church. There we descended a set of decaying steps. Blue produced keys, allowing us entry into a sort of subterranean cave with a cross above the doorway.

This underground room was not actually a cave, but rather a

plastered-over cement shell. It was meant to evoke a famous cave chapel in Manresa, Spain, where St. Ignatius of Loyola founded an order called the Society of Jesus. This Kinloch replica was the centerpiece of the Manresa Retreat House, which opened in 1941, and served as a place for St. Louis–area Black Catholic laymen to spend long weekends praying and reflecting. The faux cave included a few wooden pews, and it would have been a cozy place to read scripture seventy years ago.

Right now, however, I was happy to move along. The ceiling was literally crumbling above us.

Justine Blue ended our tour at the Horse House, a half mile north of the parish. It had wooden planks covering the windows, and acres of foliage on all sides.

Public records show the house was owned by James McCray, who is likely related to ousted Kinloch mayor Betty McCray, who was impeached in 2015 after accusations that she allowed nonresidents to vote, among other charges.

The Horse House was now unoccupied, however. "We didn't even know he was gone until we saw the house boarded up," Blue said, adding that she thinks McCray and his wife departed sometime in 2017. They left the horse when they moved, she continued, adding that it died at some point in 2018, though she wasn't sure why. (People told me the mare had been shot numerous times over the years.)

The horse's small, wooden stable across the street remained intact, however. It opened onto a paddock where she could run, ringed by a three-foot-high wooden fence.

"She wasn't the only one," Blue continued. "There were horses here for years when I was growing up. We had another house further down, he had a couple horses as well."

The Horse House was eerie. A burned-out dumpster sat in its side yard. It was easy to imagine wayward kids peddling their wares on the front steps. A 2015 Kinloch police report described the address as "known for heavy drug activity," and the house was the subject of a sting in April 2015 when an undercover officer purchased $40 of crack cocaine on the property, and discovered more inside the house. Guns were sold there as well, with frequent shootings reported.

Jorell's friend Mike Fuller visited the Horse House frequently. He said that when Jorell first started passing by on his way to Danielle's house, the locals didn't know what to make of him. For one thing, the Kinloch guys had a long-running gang rivalry with people from Jorell's block. And yet here was Jorell, strolling through their territory, carefree.

"They were like, 'Who's this young kid who don't even live in Kinloch, walking by like he own the place?'" said Mike.

Impressed with Jorell's chutzpah, they got to talking, and before long Jorell took his place alongside them on the steps of the Horse House. They spoke for hours, bonding over their mutual fascination with guns.

On the one hand, it was a nightmare scenario to imagine. Jorell should have realized it was a bad idea to spend time at a notorious criminal hangout in one of the country's most dangerous towns. Indeed, his involvement with the guys at the Horse House may have led to his demise.

On the other hand, I couldn't help but admire his ability to make friends.

CHAPTER SIXTEEN

In high school my friends and I cared more about skipping class, acquiring fake IDs, and hooking up than we did about our schoolwork.

My friend Eric, who lived across the street from my family's St. Paul home, used to house-sit for a family out in the suburbs. When they left town he'd throw huge parties; I remember dozens of teenagers showing up, overwhelming the place. We'd drink Zima in the hot tub and blast Green Day, while the guys made drunken passes at the girls. Eventually these parties spilled onto the front lawn. I was out there once with a classmate I'll call Klaus. I can't remember what we were doing; we may have been smoking cheap cigars. But just then another car full of teenage boys—locals—drove by with their windows open. For reasons unclear, Klaus called out to them. "Sup, sup!" he yelled, in a singsongy tone.

Klaus wasn't trying to start trouble. He was just doing what drunk teenagers do, yelling to hear his own voice. Only, these guys didn't take it that way. They slammed on the brakes. Leaving the car running in the middle of the street, they jumped out. There were three or four of them, and they walked stridently toward us.

"What did you say?" the leader asked Klaus.

"Nothing," he said. "I was just saying, 'What's up.'"

Without warning, the guy pulled back and popped Klaus, right in the face. He cried out and keeled over.

Then, just as abruptly as they'd arrived, they got back in the car and vanished.

I don't think Klaus was very hurt. There was blood, but we didn't call the cops, especially since we were drinking underage. Yet I was shaken by the gratuitous violence. I can still visualize the scene in my mind.

Nothing more came of it. It was just one example of the hormonal recklessness that characterized that time in our lives. We'd sleep with each other's girlfriends, steal from each other, spread mean-spirited rumors, drive while drunk, tell bald-faced lies. It's a small miracle no one ended up in the hospital.

I can only imagine if we'd had guns.

I didn't know it at the time, but Jorell owned five guns when he died. Firearms, it turns out, were his great passion. "He wanted to open a gun store," his buddy Jordan had told me. Jermaine said Jorell could "take a gun apart and put it back together, as fast as doing a Rubik's Cube."

It's clear why Jorell never told me about this hobby. He thought I would have disapproved, and he would have been right. I would have said what seemed obvious to me: that messing with illegal guns was dangerous, that someone could get hurt, or he could get arrested. My parents were gun-control liberals who wouldn't even let me play with GI Joe.

I could have shown Jorell statistics showing that gun ownership makes one less safe, not more. Yet I doubt this abstract reasoning would have worked. Jorell feared for his safety on a daily basis. Carrying a weapon made him feel more in control.

But it wasn't just about defending himself. His older brother Jermaine was a Marines paramedic who did three tours in Iraq. Jorell admired his extensive firearm training and hoped to follow him into the military after high school. Jorell also had a collector's interest, and Mike Fuller said the two of them spent hours watching YouTube videos about gun assembly.

And as Jorell's sisters Peaches and Rece explained, there was nostalgia at play as well. Jorell had first handled guns with his father, Joe, on trips back to Arkansas. Joe owns everything from handguns to shotguns to hunting rifles, and he considers himself a sportsman. He brought Jorell to the levee by the Arkansas River, where they'd set up cans and fire at them with .22s. They later went hunting and fishing on the property of one of Joe's roofing colleagues, down in the Ozarks. "Rece could out-shoot him," remembered Joe with a laugh, about Jorell.

As he got older Jorell sometimes pilfered his dad's rifles to shoot target practice in the backyard. Once Joe found an old barrel back there, riddled with bullet holes. "I had to get on him, saying, 'Don't do that,'" Joe said.

As I learned from running a public records request on the Clevelands' address, the neighbors frequently called the police over firearm usage there. According to Ferguson PD reports, neighbors complained of "multiple shots" one night in March 2014, and that October police were dispatched because of "kids shooting guns in the rear yard." In December numerous people allegedly shot guns off the balcony, and February 2016 brought a rather disturbing report: "Loud noise like a gun, then a dog crying." It's not clear which of these calls involved Jorell, but surely some of them did.

You must be twenty-one to buy handguns in Missouri, but Jorell got his from unlicensed street vendors. It was incredibly easy. Ferguson and Kinloch, like all low-income parts of St. Louis, are swimming in black-market firearms. These weapons are not necessarily sold by a nefarious criminal element. Some neighbors trade with each other out of their homes. They do it to make a few extra dollars, or even to try to keep the block safe. The Horse House, as far as I can gather, was not a sophisticated operation run by underworld bosses, but by a group of young men trying to impress each other with the latest wares.

Some of these black-market guns are manufactured in the United States. Others are made in Eastern European plants that are holdovers from the Soviet era, from when the Kalashnikov rifle revolutionized warfare. They are imported by mammoth-yet-barely-known companies like Century Arms, whose eighty-thousand-square-foot warehouse in a small Vermont town bears almost no indication from the outside that its products fuel chaos across the continent. Though military-style rifles are illegal to sell, Century Arms gets around this through a loophole: by importing "slimmed down, 'sporting' versions of their foreign rifles that can clear federal importation restrictions, then retrofitting them with U.S.-made parts, including bayonets and high-capacity clips," according to a news report.

From there, these rifles and semiautomatic pistols are sold at gun shows and shops around the country, with very few safeguards stopping straw buyers from reselling them to criminal gangs or Mexican cartels. Thus the arsenal of El Chapo's famed Sinaloa Cartel is filled with firearms purchased in America. Meanwhile this same "iron pipeline" supplies illegal guns to people in St. Louis and North County.

"In the '80s, guys had Saturday night specials," St. Louis police officer Jay Schroeder told the *St. Louis Post-Dispatch*, referring to cheap, small-caliber handguns so-named because they were supposedly used in weekend stickups. "Now guys have firearms with 30-round magazines. They're spraying bullets all over the place." George Mason University criminologist Chris Koper said the 2004 expiration of the federal assault weapons ban has led to the increasing prevalence of high-capacity semi-automatic guns on the streets, for which the state of Missouri has no restrictions. Further, Missouri's 2007 repeal of the law requiring a permit to purchase handguns appears to have had an outsized impact on Black communities, leading to a 33 percent increase in gun killings of Black men aged fifteen to twenty-four, according to a 2018 study. (The same study found "no evidence of an increase in firearm homicide among white Missourians.")

The repeal of these types of laws bewilders me. At the same time, I appreciate certain aspects of gun-rights arguments, because you can't put the genie back in the bottle. If we lived in a country where guns are scarce—like Great Britain or China—then citizen gun-ownership would be ridiculous. But in a country where there are more guns than residents, I understand why some law-abiding people would want to arm themselves against criminals who are likely to be armed.

This rationale is gaining strength in the Black community, where gun ownership is rising and support for gun control has been declining since the 1990s. In hip-hop, there's a long history of rappers espousing firearm ownership, both as a status symbol and to defend oneself against aggressors, including police. "I don't trust Black leadership that wants to de-arm Black people," rapper Killer Mike told *Yahoo News*, referencing politicians including Kamala Harris. "Gun laws affect Black people first and worst." Black gun clubs have gained popularity in recent years, like the National African American Gun Association, which said they received two thousand new members within just a few hours of George Floyd's 2020 killing.

Yet these trends may be fueling the crisis. A University of Pennsylvania study from 2009, which analyzed nearly seven hundred shootings of Philadelphia residents, found that, compared to unarmed people, those carrying guns were more than four times as likely to be shot, and were four times more likely to be killed. Further, people attempting to use their guns in self-defense usually failed. "Although successful defensive gun uses can and do occur," the study reads, "the findings of this study do not support the perception that such successes are likely."

One fact that surprised me is that the leading category of gun death in the US is not actually mass shootings, or even homicides. It's suicide.

I can imagine how possessing a gun would make one *feel* safer, and maybe for someone with extensive training in the use of firearms this may actually be the case. But for everyone else, it seems like a bad idea.

As Mike Fuller described it, Jorell gripped his roll of cash tightly as he approached the Horse House in late 2015. He'd been working long hours at the St. Louis Fish & Chicken Grill recently, and he was eager to spend his earnings in this black-market economy.

His first purchase was an inexpensive handgun, likely something unreliable, a small 9 mm or .380 perhaps. He later exchanged it, plus a small amount of money, to trade "up the ladder" for a better gun, said his father Joe. I'm not sure of the timeline, but Mike said Jorell traded a small-caliber Beretta M9, along with about $100 cash, for a .40 caliber Beretta. It's not clear which of these Berettas—both semiautomatics—

he was referring to in his December 2015 Facebook post threatening unnamed adversaries.

Jorell returned to the spot again and again, trading guns up the ladder until he acquired the handgun of his dreams, a black 1911 semiautomatic pistol with a brown wooden grip. "He was so happy to have it," said Montrel Fuller. "It was a big boy gun."

Jorell almost always had his 1911 with him. He showed it off to everyone, until Mike cautioned him against doing so, thinking someone might want to steal it.

The night before his death Jorell dropped the gun off at his friend Big Ant's house on his way to work, and then picked it up on his way home. He carried it on him when he departed the Cleveland home on the afternoon he died. "It should have been on him when they found him dead, but they never found it," said Big Ant.

The cash in Jorell's pocket was left alone, but the 1911 was stolen off his dead body.

This made some of the people I interviewed wonder: Was Jorell killed *for* his gun?

The possibility that someone would have such little regard for human life, that they would kill for a firearm, was horrifying. Jorell's gun was beginning to feel like a symbol—of everything he wanted in life, and everything that ruined him.

I needed to know: What made it so coveted?

Since I knew little about guns, I consulted Matthew Allen, a firearms expert from St. Louis who does private security in hotspots around the world and once provided "executive protection" for Anheuser-Busch. We met at Starbucks. Possessing a calming presence and a giant beard, he became immediately curious when I said Jorell had a 1911.

"Usually in the streets people have very cheap guns that are not overly reliable," said Allen. Yet a 1911, he went on, was his favorite gun in the world—in fact, he owned three. It isn't a brand like a Glock or a Smith & Wesson, but rather a style, sold by manufacturers including Colt and SIG Sauer. Designed by a man named John M. Browning, known as the Father of Automatic Fire, the pistol was adopted by the US Army in 1911, thus acquiring its name. It became beloved by gun enthusiasts, but today it is known as something of an "old man gun," Allen said.

Yet its craftsmanship is impeccable, and it maintains a retro cachet for discerning collectors like Jorell. Because it is rare, the 1911 would have stood out among the other firearms bought and sold through the Horse House, Allen added.

Allen also worked as a private investigator. I told him about Jorell's case, lamenting that the St. Louis County detectives had information that could likely help me, but were unwilling to share it. He said he knew someone in the department, and that he could potentially arrange for a sit-down.

I thanked Allen for his time, but our meeting left me slightly unnerved. I pictured Jorell beaming with pride when he acquired his 1911, showing it off to others, all the while making them jealous, and perhaps inspiring them to plot against him. I soon spoke with Mike Fuller again, who speculated that the same person who took the gun off Jorell's body might have been the one who killed him.

That made sense. So now I needed to know: Who took Jorell's gun?

Many in Jorell's circle believed the culprit was a young man named Leron White. He was a fascinating figure, a minor celebrity in Kinloch, and he became my #2 suspect.

In a town full of struggling people, White came from a respected, monied family, the son of a drug trafficker and the nephew of a nationally known rapper. A year younger than Jorell, with hazel eyes and a penetrating stare, he was a stand-out basketball player for the McCluer South-Berkeley High School Bulldogs, before getting caught up in a cycle of shootings and retaliations.

"Stalked by demons, guarded by angels," read his Facebook page.

When Jorell knew him, he ran with a crew of eighteen- and nineteen-year-old young men from Kinloch called the Gutter Crew. They were accused of stealing cars and committing other crimes, and they doubled as a hip-hop group, posting videos with high production values to YouTube, in which they boasted about eliminating their adversaries.

White's family appears to have divided their time between a home in the North County suburb of Spanish Lake and the home in Kinloch that people called the Gutter Crew House, just up Martin Luther King Boulevard from the Horse House.

The Gutter Crew House would become a focal point of my investigation. While the Horse House was falling apart, the Gutter Crew House had been recently renovated, with a manicured front yard and stately pillars by the front door. New cars and fancy SUVs lined driveways on either side of the home. The Gutter Crew House was owned by Tori White, Leron White's father. Tori was also the cousin of the former mayor of Kinloch, Keith Conway. According to *The Daily*, the Gutter Crew House was owned by the town until, in 2001, Conway held a raffle to give away the house for free—and his cousin Tori White happened to win it.

Members of the White family could be quite accommodating. Once, one of my sources pulled up with a baby in his car. Leron White's sister came out to talk to the source, and she lamented that the baby wasn't in a car seat. She excused herself and then returned with a brand new seat. "*Please* put that baby in this car seat," she said, according to the source. "There are potholes up and down the street."

But the house was also a place of chaos, with frequent shootings, drive-bys, and accusations of domestic assault and car theft. In 2016 police were called there at least six times, including once in January, when police and fire crews arrived to find a man "foaming at the mouth and unresponsive to verbal commands." EMS soon arrived, but a woman identified as Mrs. White—presumably Leron's mother—complained that one of the first responders had "searched her dresser drawers in the base-ment." An officer denied the allegation; it's unclear what happened to the unresponsive man.

Tori White has twice been convicted of federal drug crimes, receiving five years both times. Further, police lodged drug violations in connection with the Gutter Crew House at least once. (The name of the person or people charged was not included in the report.)

Really, that entire, desolate stretch of Martin Luther King Boulevard was bustling with criminal activity. Between the Horse House, the Gutter Crew House, and another property nearby, I heard reports of prostitution, a major auto theft ring, regular shoot-outs, as well as heroin, fentanyl, crack cocaine, and Xanax dealing. Kinloch's remote location and crumbling infrastructure made people feel they could commit crime with impunity.

I can't imagine a scarier place to spend time, but Jorell was there frequently in the months before he died. Possibly he didn't understand the imminent danger; then again, perhaps the danger is what drew him in. He grew close with Leron White, who became a polarizing figure among Jorell's friends and family. Some believed he was a real friend to Jorell, while others didn't trust him at all.

Leron White was never charged in Jorell's murder, or even interviewed as a suspect. But he was well known for armed, reckless behavior. Montrel Fuller called him a cowboy. When I began investigating Leron White, he was incarcerated in the county jail following three separate arrests over a short span of time. Police from Florissant cited him in November 2016—three months after Jorell's death—for "creating a substantial risk of serious injury/death" and fleeing arrest. One month later he was caught in a stolen car. "Defendant . . . took off at a high rate of speed," reads the police report, "[leading an] officer on a high speed chase through intersection disregarding stop signs and stop lights and weaving in and out of interstate traffic." The officer discharged his weapon in the process, though it doesn't appear anyone was hurt. White received five years' probation.

A year later he was arrested on more serious charges, for an alleged triple shooting in Jennings. According to a police report, on November 3, 2017, Leron White and his father, Tori White, were attending a funeral for a middle-aged man named Darrius Marks at The Ambassador nightclub—the same spot I'd once gone to see a rap show with Jorell—when an argument broke out in the parking lot. It's unclear what the argument concerned, but a law enforcement officer close to the situation said the White family had a "Hatfield and McCoy"–type relationship with the Marks family. In fact, Darrius Marks had been shot to death about a week earlier, and his body was found less than two blocks from the Gutter Crew House. (No one in the White family, nor anyone else, has been charged in Marks's death.)

"As the argument escalated, witnesses said Tori and Leron White began firing into the crowd as they retreated to their vehicle," reads the police report. "Members of the crowd returned fire. As Tori White and his son fled the parking lot by vehicle, they continued to fire into the crowd from the moving vehicle." No one was killed, though two of the three victims were critically wounded.

Leron White and his father each faced felonies including armed criminal action, assault, and unlawful weapon use. Their bond was set at $300,000.

In a chilling postscript, five months later a man was mowing his neighbor's lawn in Ferguson when he found Darrius Marks's hand lying in the backyard grass, less than a mile away from where Marks's body had been found. The man posted about it to Facebook and the police investigated. The Marks family told a local television station that Darrius's body had been found missing both hands.

According to a law enforcement source, Darrius had been punished "because he was stealing from somebody." It's unclear if the amputation occurred before or after his death.

All of this had taken place after Jorell died. While Leron sat in jail awaiting trial, Jorell's people continued talking about him. Rumors began spreading. Many believed Leron stole Jorell's 1911 off his body.

But that wasn't all. Others believed Leron killed Jorell. That's because, on the day of Jorell's death, Leron was acting extremely suspicious.

In the early afternoon of August 27, 2016, a Berkeley resident named Cecil Johnson was driving his gold Ford F-150 truck through Kinloch, when he saw a horrifying site. He slammed on the brakes.

Jorell Cleveland lay prone on the ground, his head turned to the side, his hands under his body. He was still breathing. Blood poured out of his mouth.

The thirty-seven-year-old Johnson hadn't seen the shooter, he said later, but recognized Jorell from working at St. Louis Fish & Chicken Grill. Johnson got out of his truck and called 911. Following the operator's instruction, Johnson turned Jorell over and attempted to resuscitate him.

In the process, Jorell's 1911 gun fell out of his pocket onto the pavement. Johnson picked it up and put it closer to Jorell. He told detectives he did this so police would know the gun belonged to Jorell.

Johnson continued tending to Jorell, still on the phone with 911, as three young men approached. They eyed the scene. One of the boys took off his shirt, picked up Jorell's gun with it, and wrapped it up. He did not remove the cash Jorell had in his pockets.

Johnson just watched, unsure what to do. He recognized the young man who picked up the gun, but didn't know him by name.

I later determined that this group of three included Leron White and two of his friends, Charles and Marcel. It's not clear which of the three grabbed the pistol.

Wordlessly, they hurried away. They soon drove to the Cleveland house in Ferguson—where they broke the news to Jorell's family that he was dead.

Charles was the one with the prominent neck tattoo, who yelled up to Jorell's brother Jermaine on the roof of the neighbor's house. When the three Kinloch guys spoke with Mike and Iesha at the Clevelands' front door, they said they'd found Jorell lying in the road. They did not mention his gun. "They were shaking like a leaf," Mike Fuller said.

Jermaine noticed their "nervousness" and "shakiness." There was a "stutter among their words," he went on, adding that two of them contradicted each other in their stories.

"I think those boys know more than they're letting on," Jermaine added.

Jorell was killed on the very northern edge of Kinloch, near its border with Berkeley. It wasn't immediately clear which police force had jurisdiction. Eventually Kinloch police took charge, though St. Louis County would lead the investigation.

After receiving the call from Danielle's mother, I arrived to the Berkeley side and watched as Jorell's body was taken away, and his blood was sprayed off the pavement.

The Clevelands, however, had arrived to the other side of the crime scene, where many Kinloch residents gathered. Soon Leron White and his two friends arrived back to the scene. But since they'd spoken with the Clevelands at their home, only minutes earlier, something was different.

"They had changed clothes," said Jermaine.

Also on the scene was a thirty-year-old woman named Layla Cooper. She lived on Jefferson Avenue, very close to where Jorell had been killed. She hadn't seen anything, she later told police, but her mother had "observed a person crawling on Courtney Avenue."

That person was Jorell, who had just been shot. According to Cooper, her mother next observed "a burgundy vehicle [approach] the male and one of the occupants removed an item from the victim's person prior to driving away." These people were Leron White and his two friends.

Detectives were not able to make contact with Cooper's mother, and Cooper's secondhand account differed slightly from that of witness Cecil Johnson, who seemed to imply that White's crew had arrived on foot. (Jermaine Cleveland said White and his two friends arrived to the Cleveland house in a "dark-colored sedan," which seems to match Cooper's description.)

But at the crime scene, Cooper began speaking up, Joe Cleveland told me. To anyone who would listen, she loudly proclaimed that White and his friends had taken the gun off Jorell's body.

White did not take kindly to this public insinuation.

"Shut up," White told her, in Joe's recollection.

"I know y'all ain't gon' do nothin' but jump on me," she responded. "Y'all broke my arm last week. Y'all whooped me in front of my daughter last week."

Leron White's suspicious behavior on the day of Jorell's death, coupled with the fact that he'd since been accused of a violent crime, led many in

Jorell's circle to suspect him not just of stealing Jorell's 1911 gun, but in his murder.

White emphatically denied killing Jorell. Further, neither of the two witnesses—Cecil Johnson and Layla Cooper's mother—claimed he did it.

But was Leron White telling the full story? That seemed unlikely. Many believed he was concealing critical information.

And so I dug in to Leron White's story. I learned that he had a famous uncle, a rapper named Huey who'd become a national sensation. And on his way to stardom, he'd left all sorts of clues about White and his family.

CHAPTER SEVENTEEN

If you listened to pop radio in 2007 you surely heard the Huey song, "Pop, Lock & Drop It." Maybe you even had the ringtone. Irrepressibly bouncy, full of video game bloops and bleeps, it riffed on a West Coast dance move called the pop lock and combined it with a "drop"—a quick squat. It's fun to watch, if hard on my forty-something knees.

Its title also refers to gunplay.

Huey, born Lawrence Franks Jr. and originally known as Baby Huey, wasn't exactly a gangsta rapper. Instead, he employed the template of St. Louis's biggest star at the time, Nelly, who debuted at the turn of the millennium and sold a bajillion records by appealing to the ladies, while also dog-whistling his street credentials.

Huey steered himself into the same commercial lane, crafting dance floor hits featuring videos of bouncing women and shiny jewelry. He wasn't quite as chiseled as Nelly, but he had a great ear for beats, and his infectious energy and flying dreads were a blast to behold.

On his debut album Huey told dark tales of his Kinloch upbringing. A stand-out track titled "My Zone" references the local gangs and his brother Tori White, who is Leron White's father and the owner of the Gutter Crew House. Tori White, who "sold drugs" according to the song and two federal convictions, financed his brother Huey's early rise in the music game with his drug money, say sources close to the situation.

My whole surrounding around me pump blood
Except big bruh, he was Six-Deuced up...

Even before he was arrested with his son Leron for the alleged shooting at The Ambassador nightclub, Tori White had been incarcerated for much of his adult life. At only seventeen he was charged with first-degree murder of a man named Dwayne Jackson. A witness said Tori jumped out of a car and began shooting; ultimately, he was convicted only of involuntary manslaughter. Then, in 2003, Tori was sentenced to five years in prison for conspiracy to distribute crack cocaine out of a Kinloch auto body shop. He was still on probation when, in 2009, the FBI, DEA, and local police embarked on a years-long investigation of his crew. Like something out of *The Wire*, authorities used secret video, wiretaps, and undercover buys, ultimately seizing not just heroin and cocaine but thousands in cash, SUVs, a Rolex, and eight guns, including a rifle and a shotgun. In 2013, Tori White again received a five-year sentence.

Yet Huey stuck close with his brother Tori at a time when their family was falling apart. Their parents had drug abuse problems, and Huey's grandmother saved him from the foster service system. She was active in church, and Huey attended regularly.

Huey's family moved in and out of Kinloch over the years. During his childhood the town maintained a sense of community, but upon his return as a teenager it had almost fallen off the map, with so many homeowners having accepted the airport buyout. "There was always a lot of drugs going on and, of course, a little bit of violence," Huey told the *Riverfront Times*. "But when I came back the airport thing came about, and the police was real bad. County police was coming out there, chasing people and shocking them with Tasers—all kind of stuff happened. Before you knew it was like a ghost town."

Huey attended McCluer, just like Jorell, but was kicked out after being "escorted off the premises in handcuffs because of a fight over a girl," he told the *St. Louis Post-Dispatch*. He received a gun charge and spent time in jail, his bond set at $100,000.

In the meantime music began paying dividends. He started making beats for other rappers and soon began rhyming himself, mentored by his aunt Angela Richardson, a music manager who built a studio in her house.

He wrote "Pop, Lock & Drop It" in an hour, and soon local radio caught the fever. "I've never had so many requests for a song," said one DJ. In August 2006 the *St. Louis Business Journal* reported Huey's signing of a $2.5 million record deal with the iconic hip-hop label Jive Records, a subsidiary of Sony BMG.

This didn't mean two and a half million went into his pocket; some of it went to his lawyer and manager, and some of it funded the production of his debut album *Notebook Paper*. But Huey was ecstatic. What seventeen-year-old wouldn't be? Working with a producer named Mickey "Memphitz" Wright, Huey recorded in Atlanta, recruiting stars including T-Pain, Lil Bow Wow, and the producer Jazze Pha.

Huey came home to film the "Pop, Lock & Drop It" video with a hundred of his closest friends, including two of his nephews, then elementary school students Leron White and his friend Marcel, dancing in comically oversized shirts. The song ascended Billboard's heights, peaking at #6.

Huey had defied all odds, a success story from one of the poorest towns in America. He recorded an episode of MTV's *Cribs* and began calling himself "Hue Hef" after getting his photo taken with Hugh Hefner at the Playboy Mansion.

"You can't talk about St. Louis hip-hop without talking about Huey. You just can't," says journalist Toriano Porter. "For him to come from where he came from and get to a major level and be on a major stage, it gave other kids hope."

Yet even at the height of his stardom Huey hung out in Kinloch with notorious characters amidst drug-dealing activities. It's unclear if he himself was involved in his brother Tori White's drug business. In 2017 Huey was arrested for a small marijuana charge, which was dropped.

"I never saw him on drugs," said his aunt.

Throughout Huey's young adult life Kinloch remained a drug distribution hot spot, with people throughout his neighborhood selling heroin, fentanyl, crack cocaine, and pills, all drugs that had traveled great distances.

Illicit chemicals sold in St. Louis come from across the globe: Columbian growers provide the coca leaves for cocaine, Chinese lab chemists synthesize fentanyl, and poppies for heroin are grown in the mountains of Mexico. All three drugs are processed by the Mexican cartels, who cut and package them before sending them north across the US border. So-called Xanax pills are often made in America on clandestine pill-pressing machines, and are frequently cut with fentanyl.

Once in the US, the drugs are then distributed through regional affiliates, ranging from the Salvadoran gang MS-13 in Los Angeles to West Virginian crime families to African American gangs in St. Louis. Highway drug busts occur frequently around St. Louis, as the city is on a major trafficking route between Texas (a main entry point from Mexico) and Chicago, a main distribution node.

Powerful kingpins used to coordinate street dealers, the business model of Harlem trafficker Frank Lucas as well as the Black Mafia Family. But these days the trade is largely decentralized. Nobody's really in charge in places like North County, which is a recipe for turf wars. There are exceptions, but drug dealing in St. Louis is largely done out in the open. Despite the rise of the dark web and other technology, many dealers still post up on corners, or in gas stations, flagging down anyone lingering.

In northern Kinloch, dealers just assume anyone passing through is looking for drugs. Huey's family was a major player among these operations, which fueled the area's gun violence and revolving-door incarceration. Meanwhile, Huey's descent from the heights of fame happened gradually; as the years passed, he was less like a superstar, more like a regular guy.

By the mid-2010s there was a new face on the Kinloch scene—Jorell. He became a regular presence. It's unclear if he and Huey were friendly, but they ran with the same people, and inhabited the same milieu.

As I came to learn, their tragic fates were intertwined.

CHAPTER EIGHTEEN

Jorell's close friend Mike Fuller and his twin brother, Montrel, were both being charged in the same 2017 robbery, but their cases were separate. The charges Montrel faced were more severe, since he had allegedly planned the crime, along with a woman named Christina Reed.

I met Mike and Montrel at the St. Louis County Courthouse on March 8, 2019, to offer support on a particularly fraught day. They were nervous. Reed had just been sentenced to fifteen years, and Mike and Montrel were about to learn what sort of plea bargain their lawyers had negotiated.

Mike arrived at 9:00 a.m., clad in an unlaundered white jacket and chewing on Starburst candies. He was followed by his lawyer, a burly middle-aged man named Anthony Muhlenkamp. In a small conference room, Muhlenkamp lectured Mike about money he owed him, before imparting the news: The prosecution was offering five years in prison. With good behavior Mike would do 40 percent of that, minus time already served. All told he might do less than two years.

Of course, Mike didn't want to spend any time in prison at all, and they discussed the pros and cons of taking the plea. The lawyer believed going to trial was too risky; I wondered if he just didn't want to spend more time on Mike's case, especially since Mike still owed him money.

While Mike mulled his options, Montrel's lawyer came into the room, a thin guy with a hipster aesthetic reminiscent of the actor Adam Scott. He told Montrel the prosecution was offering a favorable plea deal, similar to Mike's, but under one condition—that Montrel submit to a drug test. Staying drug-free was a condition of his parole.

The catch was that Montrel needed to submit to the test here in the courthouse. Right now.

As identical twins, Mike and Montrel are hard to tell apart at first glance. Montrel is doughier, with a hair-trigger temper and a fierce intelligence. When he's feeling philosophical he talks in thick, dense slabs of ideas, and when he's under pressure he speaks in a higher register, making his voice sound threatening.

"I'm not going to pass," Montrel said, standing up and growing agitated. "They'll put me in jail right now." The lawyer asked him to sit down. Fleeing the scene was far worse than failing the drug test, the lawyer insisted. "It's best to take your chances."

But Montrel wasn't convinced. He grudgingly followed his lawyer out of the room to discuss the idea more, but quickly returned by himself. In a huff, he began throwing his belongings into his backpack. "Let's get out of here," he said to Mike. "I just smoked some weed."

I chimed in, speculating that if he only had weed in his system, it might not be a big deal. St. Louis County's recently elected prosecutor Wesley Bell—a reformer who rode into office on a wave of outrage after the officer who killed Michael Brown wasn't charged—had announced that his office would no longer prosecute small marijuana charges. Even if this didn't apply directly to Montrel's parole, there was a chance the judge could be lenient, right? Again, I wasn't a lawyer, but running from justice seemed like a bad idea.

Mike too tried to discourage him. "C'mon," he pleaded.

But Montrel could not be convinced. He argued back, his voice growing so loud that people looked at us through the conference room window.

Montrel zipped up his backpack and stormed out. Mike—who was his ride—clearly didn't want a scene, and felt loyal to his twin. "I can't leave my brother," he told me, shrugging his shoulders and following Montrel.

I sat there for a few moments, stunned by what seemed like poor decision-making. When I finally got up to go after them, they were gone. Montrel's lawyer soon returned, frowning at Montrel's absence. He told me that, fortunately for Montrel, the favorable plea deal wouldn't be immediately rescinded after all. He had until March 13—five days away—to turn himself in and submit to the drug test.

I called Montrel to tell him this, but he didn't answer. We finally connected on the morning of March 13. He regretted his dash from justice, but said he'd been in touch with his lawyer and planned to mitigate the damage by turning himself in to authorities later that day. He had until 4:00 p.m.

Instead of hanging up the phone to prepare for his prison stint, Montrel turned ruminative. "How's your Jorell investigation going?" he asked.

I told him I was focusing on the guys from Kinloch. I talked about the Horse House, the Gutter Crew House, and Leron White, someone who claimed to be Jorell's friend but also may have lifted his prized gun off his dying body. I had several puzzle pieces, but they weren't adding up to a coherent picture. Something wasn't right.

Montrel listened while I laid all of this out. Finally, he spoke up.

"Nobody's being honest with you about Jorell," he said, before pausing. "I don't know why everybody wants to sugarcoat shit. I'm twenty-eight years old, I'm finna be thirty. I gotta go to prison for five years of my life. I'll give you the truth, even though it's gonna come with a lot of backsplash on me."

I took a deep breath. I had no idea what he was about to say.

"Did Joe show you the autopsy report about what was in Jorell's system before he died?'

"No."

"Okay, I'll give you the truth. I've been getting high since I was nineteen years old. Heroin. And Jorell was using heroin too." He paused.

"I ain't trying to diminish his name. I loved that little dude. I loved him like a brother."

Like many African Americans, Montrel pronounced "heroin" as "hair-ON." I found myself focusing on this detail. I wasn't ready to absorb what Montrel was telling me.

"How do you know?" I asked.

"Because I watched it go down," said Montrel. Jorell was introduced to heroin by people hanging around the Cleveland house, he went on. Not Jorell's family members, but by a group of twenty-somethings, whose names he didn't want to reveal.

Montrel said Jorell joined the group in taking Xanax pills and snorting heroin. Though Jorell "wasn't no junkie," Montrel said, his drug use grew increasingly problematic. He began purchasing heroin in Kinloch for $100 per gram. One time after drinking and using heroin he climbed into the bathtub and began screaming, fearing overdose.

Jorell's heroin use and his increasingly hotheaded behavior seemed linked, others told me. "He started picking up bad habits," said Jorell's sister Peaches later. "He wanted to fight with me all the time, over the smallest things ever. It be like, a pair of shoes on the floor, and he would be yelling, like, 'Why this stuff all up on the floor? Y'all just nasty, y'all don't clean up!'"

"Even me and him got into it once," Montrel went on. "So bad."

On the night in question, not long before Jorell's death, his girlfriend Danielle was staying over with him at the Cleveland house. She had just gotten off her shift at St. Louis Fish & Chicken Grill, and it was payday. Danielle had both her and Jorell's payouts in her purse; the total was around $200, in cash. When they woke up the next morning, it was gone.

Montrel vehemently denied he'd taken the money. He claimed the culprit was a mutual friend they'd been hanging out with the night before. But Jorell was unconvinced. "He was pissed off," said Montrel. "But I was pissed off too, because he was accusing me. I told him that I was gonna grab him and beat him like a child."

As their argument escalated, Jorell grabbed one of his guns and followed Montrel into Mike and Iesha's room. "He pulled the fucking trigger!" Montrel said. Fortunately, the gun didn't have its clip in, and no bullets were fired. "He was trying to scare me. Jorell had reached a point in his life, he wasn't taking no bullshit from nobody."

Montrel actually respected him for this, and, as unlikely as it sounds, the pair quickly reconciled. The very next day, in fact, Montrel was once again at the Cleveland house. He had a job interview, and although Mike wasn't home, Montrel had come to borrow a pair of his brother's black pants. Montrel went upstairs to retrieve the slacks, only to encounter Jorell once again.

"What's up 'Trel," Jorell said, startling him. Standing at the top of the stairs, Jorell wore a sheepish expression and apologized for the gun incident the previous day.

"Man, we ain't even gotta talk about that," Montrel responded. "You don't have to apologize. We brothers."

They patched things up, and before long each confirmed that he was carrying drugs; Montrel had heroin, and Jorell had marijuana. To cement their reconciliation, they shared their stashes and got high together.

"We did, like, a whole half a gram [of heroin], just me and him," Montrel told me. "And we smoked that blunt. He helped me find the iron to iron my pants."

It was a bonding experience, Montrel remembered with both nostalgia and sorrow, since it was the last time the two of them ever spoke. Soon the talk turned to their drug suppliers. Montrel had a contact who supplied him with heroin, in St. Louis proper. But Jorell had his own heroin source, in Kinloch. In recent months he'd been going there to buy the drug.

"I gotta tell you the truth, Ben," Montrel told me, almost apologetically. "Everybody else has been giving you the runaround." The narrative about why Jorell was in Kinloch at the time of his death, that he was on his way to buy chains for his brother Jermaine and his girlfriend Danielle? There may have been some truth to that, Montrel said. But another reason Jorell was in Kinloch, the main reason, was to buy heroin.

It's not clear where he got it—likely the Horse House or the Gutter Crew House—but Jorell seems to have purchased and snorted heroin right before he died.

This is what Montrel believed. And though Montrel didn't know who killed Jorell, he believed that the transaction cost him his life.

I absorbed all of this silently over the phone. When Montrel finished I thanked him for talking to me. I asked him to stay in touch while he was in prison, and we hung up.

Over the coming weeks the Fuller brothers learned their fates. Montrel actually didn't turn himself in the day of our call—more than a month later he was pulled over on a driving infraction and taken in on a fugitive warrant. This seems to have badly hurt his case, as he was sentenced to twelve years in prison. Mike, in contrast, received only five.

During this same time period, I processed the new information about Jorell.

When I'd heard that he was violent and reckless with firearms, I hadn't believed it, at least at first. But when Montrel said Jorell was on heroin, it immediately rang true.

I'd spent a lot of time around users of heroin, fentanyl, and other opiates for my book *Fentanyl, Inc.* In retrospect, I recognized the signs in Jorell. He'd often been moody around me, and prone to nodding off at odd times. Back then I'd reasoned he was staying out too late and his home life was chaotic, which is why he needed to catch up on sleep when he came to our house.

The truth is, I didn't want to see what Jorell's behavior was actually telling me. When I observed how carefully he guarded the contents of the locked Lacoste man purse he brought to our house, I assumed it contained weed. But maybe it contained heroin too.

Later, I received Jorell's autopsy. Just as Montrel said, it confirmed that he died with opiates in his system.

The idea of a young man, a teenager, lost to heroin, was as sad as anything imaginable. I fell to the depth of despair upon learning that Jorell had turned to hard drugs. I walked around numb for days. It felt like an after school special come to life, or the kind of film reels we used to suffer through in junior high, with bad actors screaming hysterically. I never thought someone so close to me would fall victim to heroin, never imagined I would become a character in one of these melodramas, playing the part of the clueless mentor completely out of touch. I'd bee-bopped through my daily life, oblivious, while the warning signs were all around me.

I felt anger toward my own stupidity. Before writing *Fentanyl, Inc.* I'd been largely ignorant of the opiate epidemic. No one I knew did heroin when I was growing up. But by the new millennium everything had changed. The overprescription of pills like Oxycontin had kicked off the plague, which segued into a heroin problem when patients' prescriptions expired and they sought opiates on the black market. Now, most of the heroin sold in the US is cut with fentanyl, a much deadlier drug, and this problem has hit low-income Black communities particularly hard. It's likely that the "heroin" being sold in Kinloch was actually heroin mixed with fentanyl.

I'm not sure if Jorell was influenced by peer pressure, or if his life was just so miserable that he used heroin to feel better. Besides the every-day indignities of life in poverty he experienced, he was also failing out of school. Further, he'd recently flunked an Army practice quiz, which meant his dream of serving in the armed forces was fading.

I should have recognized the warning signs. If I'd known he was taking heroin, I could have supported him and directed him toward services like medication-assisted treatment, which is provided for free by recovery clinics. He could have taken medicine like buprenorphine or naltrexone, which helps opiate users quit. He would have stood a chance.

Now it was too late. It just felt like another way I'd failed him.

Despite my self-pity, I made a strong effort to push those feelings aside. If I was going to solve Jorell's murder, I had to remain objective.

And so I cleared my head and looked into Montrel's theory—that buying heroin in Kinloch led to Jorell's death.

It made a certain sense. In fact, it addressed an issue that had long been nagging at me.

The issue was this: nobody understood how Jorell could have been killed at point-blank range. That's because Jorell had grown so paranoid in his final months. Fearing enemies were all around him, he didn't let potential adversaries close enough to do him harm—not without pulling out his own weapon first.

That meant he must have been killed by someone he trusted, many believed. "Whoever it was, Jorell had to know him," his sister Rece told me. "He was always aware of his surroundings."

But if he were high on heroin, that changed everything. His judgment would have been clouded. His reaction time would have slowed.

He would have been too impaired to properly defend himself. If an enemy crept up on him in this state, he would have been too high to realize it.

So, who pulled the trigger? I still didn't know.

Leron White's role in this remained difficult to understand. It seemed possible that he, or someone close to him, had supplied Jorell with heroin. And it seemed even more likely that he'd taken the pistol off Jorell's body, or at least been there when it happened.

White certainly didn't look good in all of this. But interviewing him would be difficult. He was in prison, for one thing, and the coronavirus pandemic had shut down visits. Plus, I didn't want him to know I was working on this story. Who knew how he would react? Even if he hadn't killed Jorell, he had a lot to lose, and every reason to be suspicious of a random white guy who wanted to talk about a murder.

Fortunately Mike and Montrel were doing their own investigating. Inside the penitentiary system they doubled down on their efforts to solve Jorell's case and had great access to key figures.

When it comes to sleuthing, the incarcerated are often better informed than those on the outside. That was particularly true in this case. Many of my "people of interest"—including some of those whom I suspected of killing Jorell, and associates of those suspects—were on the inside, either at the St. Louis County Jail, Missouri state prisons, or federal prisons.

The Fuller twins had talked to some of them at the St. Louis County Jail following their arrests for robbery, before their mother posted their bond. In late 2017 they encountered Leron White there, who was also locked up while awaiting trial.

It was awkward, considering many believed White killed their close friend Jorell. Nonetheless, Mike didn't hesitate to ask him tough questions.

"I heard you guys had something to do with my little brother getting killed," Mike said.

"I didn't do it," White insisted, adding that none of his Kinloch associates from the Gutter Crew House or the Horse House were responsible either. "We didn't have nothing to do with his death, I swear."

At another point, Montrel and White became cellmates. "I was in a cell with Leron for, like, a month and a half," Montrel told me. "Me and him played cards together a few times. He used to cheat."

To Montrel, Leron White also contended he hadn't harmed Jorell. How could he have? The two of them were friends, he insisted.

Indeed, by all accounts, White and Jorell spoke warmly of each other. White even attended Jorell's candlelight memorial service following his death.

And yet, according to Mike, White admitted taking Jorell's 1911.

"He said that he did steal the gun from off Jorell body," Mike said, "because he didn't want people to look at Jorell as a [criminal]. He said he wanted to give the gun back to us, but he ended up getting locked up around that time."

This was one hell of a tortured story. I found it difficult to believe. Mike and Montrel also thought it sounded suspicious.

Still, White maintained his innocence in Jorell's killing and even offered an alternate theory. The real killer, he claimed, didn't come from Kinloch at all, but from Oak Avenue in Ferguson. The culprit was someone with a hair-trigger temper they all knew, who'd had a recent, acute beef with Jorell.

Mike Fuller prides himself on being someone who doesn't suffer fools. He recognized that Leron White had a strong incentive to lay blame elsewhere.

And yet, in spite of himself, he couldn't help but believe that White was correct.

CHAPTER NINETEEN

In early 2019 I visited the cemetery where Jorell was buried. It was my first time there since his funeral.

Some people find cemeteries depressing, but I find them calming, particularly the North County cluster of graveyards along St. Charles Rock Road. They're huge green spaces within bustling residential areas, bastions of quietude where no one will bother you.

The headstone engravings reflect the decedents' quirky personalities, and tokens left by loved ones run the gamut from flower bouquets to booze bottles to—as I saw one Thanksgiving—a papier-mâché turkey. In this rapidly changing part of the county, the cemeteries evoke a feeling of permanence, especially the old mausoleums, with their exquisite stone and stained glass craftsmanship.

Jorell is buried at Laurel Hill Memorial Gardens, a nearly hundred-year-old graveyard in Pagedale, the municipality where my suspect #1, Chauncey James, happens to be from. It's well trafficked, not just by grieving widows but by young men who have lost friends. When I pulled in I saw someone had spray-painted the word Crypdale on the road, apparently to shout out a local gang.

I spoke with the cemetery's twenty-two-year-old operator, Riley, whose family has been in the business for generations. His mother, who died when he was young, is buried in his uncle's cemetery in South County. He said that because of North County's surging murder rate they were running out of space here. For that reason they were considering ending "containerless" burials. Riley lamented that they no longer offered bronze flower vases because they kept getting stolen from grave sites.

After reeling off a few other depressing aspects of the funeral business, he produced a paper map of the grounds and showed me where to find Jorell's plot. I thanked him and walked across the road, past a children's psychiatric hospital, arriving at a small, annexed burial area bordered by a mobile home park. I counted the rows until I arrived at Jorell's patch of dirt, marked only by a small cross and a red ribbon.

What are you supposed to do at a gravesite? I hadn't brought any flowers, so I just closed my eyes and tried to remember him; the things we'd done together, the times I'd been proud of him, the laughs we'd shared. After a few minutes I gave up. It felt absurd to be thinking like this.

I didn't want to dwell on memories of Jorell—I wanted to be making new memories together.

I drove home frustrated. Ruminating on the past just didn't feel therapeutic or productive. I didn't want to sit around feeling sorry that Jorell had been killed, I wanted to be *doing* something about it.

Maybe I just feared dealing with my emotions. That's what Anna suggested, and she probably had a point. I'm far from the only man with this problem, and I understand the potential negative ramifications of failing to drill down on my feelings. By denying my emotional state, I risked making unconscious decisions. As I worked my investigation, I couldn't risk any blind spots. I needed to see the world clearly, starting with myself. I needed to understand how Jorell's death affected me, and what these feelings were causing me to do. It's like I was traveling a dark highway with my eyes half closed, risking losing my bearings and getting lost.

And yet it was growing exceedingly difficult for me to navigate my feelings. For one thing, I worried about wasting time. The longer his murder remained unsolved, the more likely it would remain so, I thought.

My mind kept tracking back to his case and what I needed to do next.

* * *

Soon after visiting the cemetery I decided to get in touch with Jorell's sister Rece. We'd spoken sporadically but had never done a full-length interview. That needed to change. She was close to her younger brother in age and one of his best friends, privy to certain aspects of his life that were off-limits to others. She said she'd be happy to talk, and so one morning in March 2019, I visited her apartment.

From the highway I drove north on West Florissant Avenue, where the Michael Brown unrest had taken place five years earlier. Few visible scars remained: the burned shops had been rebuilt, or in some cases demolished. Despite the promises of revitalization, West Florissant Avenue remained a bleak expanse of fast food restaurants, beauty supply stores, and predatory loan enterprises. There were empty parking lots as far as the eye could see. Commuters raced down the four-lane road. Pedestrians cowered on stretches of sidewalk that were sometimes not ADA compliant, and the few who dared ride bikes took their lives into their hands.

I approached Canfield Drive, the street where Brown was killed. I turned right at a sign for an abandoned car wash, which featured an anachronistic cartoon chauffeur holding a bucket and a towel. Arriving a few minutes before my scheduled meeting with Rece, I stopped to examine the memorial plaque to Brown, laid into a sidewalk and surrounded by roses and a teddy bear. "In Memory of Michael O.D. Brown, May 20, 1996-August 9, 2014," it read. "He'd like the tears of those who grieve to dry before the sun of happy memories that he left behind when life was done."

This memorial had become a tourist destination of sorts, and a place where TV newscasters reported live on the anniversaries of his death. But on most days it simply faded into the landscape of this low-income neighborhood. Right now people were heading to work, walking to the bus stop, or rumbling past in pickups.

Behind Brown's plaque was a little park on a bluff. Its walking path cut through dense woods and featured remains of those '70s-era fitness stations—for doing pull-ups or sit-ups—from back before gyms were popular. No one walked the path on this chilly morning, though muddy tire tracks indicated someone had recently taken a joyride.

Just across the street was Rece's apartment complex, called Canfield Green, where she moved not long after Brown's death. (In 2021 it was renamed Pleasant View Gardens.) She now resided only a hundred yards or so from where he was killed. The proximity to this historic spot was neither draw nor deterrent for her; it was simply preferable to other nearby subsidized housing options, like the Park Ridge apartments, her previous home, which had been burgled four times in one year, she said. Fortunately she was never home when it happened, but intruders took just about everything: TVs, DVD players, baby clothes, even Pampers. These types of break-ins are commonplace in southeast Ferguson, where five low-income apartment complexes (including Canfield Green and Park Ridge) account for 25 percent of the city's violent crimes. They're the kinds of places where no one bothers to sweep up the shell casings.

"You still hear gunshots outside—at night, in the morning—but it's actually nice here. It ain't bother me yet," Rece said, after I entered the apartment. We sat down on a brown sectional sofa; clothes were scattered on the floor, and the bathroom counters were piled high with wigs and hair extensions. These were inventory for her hair-styling business, a side gig from her main job as a manager at a fast-food spot called London's Wing House.

Rece is the most social of the Cleveland children, constantly chatting on her phone, texting, and posting on social media. Though she asked me not to print her real name, she said she got her nickname because her mother ate Reese's Pieces throughout her pregnancy. "They're not my favorite, though," she added with a laugh. "That's weird to people."

Her boyfriend had lived here until recently, but now her sister Peaches was staying here and helping out with Rece's four-year-old son. Rece and Peaches shared both of the same parents as Jorell, giving them a special bond.

"He had a big heart," Rece said. "He was very sweet. He would do little simple stuff. Like, when I was in the hospital after I had my baby, and I had to have surgery, he brought a card and a teddy bear."

Rece was nine months pregnant when Michael Brown was killed. During the unrest she hunkered down inside the Cleveland house in

Ferguson, before going to the hospital to give birth just a few days later. Soon after coming home with her son, however, Rece decided to move out. A bad crowd had begun gathering there. "They'd have guns toting," she said. Making matters worse, Jorell was getting caught up in it. "They was popping pills—like Xanax." She didn't know that Jorell was using heroin, she said, but it was all too much. "I didn't want to have all that around my baby, so we moved out."

She was glad to have departed, but she no longer saw Jorell as often. When he was killed she took it as hard as anyone, and she has worked to keep his memory alive. Every year Rece and the Cleveland family go down to Arkansas to celebrate his birthday, March 15, which coincides with a festival in their hometown Dumas called the Hood-Nic, a party that raises money for education.

Rece showed me an oversize, handmade birthday card on her wall, in honor of what would have been Jorell's twenty-first birthday. It included a glossy picture of him looking fit in a pair of shorts and a T-shirt. Below that a couple dozen friends and family members had signed and offered well-wishes to Jorell, almost all of them using the phrase "Happy C-Day."

From my reporting on gangland Los Angeles, I knew exactly what this meant. Members of the Crips don't like to use the letter "B," as it's associated with their archrivals the Bloods. And so, "Happy B-Day" becomes "Happy C-Day."

I didn't ask Rece about it, but on the drive home I contemplated the possibility that Jorell was a gang member. It was hard to believe. He was too independent, I thought. Too free-thinking. But—yet again—I was being naive.

When Jorell's family moved to Ferguson in 2006 he was a scrawny nine-year-old kid. He was cute in that "pat you on the head" kind of way, and people often mistook him as younger than he actually was. As he grew older he got tired of this treatment. He wanted to be one of the big dogs.

The focus of his world grew increasingly beyond his family and his community at school, and he began spending time with the guys on his block. To the uninitiated his street, Oak Avenue, appeared like any other street. But by Jorell's teen years it had become Crips territory. Guys often wore blue clothes, hats, and bandanas; St. Louis Blues hockey paraphernalia was popular. On the other hand, in areas representing the Bloods—like Kinloch, for example—Cardinals' baseball gear was preferred.

It turns out the Crips and Bloods affiliations were imported directly from Los Angeles, circa the 1980s and '90s. Southern California gangbangers moved out here to sell drugs, attempting to expand their influence beyond oversaturated LA markets, including Compton. This trend was documented in rap songs like Ice Cube's 1991 track "My Summer Vacation," in which the drug-dealing narrator heads east.

> *Catch a flight to St. Louis*
> *That's cool, cause nobody knew us*

These dealers had limited success; in many cases the locals fought back and the Los Angeles affiliates were forced to retreat back home, leaving only their gang affiliations behind.

Yet there are differences between Los Angeles and St. Louis gangbanging. While every block in some parts of South LA have been carved out by rival gangs—and crossing the wrong street in the wrong colors can bring trouble—there's more crossover in St. Louis. Local gang members often maintain friends in other sets, and you don't hear about people being killed for colors.

As for Jorell, it soon became clear to me that he was, indeed, a Crip. But Mike Fuller said gang membership wasn't a particularly important aspect of his life. He joined because "everybody from Oak are Crips, and he liked the color blue," Mike said. He added that he didn't believe Jorell had been "jumped in"—beaten as part of an initiation ritual—or anything like that.

More than anything, Jorell identified as a member of the Oak Boys, a clique representing Jorell's block. Their membership overlapped with the Crips, though not everyone joined both. The Oak Boys were teens and twenty-somethings who hung out at Oak Park, located near the Cleveland house. On this sprawling expanse of grass—dotted by play-ground equipment, basketball courts, and soccer fields—the guys could be found listening to music, comparing guns, or just chewing the fat.

Some Oak Boys sold weed or harder drugs. They had a common enemy in a rival Kinloch gang nearby, but the Oak Boys weren't par-ticularly organized. They were mostly just a group of directionless kids who had come up together in the same crummy schools. The workforce didn't have much use for them, so they banded together for safety and camaraderie, and to perhaps make a little money. "A lot of us don't get along 100 percent of the time, but when it's needed, we come together," Jorell's friend Big Ant told me.

Big Ant is a member of the Oak Boys. He's a corpulent, affable neighborhood presence who'd known Jorell since he was young. I'd met him only a couple of times in passing, but he was glad to discuss Jorell's life. He said that Jorell certainly had a temper, but he could also be funny. "He was a silly dude, man," Big Ant said. "Anybody that can stand in there with me and crack jokes all day, that's my type of person." Big Ant also offered key insight into Jorell's trajectory within the clique, and how it affected the way he saw himself.

As Big Ant described it, when he was young Jorell watched the Oak Boys from afar, while playing basketball or riding his dad's four-wheeler in the park. He was curious about them, but intimidated.

Eventually he worked up the courage to talk with them. At first, they mocked his youth and small stature. "We do all the younger fellas like that, trying to hang with the big fellas, but you ain't old enough yet," said Big Ant.

Before long he found his way into the fold. At first he was thrilled. But though inclusion had its privileges . . . it also had its pitfalls.

The Oak Boys began calling him Lajo—Little Joe—after his father Joe, and because of his size. This light hazing was normal, but Jorell didn't tolerate being pushed around much. He gave as good as he took. Very quickly he began to demand respect, and the guys admired how he couldn't be intimidated. "Somebody like Jorell, he's gonna stand his ground," said Big Ant.

When I started high school I admired the upperclassmen guys, seventeen- and eighteen-year-olds with licenses and cars, who dated pretty girls and had access to weed and booze. They seemed to have it all figured out. Jorell looked up to the older Oak Boys in this same way. They were bigger, they had swagger, they had guns.

Those older boys I used to idolize? I don't anymore. Many of them remain caught up in the same bad habits and vainglorious pursuits from high school. Turns out they didn't really have it all figured out. And neither did the Oak Boys. They were trapped in a system that penalized anyone who played by the rules and rewarded those who lived cynically. They moved in a haze of uncertainty, fear, and mistrust.

And though the burnouts from my high school are still mostly around, many of the Oak Boys are now in prison. Or dead. Many suffer undiagnosed PTSD.

Jorell bonded with the Oak Boys through hip-hop. They enjoyed Southern rappers like Gucci Mane and Lil Boosie, and many Oak Boys were also aspiring MCs themselves. As far back as 2008 they'd been uploading videos to YouTube, showing off their handguns, rolls of cash, and ziplock bags of drugs. They shouted out incarcerated members of their crew and paid allegiance to "Oak Bloccc."

If you want the pants scared off you, watch a St. Louis rap video. Hometown heroes Nelly and Huey once dominated rotation with videos filled with buxom women and sparkling jewels, but those days are long gone.

Often set in overgrown parts of North County, today's videos document chilling aspects of street life. Teenage rappers prowl dark streets brandishing firearms. Their crews pass around blunts or Styrofoam cups of codeine-promethazine cough syrup. Everyone's packed to the gills, and their wild parties seem on the verge of devolving into crime scenes. In one video a local rapper called 30 Deep Grimeyy (named for the number of crewmates he says he travels with) carries an AR pistol in one hand and a pair of street signs in the other; the intersection displayed on the signs shows it's been stolen from a rival gang's territory.

The St. Louis scene is populated by compelling and intriguing characters, like Luh Half, a little person with a huge following, and standout female rapper Jai Ktchnz. Videos throughout the scene are technically sophisticated, made on low budgets but with high production values, which creates an unnerving verité quality. Nobody doubts that these guns are real, and they're usually pointed directly at the camera. One wonders: Aren't they worried about the police? It turns out that they should be. In fact, Baltimore cops used the drugs and guns displayed in the video of a rapper called Young Moose as probable cause for a raid in 2014, leading to his arrest. Two years earlier, in rapper Lil Boosie's murder trial in Baton Rouge, prosecutors used his lyrics against him as evidence, though he was ultimately acquitted.

Ice Cube's 1991 track "My Summer Vacation" was a morality tale; in the end, the LA dealer is put away for life. But the St. Louis rappers' songs hew closer to the present-day reality of a rotted criminal justice system. Their characters escape prosecution, and their enemies perish.

Using similarly bleak imagery, the Oak Boys hoped to be the next breakout group from the St. Louis area. Their song "Out the Mud" discusses being marginalized by society, while their video for "Monster" focuses on their outlandish arsenal, featuring AR-15 rifles about three feet long, semiautomatic pistols, and a 12-gauge pump shotgun. Some of the guns are customized with exotic accoutrements.

To me these videos are terrifying, but Jorell was captivated by it all. He did a little rapping himself, and though he was too shy to perform for me or his friends, he was on hand for the "Monster" video shoot. Fresh off a shift at Popeyes, he brought a batch of fried chicken to the set in a garbage bag. They were so happy with this gift that they filmed the delivery and put Jorell in the video. He was thrilled by his fifteen seconds of fame.

Over time, many Oak Boys developed real love for Jorell. An older member of the clique named Calvin took him under his wing. Big Ant got Jorell's name tattooed on his left hand and wore a "Lajo" memorial T-shirt in a video, after his death.

But not everyone embraced the young newcomer. An Oak Boy named Ricky Watkins chastised Jorell regularly. Because of their increasingly confrontational relationship, I came to consider Watkins suspect #3 in my investigation, the third and final person I believed could have killed Jorell.

Sharply dressed, with bright brown eyes and a drooping goatee, Watkins was five years older than Jorell, and taller. He shared his name with his father, a Kinloch native.

Ricky Watkins Sr. did time for crack cocaine dealing and armed criminal action in his day, after shooting a man he believed was a police informant. Just six months before Watkins's birth, Ricky Sr. was involved in a strange domestic incident in Kinloch, involving the mother of two of his children and his own mother, which culminated in police finding a sawed-off shotgun in a barbeque pit. A St. Louis County police investigator sought to charge Ricky Sr. with assault and burglary, but could not "due to lack of victim cooperation."

This was the world Watkins was born into. Though he graduated from high school and attended some college, like his father he faced trouble with the law. In August 2016, just ten days before Jorell's death, he was arrested after being caught by police with an unlicensed Springfield Armory semiautomatic pistol. Like many of his contemporaries he posed for social media photos with firearms, sometimes color coordinating his gun with his outfit. He was never convicted of a violent crime, but many in the neighborhood feared him. Iesha warned Jorell against hanging out with him.

From the start, Joe Cleveland didn't trust him. From what he understood, it was Watkins who drove a wedge between Jorell and his former friend Lil Glen—the guy who once slept over at the Cleveland house, but then later stole guns from the family and shot Joe in the back. Further, Joe's kids told him, Watkins spent his time menacing people and showing off his .38 at Oak Park. And so one day Joe got into his truck and drove down to the park to set a few things straight.

"I live here," he told Watkins, in front of Watkins's friends. "I ain't going nowhere. I pay taxes on this park, and my kids are gonna play here. They better be safe."

Joe warned Watkins against trying anything. He said he'd learned where Watkins kept his .38 and its three bullets—under the garbage can belonging to a household adjacent to the park.

"I better not have to come back down here on account of your stupidness," Joe concluded.

Watkins didn't take kindly to Joe's warning. He made an aggressive move, "like he wanted to walk up to my truck," Joe said.

"I pulled out my .44 and said, 'No, you ain't going to walk up to my truck,'" Joe recalled. "I had no more problems out of him after that."

Some portrayed Ricky Watkins as the bad guy, but he had deep scars of his own. Traumatized by the death of a beloved uncle in 2013, he wrote dark status updates on his Facebook page, prophesying his own death and worrying about his children.

He was also a big flirt. "Every time he saw me, he'd try to talk to me," said Jorell's sister Rece. He could really turn up the charm when he wanted to. "Get him mad, it might turn bad, but other than that, he's a funny guy," said Big Ant.

Added Watkins's friend Nett: "He was super funny—always cracking jokes, always laughing, playing. It's just that, when he get in his little ways, he can be a little disrespectful. He didn't know when to stop."

Watkins could lose his cool over the littlest slight, people said.

Kind of like Jorell.

Since Mike and Montrel were identical twins, people often got them confused. This happened one afternoon at R&R Mini Mart & Liquor, around 2016, though no one seems sure exactly when. This was the same bodega near the Cleveland house where Jorell had gotten into an altercation in the summer of 2016 with the wife of suspect #1, Chauncey James. This time, Montrel was inside the store when he was approached by Ricky Watkins. "What up, fat ass?" Watkins said.

This took Montrel aback, since he didn't know Watkins at all. It turns out Watkins thought Montrel was Mike, whom he knew from the neighborhood. He meant his comment as a joke.

Mike is the more easygoing twin; Montrel has a shorter fuse. Montrel immediately got his back up. "Who the fuck is you?" he responded. They went back and forth for a minute or so, growing increasingly inflamed.

Watkins left the store in a huff. Mike, who was waiting in Montrel's car, saw Watkins from the parking lot. He watched as Watkins retrieved his gun from his own car, and then posted up next to the outdoor refrigerated case holding ice for sale, near the bodega's entrance. He was lying in wait for Montrel.

Mike exited the car to try to defuse the situation. He approached Watkins by the icebox.

Watkins was confused. "How did you come out of the store that fast?"

"That's my twin brother," Mike explained. As Watkins shook his head in disbelief, Mike insisted it was all just a misunderstanding and asked him to spare his brother.

Just then Montrel emerged from the store, ready to fight. Mike grabbed him and hustled him into the car. "Go to the crib," Mike told Montrel. "Go!"

Montrel started the car and drove toward the Cleveland house, but he didn't understand the urgency. "Why are we running from this guy? It's 1:30 in the afternoon. You think he's going to shoot me at this time of day?"

As they parked the car in the Cleveland driveway, Mike insisted that, yes, Ricky Watkins was capable of something like that. As if to make Mike's point, Watkins roared past them on Oak Avenue at that very moment, going perhaps forty or fifty down the residential street. As Mike and Montrel ran into the house, Watkins realized he'd passed them. "Then he did a U-turn—you could hear his tires and everything—and turned back around," Montrel said.

Shortly thereafter, Mike and Montrel heard a cascade of gunshots. "He was just shooting in the air, trying to show that, 'I ain't playing,'" Montrel said. "Just trying to show out."

Nothing more came of the incident. I couldn't find a police report about it. Both Fuller brothers found it a shocking display of aggression and believed it showed that Watkins was capable of much worse.

"That man is crazy," said Montrel.

Ricky Watkins's relationship with Jorell was often civil. When the crew would hang out at Oak Park, he and Jorell frequently got along, comparing the latest guns in their collections. "One minute they was cool. One minute they wasn't," said Jorell's sister Rece.

One morning not long before Jorell's death the Oak Boys were at the park when, suddenly, cops pulled up. Perhaps summoned by a concerned neighbor who saw their guns, the police jumped out of their cars. The Oak Boys immediately scattered, running in all directions as the cops gave chase.

As Jorell described it to Mike, he found his way into a nearby vacant house. Watkins followed right after him. Once inside the home Watkins panicked, worried the police would bust him for his unlicensed gun. In a frenzied effort to hide it, he threw it down a laundry chute, and it fell into the basement.

Ultimately the police didn't catch up to them, or anyone else in the crew. Once it became clear the cops had moved on, Watkins awkwardly requested Jorell's assistance in retrieving his gun.

"Jorell, can you help me get it out?" he asked.

"Man, you don't really like me," Jorell responded. "Why should I help you? Every time I'm around, you try to embarrass me." In the end, however, Jorell came to Watkins's aid, helping him retrieve the firearm out of the basement. Jorell came home and told the story to Mike, who applauded him for his peacemaking actions.

But mistrust between the two persisted. Watkins mocked Jorell for hanging around with his girlfriend Danielle's brother. "Why you with this white boy?" Watkins would ask him, implying that Danielle's brother might be working with the police. "Don't be bringing white boys over here in the neighborhood. You don't know what we got going on." (I never encountered Watkins myself, and in fact I was almost universally accepted by Jorell's friends. I never heard of Jorell receiving any teasing for being a "Little.")

Jorell's friend Malon said things got extremely heated between Jorell and Watkins on two or three occasions. "They always used to have words, and always used to get into it, and pull guns out on each other," he said. One time at Oak Park things got particularly hairy. Malon doesn't recall the date, or what the specific argument entailed, but "they got into it about something."

Pulling out his gun, Watkins declared, "I ain't worried about nothing. I got my gun on me."

Jorell responded by producing his own firearm. "I ain't worried about nothing either," he responded.

"They ended up pointing them at each other," Malon said. "They had words, and we calmed it all down."

CHAPTER TWENTY

Mike Fuller believed Ricky Watkins, my #3 suspect, killed Jorell. He told me this soon after I got to know him, but among the myriad possibilities I wasn't sure what to think at the time.

He didn't have real evidence, but he noted that Watkins had family connections in the area where Jorell was slain—Kinloch—which meant Watkins was familiar with the landscape. Mike also pointed out that Watkins drove a Dodge Journey SUV. I would later learn the profile of this vehicle was similar to the vehicle associated with Jorell's killer, as described by an eyewitness.

Mike believed the disputes between Watkins and Jorell could have boiled over. Watkins was petty and vindictive, Mike insisted, capable of enacting deadly violence over minor slights. "I told Jorell, 'He's jealous of you, bra,'" Mike told me. "He knows what you're capable of. He's upset because you don't bow down to him like the other little guys from Oak do."

This theory made sense to Mike's twin brother Montrel, as well, who speculated that Jorell was killed shortly after transacting with my #2 suspect Leron White for some heroin at the Gutter Crew House on that fateful afternoon.

"I honestly believe Jorell went to buy some dope from Leron and was surprised to see Watkins there," Montrel told me. "They got into it and Watkins shot him."

I was skeptical. Watkins may have been my #3 suspect, but I had a hard time understanding his motive. Sure, he and Jorell clashed, and perhaps Jorell didn't pay him the respect he felt he deserved, but it didn't sound like sufficient cause for murder.

In an effort to convince me otherwise, Mike explained that inside the prison system he'd spoken to many people who implicated Watkins in Jorell's death. Mike claimed that a shotcaller—a gang leader whose influence extended far beyond the prison—said he had been asked by one of Watkins's uncles for permission for Watkins to kill Jorell, a permission the shotcaller granted. (I could not verify any of this.)

Again, none of this particularly swayed me. Further, many in Jorell's family did not consider Watkins a suspect. "I don't think they was on bad terms," Jorell's sister Rece said, noting that Watkins, like Leron White, attended Jorell's candlelight memorial following his death. Another of Jorell's sisters, Peaches, agreed with Rece.

Soon, however, my interest in Watkins as a suspect increased exponentially, after I learned about another incident on Oak Avenue, shortly after Jorell's death.

With Jorell's passing on August 27, 2016, the Oak Boys lost one of their members. To make matters worse, Jorell was the second Oak Boy to die in the span of eight days.

On August 19, 2016, a former basketball standout named Michael Ellis was killed while driving. He was near the Cleveland home when the driver of a stolen SUV slammed into his small sedan. According to reports, four young men and a woman jumped out of the SUV and fled, and Ellis died shortly thereafter.

Ellis had played basketball at McCluer High School, where Jorell went, before being shot and paralyzed. (I never learned all the details of his injury.) At the time of his death, Ellis had long dreadlocks and two children, and he made music with the Oak Boys crew. Ellis's candlelight memorial was held on Oak Avenue, in the same spot where Jorell's would later be held.

The Oak Boys felt the strain of the two untimely losses. Ellis's death was a tragedy, but since it was an accident it was easier for them to wrap their minds around.

Jorell's death, on the other hand, felt more raw. Because no one was charged, there was no closure. It became all anyone could talk about.

Who could have done it?

And then, in whispers: Could it have been one of their own? Rumors of Watkins's involvement began to circulate.

At the center of these rumors was Calvin, an Oak Boy who lived just up the block from the Clevelands. He was about nine years older than Jorell and a mentor of sorts. They got along well.

With elaborate tattoos running from his neck to his fingertips, Calvin was a complicated guy. He was both intellectual and streetwise, capable of both great kindness and callousness.

"For the most part everyone knew him for going to school," said Nett, his ex-girlfriend. He'd studied criminal justice at a historically Black state university in St. Louis, Harris-Stowe, and he'd also attended college outside of Kansas City, at Missouri Western State University. There he pledged the Black fraternity Phi Beta Sigma, and had the organization's symbol seared onto his skin with a branding iron as a show of devotion. "They stepped in a line together, and all that," said his friend Big Ant, who attended a fraternity party with him.

Calvin also had trouble with the law. In 2014 a Ferguson man accused him and his brother of robbing him at gunpoint. But Calvin sought to turn over a new leaf and get his life together. He was the father to two young children, and, according to an online registry, was engaged to be married to his girlfriend on April 1, 2017.

He seemed to see something of himself in Jorell, despite the age gap. Calvin would show up at the Cleveland house, ask for Jorell, and the two of them would smoke weed and goof around. "[Calvin] was just a solid guy, they had a solid relationship," said Mike Fuller.

Calvin and Ricky Watkins, however, had a rockier one. They'd known each other for many years and at times seemed tight. They appeared in many Facebook photos together and often hung out together with their girlfriends. One time, according to Mike, they conspired to steal a giant marijuana plant that Mike was growing in the yard behind the Cleveland house.

At the same time, Calvin and Watkins got under each other's skin. "One minute you'll catch them best of friends, the next minute they into it," said Big Ant. Nett said Watkins shot at Calvin a year or so before Jorell's death.

At one point Calvin had enough.

"Sometimes Watkins did used to take it too far," said Big Ant, noting that eventually Calvin couldn't handle any more. "He said he was a grown man, and he shouldn't be scared of him."

Mike Fuller believed that Calvin had inside information about who killed Jorell. He believed that because, not long after Jorell's death, Calvin came by the Cleveland house and talked with Mike.

"It's fucked up about who did it," Calvin told him. Mike was all ears, but before Mike could probe him further, Calvin walked off.

Soon afterward, Mike and Calvin were hanging out with Ricky Watkins, all of them smoking weed in front of the Cleveland house. Out of nowhere, Watkins and Calvin began arguing. When things became heated Calvin snarled at Watkins: "I already got unfinished business from what you did to little bruh."

"Do what you gotta do," Watkins said, pulling out his gun.

The conflict didn't escalate that day, and everyone soon went their separate ways. But in this moment everything clicked into place for Mike. "Little bruh," he posited, was Jorell. What Calvin was saying, Mike believed, was that Watkins had killed him.

Mike would never be able to verify this understanding. That's because, almost immediately, tragedy struck Oak Avenue again.

On the afternoon of October 18, 2016, less than two months after Jorell was killed, Montrel Fuller arrived to the Cleveland house. As he parked, Watkins approached his car. Though the pair had exchanged vicious words at R&R Mini Mart & Liquor, now Watkins wanted a favor. He was with Calvin, and the two of them were working on a car, a mid-2000s model Monte Carlo. It wouldn't start, and Watkins wanted to borrow Montrel's jumper cables.

"Just make sure you bring them back," Montrel said.

Watkins and Calvin were grateful for the jumper cables. But in the coming hours their good feelings turned sour. They began to argue heatedly, though what they were arguing about wasn't immediately clear to witnesses.

"They got into it," Montrel said. "They took it outside."

They moved into Oak Park. There, Watkins threatened Calvin and may have even pulled his gun on him.

This caused Calvin to boil over. He stormed off. "He wasn't just going to let Watkins put a threat on him, knowing that nine times out of ten Watkins would stand behind those threats," said one source.

Nett knew the politics of Oak Avenue well. She was a local resident, Calvin's ex-girlfriend, and also close friends with Ricky Watkins. She told me that on October 18, 2016, just minutes after Calvin and Watkins's argument, she spoke with Watkins for the final time.

She was in her car with her baby son on her way to her mother's house when she saw Watkins and some others at Oak Park. She pulled up. Not realizing anything was wrong, Nett chatted with Watkins for a moment, about nothing in particular, and then said goodbye.

As she drove off she texted Calvin to say hello. She and Calvin were no longer dating, but they were still friends, and though she expected a quick reply, she didn't receive one. Calvin, it turns out, was in a blind rage. Just moments before she had arrived at Oak Park, Calvin had left it.

Though, again, it's unclear why, Calvin was steaming mad at Watkins. He quickly went to his house and got his gun. He returned to Oak Park and, according to bystanders, before anyone knew what was happening, shot at Watkins and hit him. Watkins crumpled, pulling out his own gun and firing as he fell to the ground.

Watkins hit Calvin with a glancing shot, but Watkins had taken the worst of the damage, and the confrontation was over quickly. Watkins lay on the ground, bleeding and losing heart rate.

Nett was approaching her mother's house when she heard the gunshots. She quickly turned around and returned to Oak Park. She saw Watkins laying on his right side on the ground, against the curb. A circle of onlookers had gathered, surrounding him. Blood was all over his body and on the ground.

Nett asked what happened. "Calvin did it," multiple people told her, too shocked to impart further details. "Calvin did it."

Watkins's cousin retrieved a towel and attempted to apply aid. A moment later an ambulance arrived. Paramedics pushed through the crowd. The ambulance took Ricky Watkins away. He died soon after at the hospital.

Watkins was the third Oak Boy killed in two months. He was a father, a musician, and a dreamer with big plans. Not everybody liked him, but no one would have wished him such a quick and brutal death.

Unlike Michael Ellis and Jorell Cleveland, whose killings garnered local news coverage, Watkins didn't receive so much as an obituary. Other than some Facebook tributes, I can't find anything on the internet showing he ever existed.

"It was a tragedy," said Big Ant, the Oak Boy. "Especially to find out that one of us did it."

Two hours after Watkins's shooting, it was first dark on Oak Avenue. The temperature was dropping, and Watkins's body had gone cold.

Upon receiving word that he was dead, his associates grew furious. They wanted vengeance. NOW. And they believed they knew where to find it.

The group hastily piled into a van and drove to the home where Calvin lived with his mother and brother.

Meanwhile, Nett made her way up the block to the Cleveland house. There she met up with Jorell's sister Iesha, her good friend.

The two were standing in the front yard when they saw the van creep up to Calvin's house.

Calvin's brother Will was in the living room with his girlfriend when he peered out the window. He saw the van stop in front of his house.

Not recognizing the vehicle, but believing it might contain someone he knew, he pushed the screen door open and tentatively stepped onto the front porch. Immediately, men opened the van's door and began blasting at him.

Will hightailed it back into the house. He grabbed his girlfriend and brought her downstairs, into the basement.

The men unloaded on Calvin and Will's house—*ba ba ba ba ba ba ba*—emptying clip after clip in a haze of sparks and smoke. They shot up the front and the side of the home. Shells fell to the asphalt, handfuls of them all at once.

Iesha and Nett ducked behind a car. It was too dark for them to make out the identity of the shooters. They were petrified.

"It looked like a fireworks show," said Nett. "It was the scariest shit in my life."

Later, each shell casing would be identified by a numbered yellow marker assigned by crime scene investigators. Nett said there were more than 120. But she and Iesha didn't wait for the police to arrive. As soon as Ricky Watkins's avengers departed, Nett and Iesha ran up the street as fast as they could to Calvin and Will's house, beating on the door until they were let in.

"All of them shots—you just know nobody's living through that," Nett said. "But thank God, Will and his girlfriend, they were okay."

But where was Calvin? He was not in the house.

Shortly after allegedly killing Ricky Watkins, Calvin had fled town. Even after being hit by a glancing shot in the shootout with Watkins, he managed to get out.

When Watkins's associates fired at his house, they were gunning for a ghost.

"Everybody in the hood was like, 'Calvin killed Ricky,'" said Jorell's brother Jermaine. "Somebody shot up Calvin's house, whoever wanted revenge.

"Now Calvin on the run."

Oak Avenue was stunned. Nobody had ever seen anything like this. The deaths of Michael Ellis and Jorell still fresh in their minds, now they were forced to add Watkins to the tally. There had been no time to heal; this nightmare was playing itself out again, over and over.

Fear and panic. Agony and anger.

Repeat.

CHAPTER TWENTY-ONE

For the second time that evening, the police came to process a crime scene on Oak Avenue. Detectives asked Calvin's brother Will who might have done this. Will said he didn't know. The detectives also talked to Calvin's mother. (It's not clear where she was during the shooting.) She asked them if they had any answers. They didn't. She quickly gathered up the family and moved them out of the house before there was more bloodshed.

Meanwhile, the question remained: Why had Calvin allegedly killed Ricky Watkins? What had sparked his anger toward his former friend?

Opinions were divided. Montrel Fuller believed it was because Calvin took the Monte Carlo he'd just fixed up with Watkins out for longer than he said he would, when Watkins wanted to use the car. It was a small dispute that quickly spiraled.

But Mike Fuller believed their argument concerned something much more significant: Jorell. Calvin killed Watkins because he believed Watkins killed Jorell.

"Calvin felt like he had to do something about that," said Mike Fuller. "Calvin killed Watkins to avenge Jorell. I know that personally."

No one would be convicted of Watkins's murder. In the meantime, his associates remained frustrated. Calvin had somehow managed to slip through their fingers.

They didn't know where he'd gone, but they were determined to find out. "Watkins's family let it be known that they wasn't going to stop until they knew he was dead," Nett said. "They would be looking for people who said they had contact with him."

They weren't fooling around. When a guy on Oak claimed to be in contact with Calvin, Watkins's people shot up the guy's house, Nett said. Fortunately he was okay. Ironically, this guy hadn't *actually* talked to Calvin, but just said he did.

Calvin knew Watkins's people were after him, and he was determined to stay hidden. He ceased speaking with Nett, she said, and practically everyone else.

"Nobody had no contact with him," she said. "Nobody knew where he was, he just disappeared."

Rumor had it that he was on the other side of the state, perhaps near Kansas City. He'd gone to college just outside of town, after all, in St. Joseph, Missouri, and his dad was rumored to live in the area. "That's where I heard he was at," said Big Ant.

But Big Ant would never know for sure. He would never see Calvin again. Calvin died about five months later, on March 25, 2017.

Very little is known about Calvin's death. According to an online memorial, he died in a car accident. It apparently happened in western Missouri, and had nothing to do with Watkins's associates. Calvin was twenty-eight.

"Nobody knew where he was, so it's not like [one of Watkins's people] could go and find him," Nett said. "He was a drinker. He probably went out one night. His mom said he was by hisself—she doesn't know if he was drunk or not. I don't know what happened."

Speculates Big Ant: "He drunk himself to, just, oblivious."

Calvin's funeral was planned in secret. According to Nett, his mother told very few people about it, worried about retaliation.

Calvin's friends found out the details anyway. Nett made plans to attend. He was her old boyfriend, after all.

Around this time an odd rumor began circulating—that Calvin wasn't actually dead. This rumor picked up quite a bit of steam.

"Everybody was like, 'He faked his death, he faked his death,'" said Nett.

Since Watkins's people said they wouldn't rest until Calvin was dead, faking his death might have been the only way for him to get some peace.

"Yeah, people said that," said Big Ant. He added that Calvin's peculiar behavior in the months before Watkins's death fueled the speculation. "He was telling us he was reading a book on selling his soul to become a millionaire, and he was in the process of actually doing that," Big Ant said. He didn't know the book's name.

Faking one's death, of course, is an almost impossibly complicated logistical challenge. Nett was skeptical. Nonetheless, at the funeral—which was well attended, and peaceful—Nett nervously confirmed that it was really him there, lying in the casket. She checked for the tattoo behind his ear, the scar by his eye, the small mole on his nose. It was all there.

This turned out to be a letdown for her.

"I wish he did fake his death," she said. "So I could still talk to him."

In less than seven months, four different Oak Boys had lost their lives.

These young men grew up in a once-thriving area that had been left to rot. They went to subpar schools and had few employment opportunities. They found joy where they could. When drama was in the air, they got caught up. When the pressure was on, they tried their best to navigate through.

They confronted impossible situations. Their deaths left children and lovers and families behind, creating new cycles of pain and poverty. One death can affect a family and a community for a lifetime. Four in quick succession leaves a legacy of endless, compounded misery.

"It was like a circle of death," said Nett. "It all just happened so fast."

Though traumatizing for the people who knew them, for everyone else these killings might as well never have happened. Besides my piece about Jorell and some news reports about Michael Ellis, very little was written about these events. No gushing obituaries, no memorial scholarships, no editorials about the need to fight poverty and gun violence.

Nothing.

It's crazy that in our data-obsessed society, where every single NBA free throw is logged, where you can instantly determine your neighbor's home's value, or the name of the key grip on an obscure film, no database contains the names of the American humans who are murdered every single day.

Calvin, Ricky Watkins, Michael Ellis, Jorell, rest in peace.

Perhaps no one was hit harder by the Oak deaths than Big Ant, the genial Oak Boy who used to see the guys nearly every day. He'd known Watkins since their days attending Central Elementary School together. Still bearing a trauma that PTSD only begins to describe, his pain is difficult for him to articulate. But it's right there in his eyes.

"That type of stuff, ain't gon' never not make you feel some type of way," he told me, adding that his coping mechanism has been to smoke a lot of weed.

Nett said that after the deaths, everyone was taking sides, assigning blame and saying "what if." She had little patience for this.

"My thing is, all y'all was standing out there when they was getting into it, and nobody tried to interfere!" she said. "Nobody said, 'Alright Watkins, you trippin,' or, 'A'ight, Calvin let's go up the street.'

"Just a whole group of them stood out there and watched it all happen."

CHAPTER TWENTY-TWO

Now that I had circled my three suspects—Chauncey James, Leron White, and Ricky Watkins—I worked to determine who was most likely to have killed Jorell.

I continued consulting Jorell's close friend Mike Fuller, who was suffering through his time at the Boonville Correctional Center, smack in the center of Missouri. It was a notorious facility. Before the prison was established in 1983, it was a reform school for boys, one known for punishing members of its underage, African American population for ill-defined offenses such as "incorrigible" behavior by transferring them to a nearby adult prison, where many were raped.

Times had changed, some of it for the better. Mike was able to buy a television set, take a welding class, and communicate with loved ones over email.

But day-to-day life was miserable. The threat of violence hung in the air. "It's a straight Thunder Dome," he wrote me. I was shocked to hear he had to pay for much of his own "hygiene," like toothpaste, soap, and shampoo. Shortly after Mike's arrival in May 2019, some of his items were stolen out of his cell while he was eating.

"I caught four people running out my cell with my food and hygiene after chow," he wrote, "and my soft ass cellmate was not standing on shit so I had to step on DAT situation right then and there."

He'd fought with the offending party, and he was now writing from the hole, where he'd been sent as punishment. He'd been in isolation for two weeks, cut off from everyone. He was missing his family, losing track of the days of the week, and going crazy. He reached out to his caseworker about his mental health issues, and it took her nearly a week to respond, but she arranged for him to get out of the hole for three hours a day and to receive access to an iPad to send messages.

I sometimes wired funds for necessities to him and Montrel, who was in a state prison in Bonne Terre, Missouri. Mike was grateful for it, but it hurt him to even have to ask. "You don't understand how hard it is when you don't have a support system," he wrote. "When you're forced to do certain things just to survive in here it does something to you. When you have to beg someone for hygiene it makes you feel less than a man."

He got out of the hole, and regular prison life resumed. From Amazon I ordered books for him that he'd requested, including my own and some urban lit titles. Many of the latter weren't allowed, however; it turns out the Missouri prison system censors thousands of books. (It won't disclose the contents of its banned list.) My books *Original Gangstas* and *Fentanyl, Inc.* got through, but not long after they arrived he called and asked if I could send them again. Someone had broken into his locker and stolen them.

"Were you able to read them before they were taken?" I asked.

"Yeah. But I was charging people. If someone wanted to see them, I would charge them a dollar to read it."

Apparently there was a line to rent my books—this made me proud— and each night Mike collected them and put them in a storage locker. But the night before, someone had busted it open and stolen the books. Mike suspected one guy in particular, who'd made it known that he didn't want to wait his turn.

"So I'm finna go and whoop him, like in an hour," he went on. "I'm gonna beat him."

"Don't do it! I'll send you new ones," I said, noting that any altercation would likely get him sent back to the hole.

"That's not the point, Ben. I got to," he went on. "Because everybody gonna think I'm a ho."

"But haven't you already established yourself in there?"

"Yes…but I told everybody, I made a big announcement—" he was interrupted by the operator saying, *This call is from a correctional facility, and may be monitored and recorded* "—I'm just going to take off on the person."

My attempts to calm him fell on deaf ears. Soon afterward he emailed from the hole again. Mike had gone after the guy, they'd fought, and he was again sent to solitary. "In prison, people kill over literature," he said later.

I planned to see him and Montrel, but then coronavirus shut down visitation. By August 2020 the state prison in Bonne Terre where Montrel was in camp had sixty-six active cases of COVID-19, more than any prison in the state. These people desperately needed care, as well as smart management to prevent the outbreak from spreading. But Bonne Terre was missing more than one-third of its staff, due to the pandemic and also "longer-term, department-wide retention issues," according to a report. Employees who had a fever weren't sent home—rather, sergeants just cranked up the AC until their temperature readings lowered.

Back at Booneville, Mike came down with telltale COVID-19 symptoms: fever and a loss of smell and taste. "I really don't have appetite for anything," he wrote. Instead of giving him proper care—or even a COVID test—prison officials simply threw him in the hole again, as a form of quarantine. Meanwhile, they continued accepting new inmates from other prisons, many of whom were already infected. They lived in close quarters, making social distancing impossible.

"We're packed like sardines," Mike said.

The situation was infuriating, from both a human rights perspective and a public health standpoint. Not long afterward, in February 2021, at a downtown St. Louis city jail, more than a hundred inmates took over a section of the facility, setting fires and smashing windows, though no one escaped. According to inmate advocates, they were protesting conditions inside, including a lack of personal protective equipment. They escaped their cells by jimmying the locks, something that's common in Missouri prisons, as an inmate told me. "Guys stick socks in the lock jam and close the door, and it looks on the [electronic monitoring system] like it's closed, and even from the outside the guards can't open it," the source said. "But from the inside, if you pull the sock and give it some force, you can open it."

Around this time, Mike learned bad news: he'd "lost his date." Though originally scheduled for a March 2021 release, his release had been pushed back to August, owing to fighting and other violations.

He was promptly transferred to the Bonne Terre prison, which, in addition to the COVID-19 problems, was experiencing a rash of drug overdose deaths. This was bad news for Mike, given his history of opioid use disorder. I wondered how drugs could even get into the prison, since it was supposedly locked down for coronavirus.

A source told me that prison officers often supplied them, or that members of the work release program "keistered" bags of heroin or fentanyl (hiding it in their rear ends) upon reentry. Also common were outsiders spraying K2—a chemical known as synthetic marijuana—onto pieces of paper, and mailing them to inmates.

I checked in with Mike's twin, Montrel Fuller, who was also bouncing from prison to prison. He was now at a state prison in Bowling Green. They had no air conditioning at the facility, and he watched a sixty-something man named Terry Allen die after being callously thrown in the hole at the height of the summer heat after unjustly being accused of being on drugs, Montrel said. (A Missouri Department of Corrections spokeswoman said Allen's cause of death was unknown.)

Montrel asked me frequently for updates on Jorell's case, and said he'd recently gotten an "RIP Jorell" tattoo from a guy with a homemade tattoo gun. The device used the motor from a CD player and was somehow powered by the USB port of a prison-issued tablet.

Montrel told me that, during his time in prison, he'd gotten close to a guy called Shard who hung out at the Horse House and knew Jorell. Shard was imprisoned because of a May 2017 incident, when he accompanied an associate who killed a man in Ferguson. Soon after,

Shard was shot in the foot at a store nearby. It's not clear if the events were connected.

Montrel believed Shard could provide good information on Jorell's case. But Shard was something of a live wire. Montrel described Shard as he did Leron White, my #2 suspect, as a "cowboy," known for recklessly discharging firearms.

Both Shard and White would be emerging from jail soon, it turned out. But I wasn't exactly chomping at the bit to talk to them. These guys didn't know me, and submitting to an interview with me wasn't likely to improve things for them.

In fact, this investigation was beginning to spook me. Whenever I interviewed someone, I was worried they would tell others I was on the trail of Jorell's killer. I was an outsider to this community, and I didn't always know where peoples' loyalties lay. I was pursuing someone who thought he'd gotten away with murder, someone with very little to lose, someone who'd likely experienced a lifetime of disappointment and distrust in people. I didn't know how killing me might play into this man's calculus. If he thought I was standing between him and his freedom, it might make sense for him to silence me.

This paranoia stayed with me. If Jorell could be killed, I reasoned, then so could I or my loved ones. Sure, my neighborhood was safer than his, but I lived only a short drive away. And it wasn't just suspect #2 Leron White and the Kinloch guys I feared, it was the Clevelands' neighbor Chauncey James, suspect #1, and the friends and family members of the Oak Boy Ricky Watkins, suspect #3, and others on the periphery of Jorell's case. I didn't know who had secrets, or how far they might go to conceal them.

Walking my dog around my neighborhood, I tried to look past the tinted windows of cars creeping by, wondering who was at the wheel. I imagined slugs piercing my duck-down winter jacket, sending feathers flying. I'd lie awake sleepless, anticipating the bedroom window shattering in a hail of bullets. I thought about my dog, Pippi—our beloved Dalmatian mix rescue—serving as the first line of defense if someone came through the door. I imagined gathering Anna and the boys in the kids' room, pushing their dresser in front of the door, crawling under the bed, and calling 911. I looked up the odds of bullets hitting various vital organs.

There was so much murder, all over St. Louis. Everyone seemed armed to the teeth.

Many people of interest in this case, like Shard, had the same given names as their fathers, who themselves had gun or drug charges dating back fifteen or twenty years. I had sympathy for these kids, born into untenable situations. On social media they showed themselves living the good life, wearing fine clothes and eating rich food. Their guns, some nearly as large as they themselves, were intended to convey security in lives that fundamentally lacked it. Anyone messing with them would be blown to smithereens, they assured us.

And here I was, trying to expose them. I strongly considered abandoning the search for Jorell's killer altogether, and telling my editor I was giving up on this book.

There's a positive side of this kind of fear, however. It forces you to appreciate what you have. One morning I found myself in church with the boys, somewhere we rarely go. They fidgeted in the pews. Afterward I took them out for breakfast at a nearby diner, its walls covered by crayon scribblings. While we waited for our pancakes, the boys, armed with crayons of their own, added to the bedlam. I let them get whipped cream.

Thinking about how quickly life can be taken made me want to squeeze my own boys tight. And so I took a moment to do so.

Still, I was used to this feeling. I'd been experiencing anxiety over my reporting for many years, dating back to my alternative weekly days. Back then our editors encouraged us to be confrontational and edgy, so we stepped on toes. Along the way, I'd managed to piss off the World's Strongest Man.

The man, whose name I'll omit, earned the title by winning the championship of the World Powerlifting Organization. He couldn't wear normal T-shirts because the neck holes were too small, and he exercised by pulling a metal sled full of free weights across a parking lot. I interviewed him at his gym and penned a snarky profile for the *Riverfront Times*.

The joke was mostly on me—I could only bench-press a small fraction of his total—but I also noted in the piece that powerlifters don't share the camera-ready physiques of Schwarzenegger-type bodybuilders, and can seem, on first glance, obese. This was unwise, and upon publication he called my cell phone, saying he'd like to meet up so I could repeat that line to his face. I declined, and spent the next few days looking over my shoulder.

Following the 2016 publication of my book *Original Gangstas*, I feared reprisal from Dr. Dre, the famous rapper and producer. While digging through the LA County court archives, I learned that in the 1980s he assaulted the mother of three of his children, Lisa Johnson, numerous times, including while she was pregnant. I verified these accounts and, as I prepared to publish them, Dre's high-powered attorney threatened to sue me. This never happened, but I nonetheless feared street justice. Johnson said Dre told her he would "deal with me," and I wasn't sure how to interpret that.

My 2019 book *Fentanyl, Inc.* included even more beehive-kicking. I went undercover inside Chinese companies making and selling fentanyl, and then published the names of the CEOs profiting off the drug. I also broke the story about how the Chinese government was subsidizing the fentanyl industry. Having pieced together a conspiracy that went all the way to the top, I spent paranoid nights wondering if retribution was imminent, and what it would look like.

In both cases, my wife talked me down. Dr. Dre had recently sold his headphones company, called Beats, to Apple for $3 billion, she noted; he had too much to lose. The Chinese drug traffickers lived half a world away. Besides, they more resembled nerdy scientists and businesspeople than drug cartel members. Ultimately, violence was bad for business.

Anna was right; I never heard back from any of these people.

My search for Jorell's killer, however, was different. This investigation was taking place in our backyard. When I began this project I had no idea who killed Jorell, so it was hard to fear what I didn't know. But now the suspects had come into focus.

Matthew Allen, the private investigator and gun expert I met at Starbucks, was shocked that I walked around without protection.

"You don't have a gun?" he asked, incredulous. "This is Missouri!"

At a certain point, I couldn't let this story go.

I didn't want to live in a world of murder with impunity. I couldn't stand the idea of Jorell becoming a statistic. He deserved justice.

And yet, justice was complicated.

Jorell's killer was most likely a Black man from Ferguson or Kinloch. Was it right for me, as a white person, to try to get him thrown in prison? Especially in the post–George Floyd era, with millions demanding societal change and criminal justice reform, this was a pertinent question.

I wrestled with it, consulting the Clevelands, my family, community advocates, journalists, and others. Most everyone agreed that the concerns of Joe—Jorell's father and longtime guardian—were paramount. He wanted to know the perpetrator's identity and motive. He *needed* to know. Not knowing was affecting his health, he said.

And so I deferred to him. Since, as he made clear, he wanted to find the killer, I would try my best. If I succeeded, and Joe wanted him put in prison, I would try to help with that too. Otherwise, I would back off.

I still desperately wanted the detectives' notes for Jorell's case, the information they gathered in their investigation. I suspected this file would contain everything from interviews with eyewitnesses to the make and model of the killer's car, and information about the suspect they'd arrested, Chauncey James.

I believed this file could help me crack the case. Yet it remained under lock and key.

When I filed a Missouri Sunshine Act request with the St. Louis County Police Department, the case's "ongoing" nature was given as the reason for my denial. At first this gave me a tinge of optimism; did "ongoing" mean that they had promising leads, that the investigation was still moving at full steam? Could they be close?

I quickly realized, however, that they almost certainly weren't. Cases are considered "ongoing" until they are solved, even if they aren't active. Jorell had been dead for three and a half years by now; in reality his case was less "ongoing" than "moribund."

Again, my mind went to dark places. Did the detectives not care? Why was this case not a priority? In the same way that I was an outsider to Jorell's community, I was also an outsider to the insular world of police, an organization with its own customs, secrets, and internal priorities. I wanted to motivate them on Jorell's cause, but couldn't figure out how to do that.

And it wasn't just the police, it was the media and the culture at large. If Jorell had been a white girl from Clayton, this story would have dominated nightly news. Tips would have come pouring in. But since he was just another young Black man from North County, everyone shrugged their collective shoulders.

I began to explore back channels. The private investigator Matthew Allen said he had good contacts inside the detectives' department, and he offered to try to grease the wheels for me. I spoke with other private investigators as well. One claimed he had a "mole" inside the police force, who could potentially get Jorell's file. This sounded almost too good to be true.

Before hiring a PI, I decided to try one last approach to get the file. A Hail Mary of sorts.

In late February 2020, I emailed a records request to the St. Louis County Police Department, asking to see all cases involving Jorell Cleveland. Even though I'd researched everyone else in his orbit, I had never done a background check on Jorell himself. I'm sure that, deep down, I hadn't wanted to know the full truth about him. But the time had come and, who knew? Maybe this check would turn up something about his murder. My expectations were low, but it was important to turn over every stone.

Not long afterward the department said my files were ready, and I could come get them.

I'd picked up dozens of similar files in the preceding months, and by now the trip was routine: I parked on the street in downtown Clayton and fed the meter some quarters. I walked the couple blocks to the headquarters of the St. Louis County Police Department, a sturdy, sightly building of brick and stone. I entered and nodded to the three cops overseeing the entry. After putting my keys in a basket, I passed through the metal detector. Inside the records room I took a number, and when it was called, I approached the counter.

But unlike my previous visits to pick up records, this time I was welcomed by an unfamiliar clerk. The woman I usually dealt with was on vacation that week. Her substitute said my records would cost $46.

"How would you like to pay?" she asked.

The price seemed steep, but I gave her my credit card, and she handed me the packet of records, thicker than I'd anticipated. The packet contained five files. The first four were slim and inconsequential, involving cases I already knew about, including the Lil Glen shooting. But then—whoa, Nelly. The fifth was forty-seven pages long.

It was Jorell's homicide file.

I took the packet to a chair in the waiting room and sat down, my heart beating fast. I opened the file, expecting anything sensitive to be blacked out. But that was not the case. Nothing was redacted, not a single line.

This was it—the document nobody wanted me to see. The whole case! I was holding it in my hands. I glanced around, worried someone would realize their mistake and seize the papers back. I probably should have just left, but I couldn't bring myself to move until I'd consumed the documents' contents. The first time through I skimmed the pages quickly, and then I started reading more carefully.

It was all there: the names of the agencies and officers who responded to the original 911 call from Kinloch; the gory details, from entry wounds, to how his body was positioned when it was found, to the bullet shell casing description; the detectives' interviews with witnesses at the scene, including with me; an anonymous phone tip about the case; information about the guys who stole Jorell's gun; interviews from the following weeks and months as detectives worked the case; descriptions of cell phone pictures; a marital dispute; an emergency trip to the hospital; the arrest of a suspect; the detectives' attempts to charge the suspect with Jorell's murder; the assistant county prosecutor's decision not to take the case.

Apparently nobody told the substitute clerk that the file was off-limits. It was an unbelievable stroke of good fortune. I sat there reading until my meter expired. And then I kept reading some more. There was so much to take in. The detectives had pursued this case with more effort than I'd realized. Some key information they never uncovered—like a strong motive for Jorell's killing—but my own reporting filled in the gaps.

By the time I finished reading I felt I knew right then and there who killed Jorell. It seemed crystal clear.

Everything about the case added up for me. There was no doubt in my mind.

I felt like a tremendous weight had been lifted, that I'd found clarity that had eluded me for years. Jorell's death no longer felt like a random act of the universe. I felt I could ascribe it to one particular person. I was satisfied it had been real and deliberate, the purposeful extinguishing of a life force.

CHAPTER
TWENTY-THREE

My first thought was that now Joe Cleveland might have some closure. I was anxious to tell him what I'd learned, but he had left on
a fishing trip to Arkansas for a couple of weeks. He was in and out of cell
phone range, and we needed to have this conversation in person. I wanted
to show him the documents and give him a beat-by-beat account of what
happened in the police investigation.

In spring we finally made it happen, and Joe stepped out to greet
me as I pulled into his driveway. He was dressed for the season in
green pastel shorts and a matching checkered button-down, and his
beard had gone completely white since I'd seen him last, a contrast
to his short black hair. Still, he looked good. He'd somehow lost
weight on his coronavirus diet of grits and wild-caught fish. For our
meeting he'd cleared out the garage, which normally served as his man
cave / refuge from the children, complete with beer fridge, TV, and
power tools. Flies were swarming, so he fumigated the place with Raid
before inviting me in. "Them old flies, I cannot deal with them,"
he said.

I can't tell you how much I love Joe. Since we first met in 2005 at the
Big Brothers Big Sisters office, we've shared only good vibes. I was won
over by his charisma and warmth, and I was impressed by his abilities
as a single dad; including the children he's had in recent years, he has
raised ten kids. He trusted his son with me, a twenty-something punk

who could barely take care of himself. Somehow he believed in my heart, often more than I did myself. Finding out who killed Jorell was one way for me to pay back his trust, I believed.

We started with lighter topics, but soon got down to the business at hand. I explained how I'd finagled Jorell's report, before setting down before him the paper-clipped, forty-seven-page case file from the St. Louis County Police Department. "Have you ever seen that before?" I asked.

"Never," Joe said, looking it over. "This is all new to me."

"This was an epiphany. After all the people I talked to, all of the reporting I did, this was the missing piece," I said. "I'm sure who killed your son."

I paused.

"His name is Chauncey James," I said, explaining that he was the man who lived nearby, whom the police took into custody. He was my #1 suspect, whose wife Marsha had been (allegedly) assaulted by Jorell in front of R&R Mini Mart & Liquor. Jorell had later (allegedly) shot at Chauncey in front of his home, and Chauncey had (allegedly) told Jorell he was going to kill him.

This was Joe's first time hearing his name.

"Wow," he said.

And with that I walked him through the chain of events leading to Jorell's death. I tried to be sympathetic, while not sparing facts and hard truths. It was incredibly emotional. More than once Joe broke down in that cramped garage, crying and sobbing, tears falling into his beard.

Chauncey James was a big guy—270 pounds—a barber by trade and an aspiring rapper.

On the morning of August 27, 2016, the day of Jorell's death, Chauncey was irritated. While getting ready to leave for an early shift at work, he realized someone had broken into his car while he slept.

This had happened before. In fact, a year earlier someone took a cell phone and firearm from his vehicle.

James was not pleased. Not only had his car been robbed again—this time of a bank card, a gas credit card, and a fake silver "Jesus piece" necklace—but the thief had left the door open, killing the battery. Agitated, James knocked on the door of his neighbor. James asked if he knew anything about it, to which the neighbor responded that his dog had awakened him around three or four o'clock in the morning, perhaps barking at the thief.

Stewing, James hit up his wife, Marsha, for a ride to work. She roused herself to drop him off at 6:00 a.m. at his job near Manchester Road, on the other side of the metro area. (It's not clear what type of work he was doing there.)

Only an hour later, according to the detectives' report, James called Marsha to pick him back up. He'd been laid off, he said, for reasons unclear.

Around noon that day James texted a friend about his car being broken into. He was "pissed," he wrote.

Did Jorell break into Chauncey James's car?

Yes, according to an anonymous tip the police later received. The tipster claimed James "killed Jorell because he saw Jorell with the item stolen from his vehicle."

But this was news to me. I'd heard nothing about it previously; Joe was skeptical.

"I couldn't really see Jorell doing anything like that," he said, noting Jorell worked two jobs at the time and wasn't hurting financially. "I just can't see Jorell being greedy."

I agreed it was strange. Yet it's possible that Jorell didn't rob James to gain financially, but simply to torment him, owing to their recent dispute.

Joe and I discussed Jorell's alleged altercations with the James family, including Jorell punching Marsha at R&R Mini Mart & Liquor after she'd thrown a drink in his face, and Jorell shooting at James in front of their home on the Fourth of July. At that time, according to Mike Fuller, James had threatened to kill Jorell.

The detectives didn't know about these incidents. They believed James targeted Jorell that day simply over the car break-in. This seemed, to me, like a flimsy motive; someone breaking into your car is annoying, but it's likely not enough to inspire murder. In fact, this weak motive may explain why there was no prosecution.

One thing seemed clear, however: Chauncey James was angry.

Around 1:45 p.m. Jorell departed the Cleveland house. He, too, was unhappy, because his father wouldn't let him take his truck to run an errand.

Where was Jorell going? Though he claimed he was headed to the Airport Market bodega in Berkeley to get chains for his brother Jermaine and his girlfriend, Danielle (and perhaps he would have eventually gotten there), he likely was going out to acquire heroin in Kinloch. He had cash and his 1911 handgun on his person.

As I learned from my reporting, after stopping by his friend Malon's house and not finding him there, Jorell continued north on Oak Avenue, before turning left. This is near where Chauncey James lived, and it's possible he saw Jorell walking by.

Jorell's path would take him past a church and into Kinloch.

He soon arrived to the Gutter Crew House. According to an anonymous tip received by police, an individual at the Gutter Crew House (name not given) tried to sell Jorell a gun. "Allegedly, Jorell knew the gun belonged to an individual at" the Horse House, the detectives' report reads. "Jorell, after being offered the gun, went to [the Horse House] to tell the owner of the attempted sale. The owner went to confront the individual selling the gun and the two got into a fight. Jorell watched for a short time and walked off."

Getting caught up in this dispute seems like poor judgment on Jorell's part. It's unclear if anything more came of it, and it's awfully coincidental that he was killed immediately afterward. But there is no evidence in the detectives' report tying anyone from the Gutter Crew House or the Horse House to Jorell's death.

Detective Rodesiler spoke to a female resident at the Horse House who wished to remain anonymous. She said only that she saw Jorell going past, and he "stopped briefly to sit on her porch before continuing to walk up the street."

Jorell likely purchased heroin at the Horse House or the Gutter Crew House, perhaps snorting it immediately. His toxicology report revealed drugs in his system including marijuana, a small amount of codeine, and a large amount of morphine—indicating heroin. (It's unclear if he was tested for fentanyl.)

The autopsy indicated that the level of THC found in his blood "defines impairment." He may have smoked the marijuana at home, or somewhere along the walk.

The drugs clouded his judgment and awareness of his surroundings, which explains why he wouldn't have been ready for an ambush.

After Marsha picked up her husband, Chauncey James, from work, he moped around the house for a bit until his mother came to get him and his daughter in her white Ford SUV. She took them to her house in Pagedale.

James told detectives he spent the day Jorell was killed cutting his mother's grass and picking up some items for her from his aunt's house in Castle Point, east of Ferguson. He also cut his uncle's hair, before departing for a concert that evening.

According to the anonymous tip received by police, however, at some point James saw Jorell with an item stolen from his vehicle. Presumably this was his chain, described as a "fake beaded necklace [with] silver beads and a Jesus piece."

One possibility is that James saw Jorell walking toward Kinloch, without Jorell realizing he'd been spotted. Anticipating Jorell's route through town, James then drove to the other side of Kinloch, parked, and waited.

Jorell was killed at 2:20 p.m. James told detectives he was "nowhere near Kinloch or Ferguson" at that time, or at any time between the hours of 10:00 a.m. and 5:00 p.m., adding that his daughter was with him the whole time.

His wife, Marsha, however, contradicted this story. She told detectives that her sister-in-law dropped off their daughter at their home in Ferguson just after 2:00 p.m. Marsha said she could not account for James's whereabouts at this time, but that he returned home "shortly after her daughter had been dropped off."

According to Marsha's account, her husband lied about two things: 1) He did not have their daughter the whole time. 2) He *was* in the area between 10:00 a.m. and 5:00 p.m.

In fact, according to her timeline, he could have returned home shortly after Jorell was killed.

Considering that James's car had a dead battery, he likely would have been driving his mother's car, a white 2004 Ford Expedition.

Police spoke with a witness who said the perpetrator of Jorell's killing had arrived in a white Ford Explorer, "1998 or 1999 box body style, four door."

I looked at these two models online, and they are difficult to distinguish from one another.

This witness, named Lemarcus Winston, would prove critical to the detectives' understanding of what happened to Jorell.

A thirty-two-year-old Berkeley resident, Winston was reluctant to speak to detectives, but he eventually told them he was riding his bike at Jefferson and Courtney Avenues in Kinloch when he saw a "suspicious vehicle"—the white Ford. "The vehicle was parked in a manner that it was partially concealed by overgrown vegetation and a bush at the corner," reads the police's account of his description.

The perpetrator, said Winston, stood near the vehicle and appeared to be waiting for somebody. Winston "saw the victim walking westbound on Courtney from a couple blocks away." At that point Winston rode off in another direction and no longer had Jorell or the perpetrator in his sights. "After an estimated one or two minutes," Winston, from about two blocks away, "heard a single gunshot from the direction he just passed."

Winston turned back. He "did not see the vehicle or the [alleged perpetrator] leave the area, but upon his return, they were gone."

Jorell was shot at point-blank range, under his chin. Blood went everywhere, but he didn't die until sometime later; his brother Jermaine said he was still breathing when he arrived. A 9 millimeter Winchester shell casing was found at the crime scene. The bullet, which went clean through, was not. It's unclear what kind of gun the perpetrator used. The Jesus piece necklace was gone.

The witness, Lemarcus Winston, was nervous to cooperate with detectives. He declined, "on a number of occasions" to examine "a photo lineup to possibly identify or eliminate a potential suspect."

Winston did, however, offer detectives a description of the perpetrator: "black male, light complexion, 260–270 lbs., heavy set, not muscular, black ball cap worn backwards, no facial hair, no shirt, individual tattoos on upper left arm, upper right arm, left and right chest, blue jeans."

This description fits Chauncey James to a T.

Detective Rodesiler asked to search James's phone, to which the suspect consented. Accessing it required the passcode "Boobie."

The phone was taken as evidence. Detectives queried his phone company, T-Mobile, for cell tower records to determine where he was at the time of Jorell's death. In the meantime, they continued their investigation.

Of James's many mistruths, the easiest to puncture was that he didn't have a gun. That's what he told detectives investigating Jorell's case at the beginning of the interview. But he soon changed his story.

He'd had a gun in 2014, he told Detective Rodesiler, but it was stolen by police, "at a bus stop."

"So you're telling me that your wife has not seen you with a handgun in the last two years?" Rodesiler asked him.

"She has probably seen me with a .38, my mom's .38," he said, adding that he "used to have it all the time."

Rodesiler was bewildered. Reads the report: "Rodesiler pointed out that shortly before he had no guns, now he has a .38 'all the time.'"

In a separate conversation, Rodesiler asked Marsha if her husband, Chauncey, had guns. "Yeah, the last couple months," she responded, adding that she had seen a gun in the house. Rodesiler showed her a picture obtained from James's cell phone of "a Silver Slide and a black framed firearm." Marsha could not say whether she had seen the gun before, but said "the picture appeared to show the interior of [her husband]'s vehicle."

In his music videos, James displays a full artillery of guns. The idea that he wouldn't have one seems preposterous.

Chauncey James and his wife, Marsha, both say that they broke up and James moved out of the house the day after Jorell died. Three years later their divorce would become official.

What caused their marital rift? Marsha had no comment. "Other women," James claimed. They had gotten into it "over a girl that had called."

From the report: "Rodesiler asked if it was because James had shot Jorell the day before, James said no."

The cell tower records came back. According to the report, they placed James "near the crime scene at the time of the incident."

I paused to take a breath.

"To me, this evidence is overwhelming," I said to Joe. "What do you think? Does this all make sense to you?"

"Of course," Joe said, gathering himself. He noted the previous altercation between Jorell and James—in which James allegedly came at Jorell with his fists, and Jorell responded by shooting. It thus made sense for James to lay in wait in Kinloch, waiting to ambush Jorell. "If I think I'm gonna walk up on you, and I know you carry a gun, I'ma have to sneak attack you."

* * *

The St. Louis County Police Department sought two charges against Chauncey James: first-degree murder and armed criminal action. On December 4, 2016, three months after Jorell's killing, James was entered as a "person of interest" into the Regional Justice Information System, which serves police departments in Missouri and Illinois.

On February 26, 2017, James was shot in the left shoulder, in an apparently unrelated incident, and taken to a West St. Louis County hospital. Suffering what was described as a "through and through wound," James survived relatively unscathed. But his visit triggered the information system, and a pair of St. Louis County detectives were dispatched to the hospital. James was taken without incident to the Division of Criminal Investigation offices, where he was questioned again about Jorell's case. From there he was taken to the county jail in Clayton.

He did not stay there long. Soon St. Louis County Police Detective Ryan Wojciuch—who had since taken over as the lead detective on Jorell's case—met with Assistant Prosecuting Attorney Doug Sidel. Concludes the detectives' report about Jorell's killing: "After a review of the facts and circumstances of the case, the case was refused."

Sidel did not respond to my attempts to contact him, and the assistant prosecuting attorney's office did not immediately respond to my request for information about their decision.

I asked Joe Cleveland if anyone told him the case had been refused. He said no.

"The last detective told me that when he tried to interview some of the [witnesses] that they no longer wanted to talk to him. That was the last I've heard from him."

"Nothing can replace him," Joe said suddenly, choking back tears.

By now I'd known Joe for fifteen years, through the deaths of three of his children, but I had never seen him cry. Once he got started, the tears wouldn't stop.

"It's a lot of things that goes on in life that you try to put out your mind. Yeah, I miss my son. We had some things planned, you know. I guess God needed him back."

I asked him what they had planned.

"He was gonna go to the military, and that's what I wanted him to do. He liked dogs. He said, 'Daddy, I'ma go to the military, I'ma send you some money, we gonna buy a farm.'"

PART III

CHAPTER
TWENTY-FOUR

O nce I was convinced I knew who had killed Jorell, I called the
detective in charge of Jorell's case, Ryan Wojciuch. I was excited to
discuss the news, and see if he thought my insight into the case—
particularly Chauncey James's possible motive—could help bring James
to justice.

I left him a message. He never called back. I later found out that
both Wojciuch and the original lead detective on the case, Jason Rodesiler, had been transferred to different departments. Neither worked in
homicide anymore. It wasn't clear who, if anyone, was now covering
Jorell's case.

It was officially on the back burner.

This was frustrating, but I was soon able to make inroads with a
different St. Louis County detective. At the suggestion of a journalist
friend, I reached out to Joe Burgoon, a cold case investigator with the
St. Louis County Police. Burgoon, who had recently turned eighty, spent
more than forty years with the St. Louis city police department, as an
officer and a sergeant. Since he began working cold cases for the county
in 2005, he'd solved four murders and dozens of sexual assaults.

He was the real deal. Other detectives I'd spoken with had been
curt, but Burgoon didn't rush. In preparation for our phone call he'd
gone through Jorell's files, including infractions Jorell committed before
he turned eighteen, records I didn't have access to. Burgoon found that

he'd been arrested for receiving stolen property, and also for possessing marijuana, though the charges didn't amount to much. Burgoon listened as I described the ins and outs of Jorell's daily life.

"He sounds like a good kid," Burgoon said. "He had a job and a girlfriend."

We spoke about Chauncey James. Beyond Jorell's case, James had been arrested a half dozen times, on gun, drug, and DUI charges. He'd never been convicted of a felony, but he continued having issues with law enforcement in the years after Jorell's killing, including for possessing a controlled substance. After his divorce he moved out of Ferguson.

I believed James had killed Jorell, I told Burgoon. But I could only speculate why the assistant county prosecutor didn't charge him.

When I finished, I expected Burgoon to say he couldn't help me, that we were out of luck. But he didn't.

"If the witness or witnesses can be convinced to talk, then maybe we can get the prosecutor to bring it to the grand jury," he said. "But that's a big if. They don't want to be known as a snitch."

Burgoon said he himself likely couldn't get the job done—that he'd probably fail like the other detectives before him. "They don't know me from Adam," he said, of the witnesses.

But Joe Cleveland and I could try to appeal to the witnesses, as people who knew and loved Jorell, Burgoon went on. This personal touch might be more effective at swaying them to testify.

This seemed like good advice. I thanked Burgoon and said goodbye.

I talked with my mother about the situation. She'd received bad news in early 2020, when she was diagnosed with ALS, the neurodegenerative disorder known as Lou Gehrig's disease that causes one's muscles to waste away. She'd always been supportive of my journalism career, even when it took me in dangerous directions. But this case scared her. "What if the perp gets wind of this and comes for retribution?" she asked. "What are you trying to accomplish?"

"If this guy has killed once, he could kill again," I said. "He should be off the streets. And Jorell's family may want closure."

"I can certainly understand that. But I'm concerned about your safety. Think of your own family, your boys and Anna."

The last thing I wanted was for my mother to be filled with dread and concern for me during her short time left. Yet at the same time, letting a killer go free seemed like a poor moral choice.

I felt a strong urge to understand Chauncey James. Really, to me he was just a name on a police report, a character in a rap video. I'd never spoken to him, and neither had Joe or anyone else in the Cleveland family. This despite the fact that, at the time of Jorell's killing, he lived just a few blocks away.

He was like a black box to me, a mystery. This made it difficult to contemplate bringing a case against him. I had the strong urge to simply be in his presence, to see his face, to see what kind of man he was, as if just by breathing his air I could comprehend how he could do such a thing.

I planned to visit one of his hearings. I could take my pick: he was regularly in court, for offenses ranging from traffic violations to drug charges.

But then COVID-19 descended, and hearings moved online, with the public barred.

There was another possibility: from public records, I had his address. My first instinct as a journalist was to simply drop in on him. I could have gone over to his home at any time. But after much consideration, I decided not to meet him face-to-face. Sure, I would have learned something from the experience, and may have even acquired new information to share with Joe Cleveland.

But it was just too unsafe. I couldn't abandon my responsibility to my family—to stay safe, to stay alive. Meeting Jorell's killer in person could have compromised that. This value needed to stand above all others. I had to draw a line.

* * *

If anyone would have clear, unambiguous feelings about Chauncey James, I figured, it would be Joe Cleveland.

And yet, I was surprised to hear notes of sympathy in Joe's voice when we talked about the man we both believed murdered his son, whom he called "Mr. James." He had many questions for the man, including, most importantly:

"Did you really fear my son like that?"

Ultimately, Joe came to believe that James had good reason to fear Jorell, considering Jorell had already allegedly assaulted his wife and shot at him.

"If a person was shooting at me, then yeah I'd keep an eye on them," Joe said. "Maybe I would try to hurt them before they hurt me."

He added: "But to lay and ambush a person, I don't think that's right."

We kept coming back to the subject of justice, and what it meant in this context. I was focused on justice through the court system, but Joe mused on street justice.

"I don't think I could say, 'I want to see him murdered,'" he said. "I wouldn't say I want to see his life taken. I'd be damned if I wanna spend the rest of my life in prison. Two wrongs don't make no right." Joe speculated that, if he hired someone else to take James out, that person might later tell the cops, leading to Joe's conviction.

I emphasized my strong preference for rolling the dice, yet again, on the criminal justice system, noting that any retribution could perpetuate an endless cycle of violence.

"Exactly," Joe said. "Right, let the justice system work. I agree."

We spoke about my conversation with Joe Burgoon, the cold case detective, who believed we could potentially get the case brought to trial.

"I want to see him on the stand," Joe said of James. "I would like to hear him say something. Maybe he might have sense to say, 'Well, that was a bad decision.' He might just admit to it."

Getting James to the stand, however, would likely require the testimony of witnesses. And there was one who mattered above all others—Lemarcus Winston, the guy riding his bike through Kinloch the afternoon of Jorell's death. Winston passed the perpetrator standing near his "suspicious" white Ford, partially hidden by overgrown vegetation, and then saw Jorell. Winston continued on his way for a few more moments and then, when he heard the gunshot, backtracked and saw the perpetrator and the van gone, and Jorell lying dead.

Winston was the only person who'd seen the killer in the vicinity at the time of the killing. He'd only reluctantly told police what he'd seen, and he seemed to have absolutely no interest in testifying. He declined to pick the perpetrator out of a photo lineup.

He was thirty-two at the time Jorell was killed, and lived in Berkeley, about a mile north of the crime scene. I didn't know him, but from his Facebook page he seemed like a good guy, posting pictures of his kids, and promoting a charitable organization benefiting Kinloch children.

But that's about all I knew.

"I wouldn't know him from a can of paint either," Joe said.

Certainly, I could understand Winston's state of mind; cooperating with police could potentially lead to violent retribution. But that didn't mean it wasn't frustrating. Here was someone who had the power to get Jorell's killer off the streets, and he wasn't interested.

The cold case detective believed Joe and I, the victim's loving father and longtime mentor, could potentially persuade Winston to testify, more so than a random police detective. I asked Joe for his thoughts on this.

"I don't know what kind of heart he might have," Joe said of Winston. "Would this guy be putting himself in any danger?"

I suspected he would. If this case went to trial, and he testified, he could potentially face deadly blowback from people sympathetic to Chauncey James. Joe concurred. "He sends this guy to jail, then [James's hypothetical] cousin...might want to retaliate on him."

I also considered the possibility that Winston already knew James, and might try to protect him. Potentially, if we contacted him, he could even tell James that we were on his tail.

The thought made Joe weary.

"I'm gettin' old," he said. "All I want to do right now is try to enjoy my younger kids that I'm trying to raise, and the rest of my life. I don't want any kind of beef, no kind of drama, nothin' as far as these streets. I done got too old for that."

Whatever Joe decided, I would follow his lead, I told him.

There was no doubt that he and the rest of the Clevelands would bear most of the brunt of the emotional cost of a trial. They were the ones who would face any blowback in the neighborhood.

"If you want justice for Jorell through the legal system," I said, "I will put my full efforts into that."

"You have a dangerous enough job as it is, doing some of the things that you do," Joe said. "I wouldn't want to see you jeopardize your life or your family."

Undoubtedly, the detectives with the St. Louis County Police did a poor job communicating with the Cleveland family.

They never told them they'd tried to bring a suspect to trial. That stuck in my craw. After all, as Joe had noted, a conviction wasn't the most important thing to him. More than anything, he wanted to know who had done it, and why.

Sharing at least some of their information with the Clevelands would have been an act of human decency. I'd imagine they could have done it without compromising the case.

One thing surprised me, however. It's clear the detectives put in real effort. My impression was that the murders of young African American men often rank very low on the priority lists of law enforcement, but in this case the detectives seemed to have done much of the critical police work.

The problem wasn't the detectives—it was the justice system itself.

"If we can persuade the law to get justice, I would like to see that because that's what we pay tax dollars for," Joe said. "They supposed to work for us."

In Joe's ideal world, James would be tried for killing Jorell, and he and I wouldn't have to risk our lives to make it happen. "I couldn't live with me knowing you did something to get you harmed," Joe said. "I wouldn't want to see you go and put yourself in harm's way. I love you and care more about you than that."

I felt the same way about him.

Unfortunately, as Detective Burgoon noted, in cases like this, police often have a difficult time getting witnesses to testify.

This owed, I knew, to the well-earned African American distrust of the justice system. It was a problem going back decades, even centuries. Joe and I agreed that it would not be easy to get the witness, Lemarcus Winston, to testify. He might face repercussions from James's friends or family. Or, if his testimony wasn't sufficient to convict James, James himself might go after Winston.

"We already know he's tightened his lips up," Joe said of Winston. "I don't know much you can do behind that. It's just a shame the way people do, but I guess he got a life and stuff that he got to try to protect.

"Maybe he might get a conscience one day and decide that he wants to talk," Joe added.

I noted that we didn't have to make any decisions now. The case was cold, and would stay that way. We pledged to keep the lines of communication open.

Just then Joe grew ruminative. He speculated that Chauncey James might one day do the right thing, perhaps if he was incarcerated for another crime, and found religion.

"I don't know this guy Mr. James," he said. "But maybe if he goes to prison, he might confess. This world is funny. I know people that have done that; admitted to other murders before they got out of prison."

To my surprise, I eventually did get a meeting with the St. Louis County detectives. It happened after an influential friend of mine—Jeff Smith, a former Missouri state senator—hit up an influential friend of his, Chris King, the public information officer for the St. Louis County Prosecuting Attorney's Office.

After Smith talked up my project, King got in touch with me immediately. He said the prosecutor's office had declined to prosecute Jorell's case owing to the lack of witness cooperation, which cold case detective Joe Burgoon had suspected.

He also said he'd get me in a room with the detectives, so I could share my findings.

This was an exciting development, but it said a lot about the way things worked in St. Louis. Going through the official channels had gotten me nowhere; I'd needed to utilize insider connections.

It's always intimidating to enter a police station—*What if they know about that time I shoplifted in tenth grade?*—yet I was cautiously optimistic as I entered the county police headquarters in Clayton in June 2021. The detectives who'd originally worked on Jorell's case had long ago moved to other departments, so they weren't in attendance, but in a conference room I met with three detectives with knowledge of the case, Robert Bates, Andrew Hammel, and Matt Levy. All three were new to me, and they looked similar—white and probably in their thirties, with solid physiques and closely cropped hair.

Bates was now leading Jorell's investigation, and he displayed a good knowledge of the case. In a room full of alphas, he was the most alpha, and Hammel described him as their department's best and most experienced investigator.

I felt mixed emotions during our conversation. I maintained some animosity against the department, for not communicating with the Cleveland family about Jorell's case. Yet I also knew that these specific detectives weren't necessarily responsible, and further that acting rude wouldn't get me anywhere.

The four of us gathered around a comically large conference table. They were surprised to hear how I'd gotten Jorell's case file, but bore no ill will for my methods. They spoke candidly about the intricacies of his case, and about what would be required for a successful prosecution.

As a journalist, I was sure I had all I needed to convince my readers of Chauncey James's guilt—a strong motive, cell phone tower records placing him near the crime scene, and a matching physical description from a witness, for starters. And, indeed, all three detectives believed

James was the killer. Further, they gave tremendous credit to the witness Lemarcus Winston for offering so much insight into the case.

But when it came to convicting James in court, Winston's interview was all but worthless, they lamented.

For starters, he hadn't consented to be recorded. But even if he had, that recording couldn't be used at a trial, because the defense has a right to cross-examine, and you can't cross-examine a recording.

That was something I'd never thought of. Chris King, the public information officer for the St. Louis County Prosecuting Attorney's Office, had put it even more bluntly in an email to me: "Without an eyewitness or other definitive evidence, knowing someone is guilty is of no use in a criminal court."

Was it possible, I asked Bates, that Winston might by now have changed his mind and agree to take the stand? Bates conceded that was possible, and that he would go back and ask Winston again.

I appreciated the gesture. But even that might not be enough, the detectives conceded. They imagined a defense lawyer's version: James hadn't actually been lying in wait for Jorell in Kinloch. Rather, his car simply broke down there. And then Jorell arrived—someone who'd shot at him before, and was now even brandishing a gun.

The killing was nothing but self-defense.

We went through more details, and discussed the peripheral players, but ultimately it became clear the case wasn't going anywhere. The detectives stuck out their hands as we stood up and said our goodbyes, all of us vowing to stay in touch. As I left I felt more dispirited than ever about Jorell's case.

CHAPTER TWENTY-FIVE

Joe Cleveland was born in Chicago and named for boxer Joe Louis, he told me not long after our discussion about Jorell's killer, passing along the "Jo" to six of his children (Joseph Jr., Jovan, Jorell, Jovanna, Jo'Leigh, Josyha). To escape his dangerous Chicago neighborhood he moved in with a grandmother in Arkansas when he was a young man. He got together with Jorell's mother Dianne Robinson in Dumas, Arkansas, in the early 1990s. He said their pairing was only natural, considering he was a "hot boy" and she was a "hot girl." I asked him what he meant by this.

"That's like, dressing fancy and going to the club, showing out, driving Cadillacs," he said. "I wish I had some pictures with my hazel contact eyes and my perm and stuff. You'd say 'wow.'"

He and Dianne had three kids, Rece, Jorell, and Peaches, and never married. They both did prison time. In 1988 he was sentenced to ten years for unspecified drug charges. (Joe says he gave a different girlfriend weed, which she sold to buy crack, and he got charged in this scheme.) Dianne has had substance abuse issues, and she received an even harsher sentence of twelve years for a December 2003 charge of "delivery of cocaine," which left her incarcerated when Jorell and I were paired.

Joe received custody of their children, but he had demons of his own. He struggled to keep decent work in Arkansas—he had his own trucking company for a while, before becoming a roofer—and in 1986 had a violent encounter with a man outside a club in McGehee, a town just south of Dumas. Their dispute involved crack cocaine and their girlfriends. According to Joe, the man came at him with a knife, ruining Joe's good leather jacket, and threw the keys to Joe's new Sunbird on the club's roof.

"I got another set of keys to my car and got about six guns, and I came back and I retaliated," Joe said. "I caught him walking down the alley with two other guys. I seen him coming and I laid beside a tree. It was fall time of year, I had on my camouflage coveralls, and I waited until he got even with me and I aimed at him. I stepped out and he took off running and that's when I shot him. First time I shot him in the shoulder and he fell down. And I ran up on him and he hollered, 'Oh lord, don't let him kill me.' I said, 'I'm not gonna kill you, but I'ma make you remember,' and I shot him two more times in his butt."

Joe was never prosecuted for this shooting, but between it and his incarceration, he learned his lesson, he says, and vowed to avoid a life of violence and crime. Now in his late fifties, he's done many different kinds of work to survive over the years. Even in the face of tragedy, Joe remains openhearted, maintaining a home for an ever-expanding extended family. He still draws women's eyes.

But hearing about Joe's violent turn, and about Dianne's struggles with drugs, reminded me of Jorell's problems. His gun fetishism and substance abuse at first seemed to come out of nowhere, but clearly they didn't. They were influenced by his family and peers, and were also part of a generational cycle of poverty.

Americans often reject the idea that one's birth controls one's destiny. According to our national fairy tale, a little hard work and ingenuity can propel anyone beyond their zip code, race, and social class.

Reality, however, isn't usually like that. If you're born with money, you usually stay wealthy. If you're born poor, you usually stay poor.

There was a depressing symmetry between Jorell's life and that of his parents, except for one key difference: Joe and Dianne made it out alive, while Jorell didn't.

* * *

Soon I began telling other members of Jorell's family and his friends about James. None of them knew him, though some had heard the story about Jorell's dustup with James's wife Marsha.

Each of Jorell's siblings and friends processed the information in their own ways. "I'm really shocked, for real," Jovan told me. "You got more information than I got!" Displeased that James still walked free, he didn't believe justice had been served. Both he and Rece felt convinced of James's guilt, and wanted to know more information about the case. Mike and Montrel Fuller both concurred with my findings, even though it differed from their initial reads on the case. Mike could hardly believe the police let James go, but understood why witnesses would not want to speak with police. "It's sickening," said Jermaine, "that the [killer] is getting off scot-free."

Jorell's sister Iesha received the news serenely, telling me she had already made her peace. "At the time of the incident, for at least a month, I rode around Kinloch trying to get answers," she said. "But I let it go a while back when they kept telling my dad it was a cold case, and that nobody wanted to say anything."

I was surprised to see Iesha was Facebook friends with Lemarcus Winston, the main witness at the scene. Unfortunately, he was more of an "internet" friend than an "IRL" friend.

"He may have randomly friended me a while ago," she said, adding that she knew almost nothing about him.

I asked if she thought we should try to convince Winston to testify.

"I do feel like there should be a prosecution, but at the same time, I don't want no backfire as far as anybody being in harm's way," she said. "I don't want a retaliation." Ultimately, she added, she felt similarly to her father: legal justice for Jorell was preferable, but not if it meant anyone might get hurt.

Three of Iesha's siblings had died in recent years. The Cleveland family had been through enough already.

I lamented the fact that the criminal justice system was so thoroughly broken in St. Louis, and across the country. Why should a would-be murderer even think twice, when he could kill with impunity?

* * *

As my reporting wound down, I began thinking more about the writing of this book. When it came to Jorell, what was the narrative?

Maybe it was like a three act play. He'd started as a sweet young boy; been corrupted by guns, drugs, and local bad actors; and turned into a predator who sealed his own fate through violent aggression.

This didn't seem accurate, however. It felt more like a tragedy in one act. His fate had been sealed when he was born into a system that didn't care about him, and wasn't designed to protect him.

End of story.

In the coming months, life returned to normal. At least, as normal as possible during 2020, when the novel coronavirus killed some 350,000 Americans and caused economic and social unrest. Not long after George Floyd's killing I visited his Minneapolis memorial. Captured on film as his life was taken, Floyd put a face to the pain felt by centuries of African American victims of police repression. The ensuing protests spilled all over the Twin Cities, including parts of St. Paul where I used to spend time.

For many, Floyd's memorial came to symbolize the Black Lives Matter movement, which had gained speed in Ferguson six years earlier. Visiting the location in Minneapolis was emotional for me, as it conjured memories of both Jorell's childhood and my own. Surrounding the intersection where Floyd was killed, streets were blocked off in every direction. Mask-clad tourists quietly snapped photos of a statue of a raised fist at the memorial's center.

A makeshift coalition of activists had set up shop on the site, passing out hand sanitizer, tending to bouquets of flowers, and selling baseball hats at a Speedway gas station that had been gutted in the riots. I bought a cap reading "Floyd 8:46," which was initially believed to be the amount of time the police officer Derek Chauvin had his knee on Floyd's neck— eight minutes and forty-six seconds—though the actual number turned out to be 9:29.

I learned about Floyd's life growing up in Houston, where he had been friends with DJ Screw, an influential Southern producer who'd influenced hip-hop by slowing it down. Floyd battled an opioid addiction and had come to Minneapolis to seek treatment. At the time of his death he had fentanyl in his system, in addition to testing positive for COVID-19.

Floyd's love for hip-hop, and his opioid use, again made me think of Jorell. Though the two men came from different generations, and different parts of the country, I couldn't help but think that their fates were somehow bound together.

CHAPTER TWENTY-SIX

Breaking the news to all of Jorell's associates that I believed Chauncey James killed him took months.

One of Jorell's incarcerated friends hadn't originally believed James killed Jorell, but he found my argument persuasive.

And yet our conversation, which took place over the phone from prison, made me uncomfortable.

"Would you like to see him locked up?" I asked him.

"Me? Nah," he responded. "I want him dead."

He said this casually, in a way that shocked me, especially considering we were speaking on a recorded line.

"You might say it's ignorant, but that's the culture of the streets," he said. "I understand what you saying too, 'Let him rot in jail,' but still... I feel like he should die."

These words made me shudder. They felt at odds with my moral beliefs—that violence was wrong—and to my (perhaps naive) faith in the American justice system.

And yet, he wasn't the first person who told me this. Other young men close to Jorell concurred that, when a murder was committed, a prison sentence was not an appropriate consequence. Incarceration, they said, was a relatively easy life, one without bills, where all of your meals were accounted for.

Prisoners eventually come home. Murder victims never do. Only an eye for an eye could properly settle the score.

I tried to argue. I fully believed James should not be subjected to vigilante justice. Perpetuating the cycle of violence could ultimately blow back on him and the people he loved, I told Jorell's incarcerated friend.

"I know," he said. "But honestly, it's the code of the streets."

Then, unprompted, he began describing the time immediately following Jorell's death, when tempers were running high. "I *did* what I was supposed to do," he said. "I'm the one getting guns and trying to go to war with them."

I was aghast. No one had told me about this before. The "them" in his sentence were the various suspects in Jorell's case. Since at the time no one knew who killed Jorell, this friend had multiple targets in his sights.

I held my breath as he described assembling a party to follow him into battle. Members of Jorell's family declined to join him, but some of Jorell's other friends agreed to help seek retribution.

Under the cover of darkness, the hastily assembled crew hit the streets. I'm not sure where all they went, but eventually they got to Chauncey James's house.

Most members of the party didn't count James as their top suspect. But one did. And that was all it took.

The James house was dark. A member of the crew went to the front door and rang the doorbell. Though inhabitants could be heard inside, no one came to the door. The group drove around the block a couple of times, and then saw lights had been turned on.

And then, they unloaded.

"We shot up their house, all in the front, the windows," Jorell's friend told me. "We shot that house *up*."

Soon, he was told, police and an ambulance showed up. By then, his crew was long gone.

I could not verify this account. Ferguson police had no record of the incident. No one seems to have been caught. It's unclear if anyone was injured.

But according to Jorell's friend, their rampage continued. After stopping in Kinloch to buy and snort some heroin, "we shot up these other peoples' house too," he told me. This house, he said, was home to the wheelchair-bound man who lived in Berkeley, near Jorell's girlfriend Danielle, and was supposedly related to Chauncey James. This home was where, according to a rumor, someone speculated that "something was about to happen" to Jorell, shortly before his death.

Again, I could find no record of this, and I didn't press Jorell's friend for more details because he was speaking over a recorded line. The guy in the wheelchair was not killed in this incident, but he died at some point not long afterward. I would assume his death and Jorell's deaths were unrelated, but really I have no idea.

By now I was beginning to question everything. Why was I just now learning of these retaliatory shootings related to Jorell's death, years after the fact? What *else* didn't I know?

My unease deepened as I continued investigating Chauncey James. There was so much about him I didn't understand. He didn't post frequently about his personal life online. The best way I could get to know him was through his rap videos. This felt like an odd way to understand someone, considering he cloaked himself in the persona of a performer. Yet, it was somehow appropriate. It was as if my career as a hip-hop journalist had prepared me for this moment.

And so I listened to his songs. All of them. This was probably an unhealthy thing to do, considering his talk of gunplay and murdering his adversaries hit so close to home. Despite the tough guy bravado, every once in a while James offered deeper insight, rapping with heartfelt sentiment about his past. He said he'd been raised by a felon, and that he talked to his gun "more than the reverend."

> *My grandma saying that I need prayer*
> *But I ain't hearin'*

I'd watched a dozen or so of his videos when one of them caught me off guard. Filmed at his house on a low budget in 2018, it seemed fairly boilerplate on first glance. But as I looked closer I saw a small, intimate detail: stuck to the fridge with a magnet was a note handwritten in purple marker reading: "DADDY I LOVE YOU TO THE MOON AND BACK," signed by his young daughter.

This display of adoration gave me shivers. As a parent, I identified with this father-child bond, and became concerned for James's safety. James was only a bit younger than I was, and I tried to put myself in his shoes, tried to understand how he might have felt when Jorell began antagonizing him and his family, back in 2016.

I became even more concerned after watching a new video James posted to Facebook, in April 2021. Entitled "First steps since 10 days ago," and filmed at The Rehabilitation Institute of St. Louis, it showed him re-learning to walk with the assistance of a physical therapist while wearing a hard-plastic cervical collar. His left arm was in a sling. He'd clearly been in some kind of horrible accident. I wondered if his injury was related to the death of a close friend and musical collaborator, who, as I learned from his social media feeds, had been killed around the same time.

This information humanized James to me. He had a family who loved him, and was just as vulnerable as anyone else. He'd come up in the same trying circumstances as Jorell, and could potentially have the same fate. Even if he had killed Jorell, that didn't mean his family wouldn't be heartbroken if something happened to him.

I wondered: Had he been shot again? Maybe he had an enemy I'd never heard of, or maybe it was someone close to Jorell, who did so as retaliation. None of Jorell's associates would admit to it, but why would they?

The whole business made me anxious. And Chauncey James wasn't the only suspect in Jorell's case who remained in the line of fire.

CHAPTER TWENTY-SEVEN

The St. Louis County detectives' report about Jorell's death helped convince me of Chauncey James's guilt.

It also helped exonerate my two other suspects: Ricky Watkins, the Oak Boy who often had an adversarial relationship with Jorell, and who was murdered himself not long after Jorell passed, and Leron White, who was closely associated with the Gutter Crew in Kinloch.

Nonetheless, White still figured prominently in the case. He'd been in the middle of everything on the day of Jorell's death. He or one of his companions took the 1911 off Jorell's body. And then, after informing the Cleveland family Jorell was dead, they changed clothes before returning to the crime scene—at least according to Jorell's brother Jermaine.

At the scene, according to Joe Cleveland, when a woman spoke up accusing White and his buddies of taking Jorell's gun, White tried to silence her.

I still didn't fully understand his relationship with Jorell. Were they truly friends? Or had White secretly had it out for him?

Not long after receiving the detectives' report and speaking with Joe, I learned some surprising news: Leron White was free.

In early 2020 he'd emerged from the St. Louis County Jail, after a jury acquitted him in the 2017 shoot-up of the funeral reception at The Ambassador nightclub in Jennings. For his other charges, he was given probation and credit for time served.

I was surprised by his acquittal, and that the charges against his dad, Tori White, had been dropped altogether. I don't know the specifics because the St. Louis County courts sealed documents relating to the case.

But White didn't have much time to enjoy his homecoming. That's because violence soon came for him, along with his famous uncle, the rapper Huey.

When Huey signed his $2.5 million record deal in 2006, he traveled to Atlanta to record. His manager and aunt, Angela Richardson, came with him and ended up staying there. Often referred to as the Black Holly-wood, Atlanta was the epicenter of the hip-hop scene. Richardson urged Huey to move there permanently as well, not just for networking, but to escape the violence of Kinloch.

"I was trying to take him out of the hood," she said. "Some people can never see the light, even with money."

Instead, Huey returned to St. Louis, getting a loft downtown near the ballpark where the Cardinals play. He also lived in exurban St. Charles at one point. But trouble quickly resumed. One late night in May 2009 he left a party and was driving his Jaguar downtown, behind an SUV full of his friends from North St. Louis, when a car pulled up and unloaded on the SUV, killing three people inside.

Huey made it out safely. He denied the bullets had been intended for him, but the incident had repercussions for his career. He was soon dropped from a big show he was scheduled to perform with Nelly; organizers worried he might inspire violence at the event.

Huey never had another hit as big as "Pop, Lock & Drop It." His 2010 follow-up album *Redemption* didn't get much traction, and a new deal he signed in 2013 with a label owned by rapper Waka Flocka Flame didn't amount to much either.

Still, things were better in his personal life. His mom stopped taking drugs, and he got back in touch with his father, from whom he'd been estranged.

In the ensuing years he largely disappeared from the public eye. That is, until the night of June 25, 2020, when he was congregating with his nephew Leron White and others in front of the Gutter Crew House in Kinloch.

Huey's brother Tori White owned the house, and on police records, Huey listed it as his primary residence.

Everyone knew something was amiss when a vehicle drove slowly by. Its occupants unloaded multiple shots. In the hail of gunfire, Huey was hit. He was rushed to the hospital.

Leron White also took a bullet in the chest. His cousin put him in his car and drove him to the Ferguson police station, where EMS was called. White made it to the hospital and survived.

Huey was pronounced dead around eleven o'clock that night.

St. Louis cried out in anguish. "They killed my lil cousin," wrote Bruce Franks Jr., a former Missouri state representative, on Twitter.

"My dawg Huey is gone forever," lamented Jaylien Wesley, a collaborator.

"You're talking about a young man who still had a lot of life to live," Huey's first manager, Enrico Washington, told the *St. Louis Post-Dispatch*. "Kinloch is no easy place to live. It's tough. But he was...doing it the right way."

"It wasn't god it was the gunman [who] took his life," said the rapper Chingy.

Huey was thirty-two, and his death made international news. His memorial service was packed with admirers. They put carnations atop his casket, which was wrapped in life-sized, full-color images from his life.

"I'm not crying about it," his aunt Angela Richardson said of Huey's death, "because if there's one thing I instilled in the kid, you have to know God. And I know Huey know God. I'm not worried because Huey in a better place."

For many rap fans the incident was simply a passing curio, something all-too-common in the rap world. That no one was charged shocked nobody.

But the case intrigued me. Huey's death and Jorell's death had much in common. For starters, Jorell had walked by the Gutter Crew House—where Huey was gunned down—just minutes before his death.

Then there was the fact that Huey was an uncle not just to Leron White, but to another person of interest in Jorell's case—Marcel, who was with White when they took the gun off Jorell's body. The third guy with them, Charles (with the prominent neck tattoo) had also recently been killed, in January 2020, in an unrelated incident.

Huey was a decade or so older than his nephews, but they were close. Marcel posted photos to Facebook of himself wearing Huey's diamond chain, and all three men hung out at the Gutter Crew House.

Huey's death didn't traumatize me, as Jorell's had. But it seemed equally senseless, equally depressing. It was hard to believe that a man who'd become so famous as a rap artist wasn't insulated from neighborhood violence.

Yet again, no one was being held responsible for a killing. Further, I couldn't help wondering what Huey's death might have to do with Jorell's. Though the two weren't necessarily friends, they were killed just a few blocks apart.

They knew the same people and inhabited the same world.

In St. Louis, the killing of this local celebrity didn't inspire the coverage you might expect. The *St. Louis Post-Dispatch* posted a photo of the Gutter Crew House on their website and noted that police were asking witnesses to call the department or Crime Stoppers to potentially receive a reward. But there was no deep dive from that publication or any other.

No motive for the shooting was given, and county police were stymied in their search for Huey's killer, despite the fact that, according to a press release, "investigators believe as many as ten other individuals were present in and around the crime scene." A law enforcement source told me that one of the witnesses even took video footage of the killing. As weeks turned into months, it again seemed unlikely the case would be solved.

Still psychically fatigued from my investigation of Jorell's death, I didn't want to dive into Huey's case, but I poked around a bit, working with my research assistant Noah Brown. We spoke with folks from Kinloch and Ferguson who knew Huey, trying to get a sense of why they thought he was killed.

No one seemed sure, but they all agreed on one thing: Huey hadn't been the intended target of the shooting that killed him. He was simply collateral damage.

"The word on the street is that the bullet wasn't for Huey, it was for Leron," Jorell's sister Iesha told me.

"The hit wasn't on Huey," his aunt Angela Richardson told Noah Brown. "He was in the wrong place at the wrong time." Instead, Richardson agreed, the target was Leron White, who had been shot in the chest but survived.

This wasn't completely surprising. White had been in lots of hot water over the years. He'd been charged in gunplay crimes and had been shot "a half dozen times," according to a law enforcement source.

The White family also had a home in Spanish Lake, and on the night of January 11, 2017, about four months after Jorell's death, this house was hit by a drive-by. White's father Tori—Huey's brother—called in the shooting, and the police found "bullet holes in the residence and windows." That August the Gutter Crew House in Kinloch also took gunfire. Residents reported hearing about twenty shots, according to a police report. Both the home and a BMW parked in the driveway were riddled with bullets.

In November 2017, Leron White went to jail for the funeral reception shooting at The Ambassador. Very soon after his acquittal and release in early 2020 he was hit in the shooting that killed Huey.

To me, it almost seemed as if someone were waiting for Leron White to get out of jail, so they could try to kill him.

I didn't know what to make of all of this. I initially assumed this drama must have something to do with the killing of Darrius Marks, the man found shot to death and missing his hands, whose family was said to have a "Hatfield and McCoy" type relationship with the White family.

But one of my sources suggested that this most recent shooting— intended for White, but resulting in Huey's death—may have been attempted payback for Jorell.

Wait, what?

"Yeah it could be," my source said. "Most definitely, yeah."

I was stunned.

"Jorell was well loved," the source continued. "A lot of people still thought Leron had something to do with Jorell's killing."

Who killed Huey?

My source speculated it was a friend of Jorell's. This person is someone I know. I'm not going to say who, because I don't have any proof, and because it's just too heartbreaking to bear.

I didn't ask this person about these allegations, because I didn't have the energy or will for another investigation. My head was spinning, and I felt deflated.

Meanwhile, however, the pent-up negative energy on the streets seemed to be gaining momentum. "All I know is Jorell was murdered in Kinloch, and Leron was the last person to see him," another of Jorell's friends told me. "So he will *see* me!"

Jorell's friends weren't the only people upset with Leron White.

"There's a lot of attention on him right now," another source told me. "He might not live to see next year."

I tried my hardest to discourage any attempts at retaliation. Particularly since I believed White hadn't killed Jorell.

Meanwhile, White was hell-bent on "trying to get revenge for his uncle" Huey, my source said, riding around Ferguson and Kinloch carrying two Dracos, semiautomatic pistols known as baby AKs, which are small but possess incredible firepower. The gun is manufactured by the Romanian company Cugir, and its nickname comes from the country's famous villain, Dracula. They're currently ubiquitous in rap videos; even the rapper Soulja Boy—whose "Superman" dance Jorell had shown me as a boy—was now calling himself Draco.

I worried that Jorell's friends could be in White's crosshairs. The situation was depressing beyond belief. Jorell's killing seemed to have begotten another killing, which could soon beget another, like a mandala of mayhem.

Mike Fuller heard these rumors in prison, a place where the deadly drama of others' lives was a topic of everyday conversation.

"A lotta folks are saying, 'Somebody gotta pay for that,'" Mike told me. On May 7, 2021—five years after Jorell's killing, and nearly a year after Huey's death—Leron White's cousin Godrell White was shot down in Kinloch, during a neighborhood block party. More than a hundred people had gathered for the event, held for Kinloch's "hood day," featuring residents past and present. It was still daylight in the early evening when a "full-out gang war" broke out. Hundreds of shots were fired, according to an estimate; people ran for their lives, while two men including Godrell were killed. Leron was shot during the melee as well, according to a source who asked not to be named. It's unclear if either Leron or Godrell helped initiate the violence, or if they were simply attending the party. It's also unclear if Godrell's death was related to Huey's or Jorell's, or to any ongoing dispute with the family of Darrius Marks, the man who had his hands cut off.

I could barely keep track of all these deadly cases anymore.

And then, in mid-October 2021, the hammer fell. Following a nearly year-long investigation by the ATF—as well as raids on four- teen homes and businesses—Leron White and two of his associates were indicted. Investigators used "wiretaps, GPS tracking devices, hidden cameras and drug buys using confidential sources," according to a news report, and White faced drug distribution and firearm charges. At a court hearing, the assistant US attorney referenced the White family's drug trafficking organization and called the Gutter Crew a "notorious and violent" gang. He called Leron White a "very dangerous individual" and said he had been seen "randomly firing guns" while walking through a North County neighborhood.

The investigation seemed similar to the one Leron's father, Tori White, had faced more than a decade earlier, resulting in his receiving a five-year sentence in 2013.

Leron White pled not guilty to the 2021 charges, and his case had not been adjudicated as this book went to press.

The violence wouldn't cease. No one seemed to know how to stop it. Some didn't even seem interested in trying.

On that same phone call from Boonville prison, Mike said Jorell had recently appeared to him in a dream.

"He was talking about that I need to get out of prison and do right, stop getting high," Mike said.

I was happy to hear about this good influence from beyond the grave. But that wasn't all Jorell told him, Mike went on.

"He was telling me that we need to get even."

Apparently this had been recurring since Jorell died. "Even the night Jorell passed away, he was telling me in my dreams, 'Twin? You ain't gonna do nuthin'? You ain't gonna step behind me?'

"Because, if something happened to me, I know Jorell would have done something about it."

This rattled me. I told Mike my fears that, if Jorell's killer was murdered, Mike himself would be a prime suspect. I again made my case that perpetuating the cycle of violence was a terrible idea for everyone involved.

"You gotta promise me you aren't going to do anything," I said.

"I'm not," Mike said, after a pause. "I promise you."

I wasn't completely convinced. But there was nothing more I could say. Mike clearly wanted his own kind of justice for Jorell, someone who never received any sort of justice from anyone.

I wondered silently if my involvement in Jorell's case was helping anything, or if it was only making things worse.

My initial intentions had been pure, I believed. My love for my mentee, my friend—my brother—had spurred me to great lengths to find the truth. But it was now clear that his killing was only one small cog in this ever-turning wheel of violence. The socioeconomic factors that led to his death appeared long before his birth, and the repercussions of his death, it seemed, would continue long after he was gone.

Was the story over, or was it only beginning?

EPILOGUE

In January 2021, I read another distressing news story, unrelated to Jorell.

Police had found the body of a thirty-year-old woman named Ariel Brooks in her car in North County. She'd been shot in the head. Her baby girl was discovered in the back seat. "She wasn't harmed but was in the vehicle for about twelve hours before she was found," read the news report. Brooks had three other children, and her sister, Capri, spoke with a reporter. Though a suspect had been arrested in the killing, Capri wasn't taking any chances. "[S]he doesn't think St. Louis is a safe place for her nieces and nephew to grow up," read the story. "She wants her mother and the kids to move to Dallas where she lives."

I'd heard this before. Even well-known rappers were leaving town, afraid for their own lives. St. Louis had become so dangerous, survival could no longer be taken for granted.

I thought about my story subjects, and how much death they have faced. Like Jorell's brother Jovan Cleveland, who lost three siblings, his mother, his grandfather, and his uncle over a short span. Like Leron White, who lost his uncle, cousin, and more friends than I could count, or the Oak Boys, who lost four of their own in seven months. When considering the plight of the poor, we tend to talk about factors like wages and access to housing and health care. These are undoubtedly important, but what about constant trauma and PTSD? "I don't get OVER shit, I just get PAST it," wrote Jorell's sister Rece on Facebook in July 2021. "I haven't healed from a lot of shit, I just accepted it for what it is and keep pushing."

My goal with this book was not just finding out who killed Jorell, but understanding why violence in places like St. Louis was rising, and how to slow it. Deadly crime soared across the country during the COVID-19 pandemic. In 2020, St. Louis had its highest murder rate in fifty years and by year's end had solved less than 30 percent of the killings.

Yet there was no national conversation about the problem, no big-picture initiatives, just a lot of finger-pointing across the aisle.

This was hard for me to believe. An epidemic of murder! What could be worse than that?

I don't think nobody cares. It's just that nobody knows what to do. And so, after more than three years studying crime in St. Louis, I'm prepared to make a few suggestions.

I believe the biggest problem is poverty. Violent crime is born out of hopelessness and despair, but it slows when people have good educations, good jobs, and something to live for. Surely murders would drop if we could eliminate most poverty. But that isn't happening, particularly in Midwestern cities like St. Louis. African Americans in St. Louis County are more than twice as likely to live in poverty as whites, with Black people in the city more than three times as likely.

I believe simply giving money to low-income people is a good idea. Call it welfare, call it a stimulus, call it universal basic income, whatever label you choose. We can hope, pray, and wait another few decades for the invisible hand of the markets to do its magic, or we can simply prioritize the well-being of the people who need it most. I think America can afford to do it, and I think we should.

Next, we must reduce the easy availability of illegal firearms. It's possible that the loosening of Missouri gun laws led to Jorell's death, and I'm almost certain he'd still be alive today if he hadn't fooled around with guns. I realize many Americans, and African Americans in particular, believe that since criminals will always have guns, citizens should be able to defend themselves. And yet, the armed good guy defeating the armed bad guy isn't usually how things play out.

Gun rights are a foundational aspect of American culture, but that shouldn't preclude universal background checks, not to mention higher penalties for straw buyers, those who buy guns legally and then sell them to criminals. That's how illegal guns end up on the streets of Ferguson (not to mention in the hands of Mexican cartels), but straw buyers are usually just punished by probation. Another important step would be actually empowering the ATF to do its job; I was shocked to learn in Ioan Grillo's *Blood Gun Money* that the organization is not permitted to keep a computerized database of all guns sold. Instead, due to a Reagan-era law, the ATF relies on boxes and boxes of paper records that must be searched by hand, hampering police investigations.

Then there's the issue of policing. Following the killing of George Floyd, the movement to defund the police took speed, in Minneapolis, St. Louis, and many other areas around the country. It's easy to understand why. Any killing of an unarmed African American person by police is not only a tragedy, it also evokes our country's shameful history of racial power imbalances. Further, as someone who has written extensively about the opioid crisis—which is decimating African American populations— I believe that incarcerating drug users only exacerbates problems like addiction, crime, and violence. When it comes to nonviolent drug crimes, I support sending drug counselors to help with the first response, rather than just police, who often aren't well trained in these matters. I'm also a strong proponent of criminal justice reform, and I have been glad to see incarceration rates falling in places like St. Louis.

Yet I support more police in high-crime areas, not less. I have come to this conclusion after reviewing the data and speaking with many Black residents of St. Louis city and county, including aging people who sometimes feel trapped in their own homes. Following the double murder at the Kinloch block party in May 2021 that killed Leron White's cousin Godrell, the Kinloch mayor—who lives adjacent to where the incident happened—called for more patrols. People living in the most dangerous neighborhoods consistently tell me the same thing. The last thing they want is to be abandoned by law enforcement. No one wants police to abuse their power, but no one wants to be victimized by violent crime either. National public opinion polls also show that the vast majority of African Americans want the same amount of police patrolling their neighborhoods, or more.

I also support "community policing" efforts, such as beat cops on bikes or on foot. Prejudice and fear are born out of the unknown, and any opportunities for cops and community members to interact will have positive effects.

Finally, I propose a publicly accessible, national database tracking murders from around the country, with the goal of figuring out who is being killed where, and why, both to help solve outstanding murders, and to prevent others. One of the most difficult parts about Jorell's case was a lack of information. There was almost nothing available about the deaths of his peers—not in newspapers, not on the internet, not from police departments. Coroner information is often restricted only to families. Knowing who's dying, and why, is a vital tool in preventing future deaths. In the era of big data, I can only imagine this is a solvable problem.

I have a friend named Travis Whitener who lives in the St. Louis suburbs. We were put in contact by Big Brothers Big Sisters a few years ago, because he also had a "Little" die from gun violence. His name was Sam. Together with our wives, we've had nice chats over dinners, but there's always sorrow lurking beneath the surface, and the conversation often turns to bittersweet memories of our lost Littles. Not long ago, Travis talked to me about how he's reluctant to take on a new mentee, because he believes he failed Sam so badly.

I relate to these feelings. For years after Jorell's death I believed I was responsible, that I didn't provide him with the tools to keep him safe. I couldn't get past it, despite everyone insisting it wasn't my fault. What else were they going to say? I believed that if I had tried harder I could have stopped this from happening. Jorell would still be alive today.

But I'm finally seeing things differently. In Jorell's final months he had become someone unrecognizable. The pressures and trauma had made him snap. The suicide (or police killing?) of Peaches' ex-boyfriend Amonderez Green, the murder of the rapper Swagg Huncho, and the death of his brother JoJo—all of this was swirling around him. There were also Jorell's failings in school, the times he'd been shot at, the times he'd shot at others, and the fear that someone might be gunning for him at any given moment.

The fact is that Jorell could have killed someone. He apparently shot at two people—Chauncey James and Poncho, the guy from the bus stop incident—and there may have been others. In an alternate universe, Jorell wouldn't be dead, but rather be on trial for murder.

I know in my heart that I gave Jorell my best efforts. From my own, flawed perspective, I tried to teach him what was beautiful about the world and what was treacherous. I tried to unite with him in our shared humanity.

Maybe I failed. Maybe I made a difference. It's impossible to know. I tried to do the right thing, but is that, in itself, noble? What use are good intentions if they lead to bad outcomes?

I have, however, gradually shaken off my fears that I don't have what it takes to be a dad. I no longer focus on my inability to keep Jorell safe—I focus on how much he taught me about parenting.

As I write this my older son is the same age as Jorell when we were paired—eight—and he reminds me of Jorell, particularly when he's dragging his shovel around the neighborhood after a snowfall, asking to shovel driveways for a fee. My two boys drive me crazy sometimes. They leave stuff all over the house, evade their responsibilities, and demand my attention when I'm trying to get work done.

But it's not my first rodeo. Watching Jorell grow up has helped me understand the psyche of a boy heading into maturity, the struggles and the triumphs. Through Jorell I learned that a child's true development happens almost invisibly, in the background. It's what's going on in the midst of all the frustrating stops and starts.

* * *

The loss of Jorell helped me learn a larger lesson: that it's too simplistic to divide the world up into "good guys" and "bad guys."

Everyone is shaped by their environment, and everyone is trying their best. The "good guys" are often simply lucky enough not to find themselves in desperate circumstances, while the "bad guys" often must choose between dreadful options, just to survive.

The path to creating a more just and safe world starts with abandoning the idea that we are "good" and our opponents are "bad." Because, in reality, each of us are both. True sociopaths are very few in number. The vast majority of us are trying to do right, even if we stumble.

Jorell certainly was trying, even as he became overwhelmed by a world crumbling around him. He drifted away from me; I forgive him. How could I not? He introduced me to people, places, and cultures I would have never otherwise known. He broadened my understanding of the human condition. He helped me appreciate music, he helped my journalism, and, by forcing me to look deep within myself, he made me a better writer.

He opened me up to the idea of unqualified, unconditional love. He didn't care about my personal failings. He loved me no matter what. He taught me to not be embarrassed to say, "I love you." I now say it to my own kids, all the time.

It even appears that Chauncey James, the man I believe killed Jorell, was trying his best. I obviously take issue with him, but I try to put myself in his situation. I've never had someone bring menace to my front door, never had someone shooting at me, never had someone threatening the people I hold dearest. There's every reason to think James feared Jorell and was simply trying to protect his family.

I forgive him.

If it sounds like I'm letting him off the hook, understand that I'm not doing it for him. I'm doing it for myself. Because nothing is going to bring Jorell back, nothing is going to give us more time together. I'll never get another chance to be a better mentor to him, to pay attention to the warning signs, to stop talking when I should be listening. The only thing I can do is expel the hate and the anger—and the blame—from my head.

I forgive him just as I hope that Jorell, Jorell's family, my family, and everyone else I've wronged forgives me for my own shortcomings.

I forgive him because it's never too late for redemption.

I forgive him in the hopes that, now, finally, healing can begin.

ACKNOWLEDGMENTS

This book was difficult to write, but the silver lining was getting to know the Cleveland family better. For his grace and guidance, I am particularly thankful to Joe Cleveland. I hope our friendship lasts the rest of our lives.

I'm grateful to Jorell's siblings Jermaine, Jovan, Iesha, Rece, and Peaches, as well as Dianne Robinson and Tonya Walker. They revisited some of the most difficult times in their lives for the sake of this story.

Perhaps my most important source was Mike Fuller, who, along with his twin brother Montrel, pursued the truth with dogged persistence. Their help was immeasurable, and it has been a pleasure knowing them both.

Thanks to my literary agent, Ethan Bassoff, who had the idea for this book and has been a wonderful sounding board for over ten years, my esteemed editor, Brant Rumble, for seeing the vision very early in the process, and my copy editor Mike van Mantgem.

I'm not sure if it always came across, but St. Louis is incredible and everyone should move here. Cheers to locals who were great resources: Aisha Sultan, Chris Naffziger, Kosta Longmire, Jesse Bogan, Ethan Leinwand, Roo Yawitz, Matthew Allen, Tobi Owolabi, Jeannette Cooperman, Sarah Fenske, Courtney Maguire, and Percy Menzies. Special shouts to my friends Jeff Smith and Ryan Krull, with whom I've seen much of the city on jogs or on bike.

Kudos to my research assistants: Nia Plump, Noah Brown, Caroline Dempsey, and Katie Liguori, who did incredible work. For various efforts I'd also like to thank John Happel, Imade Nibokun, Toriano Porter,

Eric Royce Peterson, Joe Kessler, and Eleanor E. Artigiani, as well as my amigo Kai Flanders, for encouraging me to be bold and honest in this project.

Anna Westhoff, my wife, offered extraordinary feedback, pushing me to bring my feelings and emotions forward. She and Jorell had their own, special relationship, and he and I have both been blessed to have her in our lives.

I read my mother, Catherine Reed, a rough draft of this book during her final days, and she passed before its publication. She helped me describe the landscapes, animals, and plants in the text. I owe everything to her.

I saw an incredible sunset right after she died, and a rainbow right after Jorell died. When I see these natural phenomena now I remember these two people I love so deeply.

Jorell and Ben in 2009

ENDNOTES

INTRODUCTION

1 **"a news story about a Big Brothers Big Sisters program"**: Daphne Duret, "Program Nurtures Children of the Imprisoned," *St. Louis Post-Dispatch*, June 9, 2005.

8 **"As measured by per capita homicides per year, [St. Louis is] thirteenth in the world"**: "Ranking of the Most Dangerous Cities in the World in 2020, by Murder Rate per 100,000 Inhabitants," Statista, July 30, 2021.

CHAPTER ONE

13 **"We attended as part of a unique desegregation program"**: Elizabeth Lorenz-Meyer and Nancy O'Brien Wagner, "Onward Central: The First 150 Years of St. Paul Central High School," spps.org, September 12, 2016.

14 **"After falling in love with a Christian man originally from Germany"**: Ben Westhoff, "A Family Rift and a Cautionary Tale," *Harvard Divinity Bulletin*, Spring/Summer 2007.

14 **"Her dad, Grandpa Shelly, was...a celebrated University of Minnesota genetics professor"**: V. Elving Anderson, "Sheldon C. Reed, Ph.D. (November 7, 1910–February 1, 2003): Genetic Counseling, Behavioral Genetics," *American Journal of Human Genetics*, July 2003.

17 **"St. Louis felt such an inferiority complex"**: Bob Costas, interview by Ben Westhoff, "Costas Talks About Rams, Uecker and Richard Jewell," *St. Louis Post-Dispatch*, November 2, 1997.

17 **"I interviewed the lead singer of The Samples"**: Unreal (staff writer pseudonym), "Red Rocks," *Riverfront Times*, August 20, 2003.

19 **"enslaved people were sold on the steps of downtown St. Louis's Old Courthouse"**: "Slave Sales," National Park Service, nps.gov, April 10, 2015, www.nps.gov/jeff/learn/historyculture/slave-sales.htm.

19 **"the local slave trade was particularly fraught"**: Walter Johnson, *The Broken Heart of America* (New York: Basic Books, 2020), 92–95.

19 **"The American Catholic Church...was the largest slaveholder in the country"**: Miranda Bryant, "Catholic Order Pledges $100m in Reparations to Descendants of Enslaved People," *The Guardian*, March 16, 2021.

19 **"slave labor was used to build local institutions including the Old Cathedral"**: Andrew Theising (Florissant Valley Historical Society, Florissant, Missouri), email interview with author, May 19, 2021.

19 **"Have pity on us, let us go free for one hundred dollars"**: Thomas Brown, *In the Walnut Grove*, ed. Andrew Theising (Florissant, MO: Florissant Valley Historical Society, 2021), 33.

20 **"all within a single hour from the time he had been a freeman"**: Abraham Lincoln's Lyceum Address, January 27, 1838, transcribed on abrahamlincolnonline.org.

20 **"Annie Malone...possibly the first female African American millionaire"**: Patti Wetli, "Annie Malone Was a Millionaire Black Hair Icon Whose Mansions Were Listed in the Green Book—But Her Legacy Is Often Overlooked," Block Club Chicago, blockclubchicago.com, February 21, 2019.

CHAPTER TWO

22 **"bricks, made by European immigrants and enslaved workers"**: Valerie Schremp Hahn, " 'We were a hammer. We were a saw.' House, New Book Tell of North County's Ties to Slavery," *St. Louis Post-Dispatch*, February 8, 2021.

24 **"St. Louis, which has one of the highest rates of minority residential segregation in the nation"**: Alison Gold, "Segregation Levels in St. Louis Remain High, Study Finds," *Riverfront Times*, May 25, 2018.

24 **"Black St. Louisans below the poverty line are nearly twenty times more likely to live in concentrated poverty"**: Jacob Barker, "Racial Disparities in Income and Poverty Remain Stark, and in Some Cases, Are Getting Worse," *St. Louis Post-Dispatch*, August 7, 2019.

24 **"someone born in...Clayton has a full eighteen-year-longer life expectancy"**: Walter Johnson, *The Broken Heart of America* (New York: Basic Books, 2020), 3.

25 **"blunt assertion of social hierarchy"**: Tim O'Neil, "How the Veiled Prophet Got Its Start: An Era of Class Division in St. Louis in 1878," *St. Louis Post-Dispatch*, October 8, 2020.

25 **" 'fairest maid of his beloved city'...crowned and sits on a throne"**: William Powell, "Behind the Scenes with the Veiled Prophet Maids," *St. Louis Magazine*, January 14, 2016.

25 **"its young 'maids' have logged thousands of volunteer hours"**: No byline, "Community Service," veiledprophet.org, undated, https://veiledprophet.org/community-service.

CHAPTER THREE

27 **" 'pinks,' 'pacifists,' and 'crackpots' "**: Ernest K. Coulter, Letter to the Editor, *The New York Times*, June 24, 1942.

27–28 **"God did not create all men equal"**: Irvin F. Westheimer, Obituaries, *The New York Times*, January 1, 1981.

28 **"The child views it as, yet again, they are not a good person"**: Daniel J. Wakin, "Volunteers; For a Youngster Who Needs It, an Adult with Attention to Spare," *The New York Times*, November 12, 2001.

28 **"Big Brothers Big Sisters maintains an A+ rating"**: No byline, "Big Brothers/Big Sisters of America (National Office)," charitywatch.org, February 2019.

31 **"Riverfront Square...would have been enclosed in a five-story building two blocks long":** David Nicklaus, "No, Disney Didn't Spurn St. Louis over Beer," *St. Louis Post-Dispatch*, May 8, 2013.

31 **"per capita income was a respectable 89 percent of New York City":** Brian S. Feldman, "A Rift in America's Heartland," audio on *Innovation Hub*, accompanied by article by Ben Kesslen: "How the Coasts and the Heartland Diverged," June 24, 2016.

31 **"But with the relaxation of federal antitrust rules in the 1970s and '80s":** ibid.

31 **"St. Louis is still the premier example of urban abandonment in America":** Robert Reinhold, "In St. Louis Even the Old Bricks Are Leaving Town," *The New York Times*, July 9, 1978.

32 **"half of whom reside in poverty, and...comprise the vast majority of murder victims":** Bill Beene, "Poverty, Racial Divide Contribute to High Homicide Rate," *Metro STL*, February 11, 2020.

32 **"African American Missourians are murdered at almost triple the national average":** Ted Gest, "Unique KC Star, Post-Dispatch, News-Leader Project on Epidemic of Missouri Gun Deaths," *Gateway Journalism Review*, December 8, 2020.

33 **"It is certainly possible that there was an illegal eviction involved":** Chris Naffziger, email interview with author, October 6, 2020.

34 **"most Ferguson media coverage focused on the racist local officials":** Editorial Board, "The Lingering Damage of Ferguson's Racism," *The New York Times*, September 19, 2017.

35 **"A small section of town was known as Little Africa":** Ferguson Historical Society committee, *Ferguson: A City Remembered* (Ferguson, MO: Ferguson Historical Society, 1994), 109.

35 **"Grocery stores took orders over the telephone":** Ferguson Historical Society committee, *Ferguson: A City Remembered* (Ferguson, MO: Ferguson Historical Society, 1994), 25.

CHAPTER FOUR

44 **"I told you that no police could keep me away from you":** Bennie Cleveland, "Cleveland v. State," Supreme Court of Arkansas, September 22, 1996.

44 **"if she did not do so, she would never see her daughter again":** ibid.

45 **"Gaddy said she and Thrash had been living together in Dumas":** Mara Leveritt, "A Slippery Truth," *Arkansas Times*, October 9, 2008.

46 **"Thrash put on a blue jumpsuit":** ibid.

CHAPTER FIVE

52 **"Glen's mom later told police he had a 'mental disability'":** Ferguson Police Department report, complaint number 13-06184, April 29, 2013.

53 **"Cleveland had a small bullet wound on the right side of his lower back":** Ferguson Police Department report, complaint number 13-10968, July 11, 2013.

CHAPTER SIX

55 **"an interstate was built directly through the county's most important African American cemetery"**: Willis Arnold, "'Something Has to Be Done': Telling the Story of One of the Oldest Black Cemeteries in St. Louis," *St. Louis Public Radio*, March 2, 2017.

55 **"James Jennings...purchased three thousand acres with $15 in gold"**: Andrew Theising, *In the Walnut Grove* (Florissant, MO: Florissant Valley Historical Society 2021), 25.

56 **"Resident Robert Ellis remembered jumping from building to building"**: Robert Ellis with Marianna Riley, *Caring for Victor* (St. Louis: Reedy Press, 2009), 38.

57 **"Sometimes, agents hired black youth to drive around blasting music"**: Richard Rothstein, "The Making of Ferguson: How Decades of Hostile Policy Created a Powder Keg," *The American Prospect*, October 13, 2014.

57 **"There was an influx of Black residents"**: Dorothy Seiter, *Where the Pavement Ends*, film by Jane Gillooly, 2019.

57 **"Samuel Kye...calls [these municipalities] 'ethnoburbs'"**: Samuel Hoon Kye, *Contexts*, "The Rise of Ethnoburbs," December 13, 2018.

58 **"Much quieter was their operation running hundreds of kilos per week"**: Jerry Haymon, *Black Mafia Family, St. Louis: The Untold Story* (Carmel, IN: Dog Ear Publishing, 2014), Kindle edition, page 6706.

59 **"Lots there were sold for as little as $25 in the 1890s"**: Colin Gordon, *Citizen Brown: Race, Democracy, and Inequality in the St. Louis Suburbs* (University of Chicago Press, 2019).

59–60 **"I wouldn't have purchased a home in this area"**: Patrick M. O'Connell, "Old Chemical Spill Worries Residents," *St. Louis Post-Dispatch*, August 10, 2012.

63 **"It was something about the way they let him lay there"**: Unpublished essay by Nia Plump, May 26, 2020.

64 **"land once owned by wealthy slave owner and physician Bernard Gaines Farrar"**: Andrew Theising, *In the Walnut Grove* (Florissant, MO: Florissant Valley Historical Society, 2021), 35.

64 **"I remember seeing tanks"**: Jim Fenton, "Sending a Message," *Milford Daily News*, July 31, 2020, www.milforddailynews.com/story/sports/pro/2020/07 /31/celtics-notebook-st-louis-native-jayson-tatum-reflects-on-ferguson-mo -protests-following-death-of-mi/42570293/.

65 **"chants of 'Hands up, don't shoot' gave way to 'Fist up, fight back'"**: Marcus Stewart, unpublished interview with Nia Plump, May 2020.

65 **"A group of five or six men they didn't know pulled the ATM off the wall"**: Author interview, Jermaine Cleveland, July 4, 2019.

65 **"their Tahrir Square, their Tiananmen Square"**: Wesley Lowery, "The QuikTrip Gas Station, Ferguson Protesters' Staging Ground, Is Now Silent," *The Washington Post*, August 19, 2014.

65 **"That was the worst show in the tour, because you could tell people was on edge"**: Ben Westhoff, "Black Lives Matter: In a Year When Many Rappers Were Politically Silent, Jeezy Stepped Up," *Village Voice*, January 13, 2015.

66 **"St. Louis County Police Chief Jon Belmar said there was basically 'nothing left'"**: From staff reports, "IN FERGUSON: Businesses Burn, Police

Cars Torched as Violence 'Much Worse' than August," *St. Louis Post-Dispatch*, November 25, 2014.

66 **"Killer Mike...offered 'thoughts and prayers'":** Ben Westhoff, "Killer Mike's St. Louis Blues: Live From Tuesday's Run The Jewels Show," Deadspin, November 25, 2014.

66–67 **"The US Justice Department's investigation supported Darren Wilson's account":** No byline, "Department of Justice Report Regarding the Criminal Investigation Into the Shooting Death of Michael Brown by Ferguson, Missouri Police Officer Darren Wilson," justice.gov, March 4, 2015.

67 **"Department of Justice's hundred-page investigation of the Ferguson police department":** United States Department of Justice Civil Rights Division, "Investigation of the Ferguson Police Department," justice.gov, March 4, 2015.

67 **"Missouri State Senator Jamilah Nasheed was arrested":** Paul Wilson, "Paul Wilson: Ferguson Will Not Go Gently into That Good Night," KC Confidential, October 23, 2014.

CHAPTER SEVEN

69 **"St. Louis County Executive Steve Stenger hyped a massive revitalization project":** Steve Giegerich, "'Great Streets' Plan Advances for West Florissant," *St. Louis Post-Dispatch*, June 22, 2015.

70 **"Marohn calls this phenomenon the 'suburban Ponzi scheme'":** Ben Westhoff, "Ferguson, Five Years Later," The Verge, August 6, 2019.

70 **"TIF bonds are serviced by regressive taxes and fines levied on black motorists":** Walter Johnson, "Ferguson's Fortune 500 Company," *The Atlantic*, April 26, 2015.

72 **"I interviewed [3 Problems] for a *Rolling Stone* profile":** Ben Westhoff, "Hot Rhymes in a Hard Place: Meet the Teen Hip-Hop Heroes of 3 Problems," *Rolling Stone*, May 14, 2015.

74 **"This school is far below the state average in key measures":** No byline, "GreatSchools Summary Rating: McCluer High," greatschools.org, accessed May 12, 2020.

74 **"We chose Ferguson for the good school system":** Ferguson Historical Society committee, *Ferguson: A City Remembered* (Ferguson, MO: Ferguson Historical Society, 1994), 51.

74 **"[They] named me 'Ferguson's own Annie Oakley'":** Ferguson Historical Society committee, *Ferguson: A City Remembered* (Ferguson, MO: Ferguson Historical Society, 1994), 50.

75 **"2014 lawsuit from the ACLU":** Blythe Bernhard, "City of Berkeley Sues Ferguson-Florissant School District over School Closures," *St. Louis Post-Dispatch*, April 10, 2019.

79 **"I knew that it was only a matter of time before I would have to kill or be killed":** Shaka Senghor, *Writing My Wrongs* (New York: Crown, 2016), 91.

CHAPTER EIGHT

84 **"According to the police report, his family believed he was suicidal":** Danny Wicentowski, "Amonderez Green's Father Says Ferguson Police Shot His Son," *Riverfront Times*, October 29, 2015.

85 **"The police officers was not even six, seven feet away":** ibid.

85 **"six local activists connected to the Ferguson protests...died under suspicious circumstances":** Associated Press, "Deaths of six men tied to Ferguson protests alarm activists," nbcnews.com, March 17, 2019.

85 **"Green had tested positive for HIV":** No byline, "Autopsy Reveals Amonderez Green Tested Positive for HIV," fox2now.com, November 24, 2015.

86 **"Premature babies were displayed at the Incubator Exhibit":** Aisha Sultan, "Secrets, Scandals and Little-Known Stories About the 1904 World's Fair," *St. Louis Post-Dispatch*, October 13, 2019.

86–87 **"The first high school yearbook, *Miaketa,* was named for the Chief of 'Ferguson's Indians'":** Ferguson Historical Society committee, *Ferguson: A City Remembered* (Ferguson, MO: Ferguson Historical Society, 1994), 44.

CHAPTER NINE

91 **"[Swagg Huncho] was shot very early Sunday morning, in midtown St. Louis":** Ben Westhoff, "The Death of Swagg Huncho: Loyalty, Hip-Hop and the North County Nightmare," *Riverfront Times*, December 16, 2015.

94 **"Tupac Shakur and Biggie Smalls...were friends before a dispute":** Ben Westhoff, "How Tupac and Biggie Went from Friends to Deadly Rivals," *Vice*, September 12, 2016.

CHAPTER TEN

105 **"Every time we talked, he ended with, 'I love you'":** Ben Westhoff, "RIP Jorell Cleveland, 19—My Little Brother," *Riverfront Times*, August 30, 2016.

105 **"In quick soundbites I tried to explain what made Jorell special":** Gerron Jordan, "Family and Friends Say Ferguson Teen Gunned Down Had Big Goals and a Big Heart," fox2now.com, August 30, 2016.

CHAPTER ELEVEN

113 **"I got in a car with the owner of a fentanyl operation":** Ben Westhoff, "How I Infiltrated a Chinese Drug Lab," *Vice*, September 3, 2019.

116 **"[Jason Rodesiler] was from Michigan originally and served in the Navy":** No byline, "Rodesiler Is Now a Detective," *The Daily Reporter* (Michigan), August 4, 2010.

116 **"The St. Louis County Police Department says its detectives each handle six to eight homicide cases per year":** Erin Heffernan, "As St. Louis Killings Mount, City Detectives Face 'Overwhelming' Caseloads," *St. Louis Post-Dispatch*, March 14, 2021.

116 **"A Department of Justice study recommended detectives be assigned only three per year":** ibid.

116 **"a 2018 *Washington Post* investigation...showed that only about half of murders...get solved":** Wesley Lowery, Kimbriell Kelly, Ted Mellnik, and Steven Rich, "Where Killings Go Unsolved," *The Washington Post*, June 6, 2018, www.washingtonpost.com/graphics/2018/investigations/where -murders-go-unsolved/.

116 **"The [murder clearance] rate in St. Louis was a dismal 36 percent in 2020":** Erin Heffernan, "As St. Louis Killings Mount, City Detectives Face 'Overwhelming' Caseloads," *St. Louis Post-Dispatch*, March 14, 2021.

117 **"Campbell studied 1,600 Black Lives Matter protests around the country":** Jerusalem Demsas, "The effects of Black Lives Matter protests," *Vox*, April 9, 2021.

CHAPTER TWELVE

125 **"The Ferguson Police Department's report deviated sharply from Jorell's account":** Ferguson Police Department report, complaint number 15-00953, January 21, 2015.

CHAPTER THIRTEEN

131 **"Surveillance footage captured the presumed shooter":** Joel Currier, "Surveillance, DNA Link Woman to Killing Outside a Ferguson Convenience Mart, Charges Say," *St. Louis Post-Dispatch*, March 13, 2018.

CHAPTER FOURTEEN

140 **"James Lucas Turner, a Virginia-born West Point alum...jailed for his Southern sympathies":** Col. Wm. F. Switzler, *History of Boone County, Missouri*, Genealogy Trails, 1882, sourced from http://genealogytrails.com /mo/boone/bios_t.htm.

140 **"[Turner] brought his farm to [Kinloch] around 1883":** Andrew Theising, *In the Walnut Grove* (Florissant, MO: Florissant Valley Historical Society, 2021), 71.

140 **"J. Arthur Headon, gave a flight exhibition":** ibid, 73.

140–141 **"Others arrived as a result of the East St. Louis massacre of 1917, which included lynchings":** *Black Past*, "East St. Louis Race Riot, 1917," by Tabitha Wang, June 1, 2008.

141 **"in some cases African Americans were charged twice the price":** No byline, "Lots White Men Buy Doubled In Price to Negroes," *St. Louis Post-Dispatch*, January 24, 1917.

141 **"The Kinloch of my childhood consisted of little wood houses":** Jenifer Lewis, *The Mother of Black Hollywood* (New York: Amistad, 2017), 172.

142 **"hundreds protested and rioted for days":** *Colorado Public Radio*, "An Officer Shot a Black Teen, and St. Louis Rioted—In 1962," NPR, August 21, 2014.

143 **"A Saint Louis University study showed [Schoemehl pots] don't actually reduce crime":** Leah Thorsen, "To Make St. Louis Safer, Hundreds of Streets Were Closed. What if That Was a Mistake?" *St. Louis Post-Dispatch*, February 25, 2019.

143 **"In 1975 a Ferguson city councilman proposed erecting a ten-foot fence":** Ferguson Historical Society committee, *Ferguson: A City Remembered* (Ferguson, MO: Ferguson Historical Society, 1994), 80.

144 **"We got what we wanted, which was the freedom":** Dorothy Squires, *Where the Pavement Ends*, film by Jane Gillooly, 2018.

144 **"In 2015 I profiled Kinloch for *Vice*"**: Ben Westhoff, "The City Next to Ferguson Is Even More Depressing," *Vice*, June 2, 2015.

145 **"They're crazy-ass motherfuckers"**: ibid.

145 **"when a TV news reporter tried to report on this…he was handcuffed"**: Chris Hayes, "FOX 2 Reporter Placed in Handcuffs for Attempting to Cover City Meeting," fox2now.com, June 30, 2016.

145 **"Kinloch's violent crime rate [reached] almost three incidents per one hundred people"**: Police Executive Research Forum, "Overcoming the Challenges and Creating a Regional Approach to Policing in St. Louis City and County," policeforum.org, April 30, 2015.

145 **"Kinloch's unemployment rate is a staggering 55 percent"**: Kaitlyn Schallhorn, "Raychel Proudie Is on a Mission to Clean Up Kinloch—And She's Just Getting Started," *The Missouri Times*, June 24, 2020.

145 **"We don't say we're from St. Louis, we say we're from Kinloch"**: Author interview, Justine Blue, July 15, 2020.

CHAPTER FIFTEEN

147 **"NorthPark…has brought more than $2 million to Kinloch"**: Stephen Deere, "Kinloch's Leaders Put Hope in Small Steps," *St. Louis Post-Dispatch*, June 25, 2010.

147 **"Conway 'doled out city property to his inner circle'"**: Sarah Ryley, "City Haul: Indicted Mayor Used Small St. Louis Suburb for an Epic Corruption Spree: Feds," *The Daily*, May 31, 2011.

148 **"the church sanctuary featured a seven-foot-tall statue of the Black Virgin Mary"**: John A. Wright Sr., *Kinloch: Missouri's First Black City* (Mount Pleasant, SC: Arcadia Publishing, 2000), 85.

149 **"Manresa Retreat House [served] St. Louis–area Black Catholic laymen"**: John A. Wright Sr., *Discovering African American St. Louis: A Guide to Historic Sites* (St. Louis: Missouri History Museum Press, 2002), 116.

149 **"known for heavy drug activity"**: Kinloch Police Department Municipal Ordinance Violation Report, complaint number 15-254, July 22, 2015.

CHAPTER SIXTEEN

153 **"Loud noise like a gun, then a dog crying"**: Ferguson Police Department, event number 2016-004875, February 20, 2016.

153 **"Some of these black-market guns are manufactured…in Eastern European plants"**: Ioan Grillo, *Blood Gun Money* (New York: Bloomsbury, 2021), 43.

153 **"Century Arms [has an] eighty-thousand-square-foot warehouse in a small Vermont town"**: Ken Picard, "In Franklin County, a Global Arms Dealer Quietly Makes a Killing," *Seven Days*, January 23, 2013.

154 **"Century Arms gets around this through a loophole"**: ibid.

154 **"the arsenal of El Chapo's famed Sinaloa Cartel is filled with firearms purchased in America"**: Kevin Sieff and Nick Miroff, "The Sniper Rifles Flowing to Mexican Cartels Show a Decade of U.S. Failure," *The Washington Post*, November 19, 2020.

154 **"In the '80s, guys had Saturday night specials"**: Joel Currier, "Stronger

Firepower a Factor in Deadlier Street Violence, Experts Say," *St. Louis Post-Dispatch*, November 15, 2020.

154 **"the 2004 expiration of the federal assault weapons ban has led to the increasing prevalence of high-capacity semiautomatic guns on the streets":** ibid.

154 **"a 33 percent increase in gun killings of Black men aged fifteen to twenty-four":** Morgan C. Williams Jr., "Race and Gun Violence in the United States: A Case Study of Policy Reform in Missouri," City University of New York, 2018.

154–155 **"in the Black community…gun ownership is rising":** Melissa Chan, "Racial Tensions in the U.S. Are Helping to Fuel a Rise in Black Gun Ownership," *Time*, November 17, 2020.

155 **"[African American] support for gun control has been declining since the 1990s":** Tariro Mzezewa and Jessica DiNapoli, "African-Americans Still Favor Gun Control, but Views are Shifting," *Reuters*, July 15, 2015.

155 **"I don't trust Black leadership that wants to de-arm Black people":** Kadia Tubman and Marquise Francis, "Rapper Killer Mike: 'I Don't Trust Black Leadership That Wants to De-arm Black People'," *Yahoo News*, August 2, 2019.

155 **"the National African American Gun Association, which said they received two thousand new members":** "With Guns in Their Lives, African Americans Bear Arms—and Take Lessons," *New York Daily News*, Herb Boyd, February 3, 2021.

155 **"A University of Pennsylvania study from 2009…analyzed nearly seven hundred shootings":** Charles C. Branas, Therese S. Richmond, Dennis P. Culhane, Thomas R. Ten Have, and Douglas J. Wiebe, "Investigating the Link Between Gun Possession and Gun Assault," *American Journal of Public Health*, November 2009.

156–157 **"John M. Browning, known as the Father of Automatic Fire":** Scott Engen, "The History of the 1911 Pistol," browning.com, January 24, 2011.

CHAPTER SEVENTEEN

165 **"There was always a lot of drugs going on and, of course, a little bit of violence":** Keegan Hamilton, "Rapper Huey Looks to Shake Off the Past with a Mature Outlook and a New Album," *Riverfront Times*, August 18, 2010.

165 **"escorted off the premises in handcuffs because of a fight over a girl":** Kevin C. Johnson, "'I Got Better' Than That, Young St. Louis Rapper Pledges," *St. Louis Post-Dispatch*, June 17, 2007.

166 **"I've never had so many requests for a song":** ibid.

166 **"the *St. Louis Business Journal* reported Huey's signing of a $2.5 million record deal":** Christopher Tritto, "Baby Huey Lands $2.5 Million Record Deal with Sony BMG," *St. Louis Business Journal*, August 13, 2006.

166 **"You can't talk about St. Louis hip-hop without talking about Huey":** Toriano Porter, unpublished interview with Noah Brown, July 8, 2020.

166 **"I never saw him on drugs":** Angela Richardson, unpublished interview with Noah Brown, July 2, 2020.

CHAPTER EIGHTEEN

174 **"Now, most of the heroin sold in the US is cut with fentanyl":** Dave Davies, "Fentanyl as a Dark Web Profit Center, from Chinese Labs to U.S. Streets," NPR *Fresh Air*, September 4, 2019.

CHAPTER NINETEEN

180 **"Pedestrians cowered on stretches of sidewalk that were sometimes not ADA compliant":** Ben Westhoff, "Ferguson, Five Years Later," *The Verge*, August 6, 2019.

181 **"five low-income apartment complexes…account for 25 percent of the city's violent crimes":** Jesse Bogan, "Troubled Ferguson Apartment Complexes Change Hands, but Owners' Plans Are Unknown," *St. Louis Post-Dispatch*, May 4, 2018.

182 **"a festival in their hometown Dumas called the Hood-Nic…that raises money for education":** No byline, "The Hood-Nic Foundation," facebook.com/TheHoodNicFoundation, undated.

183 **"Crips and Bloods affiliations were imported directly from Los Angeles":** Ben Westhoff, "Cold as Ice: Two St. Louis Rappers Deconstruct an Early-'90s Classic," *Riverfront Times*, August 31, 2005.

186 **"Baltimore cops used the drugs and guns…as probable cause for a raid in 2014":** Ioan Grillo, *Blood Gun Money* (New York: Bloomsbury, 2021), 144.

186 **"in rapper Lil Boosie's murder trial…prosecutors used his lyrics against him":** Jeff Weiss, "Inside Louisiana Rapper Lil Boosie's Grisly Murder Trial," *Rolling Stone*, May 9, 2012.

CHAPTER TWENTY

193 **"Michael Ellis was killed while driving":** Nassim Benchaabane, "Police Looking for 5 People from Stolen SUV Involved in Fatal Hit-and-Run Crash," *St. Louis Post-Dispatch*, August 20, 2016.

CHAPTER TWENTY-TWO

204 **"underage, African American [prisoners] raped":** Jeannette Batz, "The Boys from Boonville: In 1963, a Group of African-American Runaways and Truants Was Sent to a Rural Reform School. Then the Nightmare Began," *Riverfront Times*, March 15, 2000.

206 **"Bonne Terre [prison] was missing more than one-third of its staff":** Ryan Krull, "Understaffed During COVID-19, Missouri Prison Is a Danger, Union Says," *Riverfront Times*, September 1, 2020.

206 **"sergeants just cranked up the AC until their temperature readings lowered":** ibid.

206 **"[inmates] were protesting conditions inside":** No byline, "St Louis Jail Riot Prompts Calls for Better Prison COVID Measures," Al Jazeera, February 8, 2021.

CHAPTER TWENTY-FOUR

227 **"[Joe] Burgoon...spent more than forty years with the St. Louis city police department"**: Jeannette Cooperman, "Q&A: A Conversation with Veteran Homicide Detective Joe Burgoon," *St. Louis Magazine*, November 17, 2016.

CHAPTER TWENTY-FIVE

236 **"[Joe Cleveland] sentenced to ten years for unspecified drug charges"**: Desha County (Arkansas) Criminal Records, Case ID: 21MCR-88-6, December 30, 1987.

236 **"[Dianne Robinson] received an even harsher sentence of twelve years"**: Desha County (Arkansas) Criminal Records, Case ID: 21ACR-05-104, December 11, 2003.

240 **"[George Floyd] had been friends with DJ Screw, an influential Southern producer"**: Gabrielle Banks, Julian Gill, John Tedesco, and Jordan Rubio, "George Floyd: 'I'm Gonna Change the World'," *San Antonio Express News*, June 9, 2020.

CHAPTER TWENTY-SEVEN

246 **"I was trying to take him out of the hood"**: Angela Richardson, unpublished interview with Noah Brown, July 2, 2020.

246 **"a car pulled up and unloaded on the SUV, killing three people inside"**: Keegan Hamilton, "Rapper Huey Looks to Shake Off the Past with a Mature Outlook and a New Album," *Riverfront Times*, August 18, 2010.

246 **"[Huey] got back in touch with his father, from whom he'd been estranged"**: Kevin C. Johnson, "'I Got Better' than That, Young St. Louis Rapper Pledges," *St. Louis Post-Dispatch*, June 17, 2007.

247 **"You're talking about a young man who still had a lot of life to live"**: Kim Bell, "St. Louis Rapper Huey Killed in Double Shooting in Kinloch," *St. Louis Post-Dispatch*, June 26, 2020

247 **"It wasn't god it was the gunman [who] took his life"**: Chingy, Instagram.com/Chingy, June 26, 2020.

247 **"I'm not crying about it"**: Angela Richardson, unpublished interview with Noah Brown, July 2, 2020.

250 **"Soulja Boy...was now calling himself Draco"**: Sheldon Pearce, "Why Rap Is Obsessed with Dracos," *Pitchfork*, February 21, 2019.

251 **"a 'full-out gang war' broke out"**: Jesse Bogan, "'Full-Out Gang War' Kills 2, Injures 3 in Kinloch," *St. Louis Post-Dispatch*, May 8, 2021.

EPILOGUE

253 **"Police had found the body of a thirty-year-old woman named Ariel Brooks"**: No byline, "Arrest in Shooting Death of Missouri Woman Found with Baby," Associated Press, January 20, 2021.

253 **"[S]he doesn't think St. Louis is a safe place for her nieces and nephew to grow up"**: Katherine Hessel, "Sister of Woman Killed in Spanish Lake Says St. Louis Not Safe to Raise a Family," fox2now.com, January 25, 2021.

254 **"In 2020, St. Louis had its highest murder rate in fifty years"**: Associated Press, "St. Louis' 2020 Homicide Rate Is Highest in 50 Years," abcnews.go.com, January 3, 2021.

254 **"[St. Louis] solved less than 30 percent of the killings"**: Danny Wicentowski, "Reckoning with St. Louis' Historic Year of Homicides," *Riverfront Times*, December 29, 2020.

254 **"African Americans in St. Louis County are more than twice as likely to live in poverty"**: Jacob Barker, "Racial Disparities in Income and Poverty Remain Stark, and in Some Cases, Are Getting Worse," *St. Louis Post-Dispatch*, August 7, 2019.

255 **"the [ATF] is not permitted to keep a computerized database of all guns sold"**: Ioan Grillo, *Blood Gun Money* (New York: Bloomsbury, 2021), 97.

255 **"the Kinloch mayor…called for more patrols"**: Robert Townsend, "Kinloch Mayor Seeks Safety Changes After Deadly Double-Shooting at Park," ksdk.com, May 12, 2021.